INTERNATIONAL LAW AND THE SUPERPOWERS

NORMATIVE ORDER IN A DIVIDED WORLD

INTERNATIONAL LAW AND THE SUPERPOWERS

Normative Order in a Divided World

ISAAK I. DORE

Rutgers University Press
New Brunswick, New Jersey

Library of Congress Cataloging in Publication Data

Dore, Isaak Ismail, 1950–
International law and the superpowers.

Bibliography: p.
Includes index.
1. International law.   2. Aggression (International
law).   3. Pacific settlement of international disputes.
4. United States—Foreign relations—Soviet Union.
5. Soviet Union—Foreign relations—United States.
6. World politics—1945–   I. Title.
JX3110.D59155   1984   341.7   83–9738
ISBN 0-8135-1014-7

FOR MICHÈLE

The Passions that encline men to Peace, are Feare of Death; Desire of such things as are necessary to commodious living; and a Hope by their Industry to obtain them.

Hobbes, *Leviathan*

Contents

CONTENTS

NOTES

FIGURE

Acknowledgments

This book has crystallized from several previous drafts, one of which was submitted to the Yale Law School in partial satisfaction of the requirements for the degree of Doctor of Science of Law. I would like to acknowledge at the outset an intellectual debt to Professor Leon Lipson of Yale Law School for painstakingly reading and commenting on earlier drafts. Special thanks are also due to Professor Richard Falk of Princeton University and to Dr. Maria Frankowska for their comments.

A number of institutions were generous enough to provide the funds and facilities without which this book could not have been written. Initial research on the book was made possible by a fellowship from the Institute for the Study of World Politics, New York. Research was continued at Yale under a Sterling fellowship from Yale Law School. I also had the benefit of the resources of the United Nations Library, Palais des Nations, in Geneva, Switzerland.

In the summer of 1981 I had the pleasure of returning to Yale Law School as a visiting scholar to do some further revision and updating of the book. I am indebted to Associate Dean James W. Zirkle of Yale Law School; to Carl F. Lamers, the Foreign Law Librarian at Yale; and to Professor Leon Lipson for providing encouragement as well as the facilities for the final stages of research.

Finally, I would like to thank Janet Weiler of the United Nations Secretariat, Geneva; Vera Felts, Elizabeth Rodgers, D. Michael Helm, Dean Jackson, Christine Szaj, Patrick Fister, and Keith Williams, for their considerable assistance in the typing, proofing, and preparation of the notes and the manuscript for purposes of publication.

Preface

It is widely recognized that international society, as presently constituted, is neither politically centralized nor regulated by a highly structured legal system. The constitutional structure of world society is at best amorphous, with no entrenched divisions of competence among the agencies that make the law or those that apply and enforce it. Political interference is endemic in those agencies that do exist: indeed, considerations of political expediency predominate over considerations of strict legality. Very often, there is, in fact, no clear standard of legality to which state conduct may be compared. In these circumstances, states arrive at canons of international conduct through a process of autointerpretation of what the pertinent norm of conduct is or should be, and if that norm is transgressed, they have resorted to self-enforcement of the norm through the extraterritorial use of force. Among the most important of the general aims of this study is the investigation of the possibility of, or potential for, disciplined normative conduct and interaction between states in the absence of formal executive, legislative, and judicial organs at the international level. Specifically, it is intended to explore the link between the creation of norms, their enforcement, and the extraterritorial use of force.

Examining the problems of superpower coexistence is one potentially fruitful approach to the problem. It should be emphasized that it is but one among several equally viable approaches, and the choice of this one does not imply that international conduct is, or should necessarily be, bipolar in essence. The choice here was influenced by the fact that in the contemporary era, the United States and the Soviet Union are among the strongest of those powers that perceive their own individual national and security interests as extending beyond their territorial boundaries. Both have used or threatened to use large-scale extraterritorial force in peacetime to protect these interests and to induce certain patterns of norm-conformity among other states as well as between themselves.

Many of these patterns have emerged, as will be seen in due course, through crisis management—i.e., situations in which one or the other power has seen its interests or security threatened by the conduct of some third state and has used force to compel a pattern of conduct that is compatible with its own political security. The following chapters explore what rules, written or unwritten, govern the use of such force and what policy considerations are taken into account in deciding whether or not to use force. Among the issues that will receive close scrutiny are the proportion or scale of severity of force, the impact any use of force is intended to have on the rival and for what purpose, and, finally, the determination of the links, if any, among these individual considerations.

Several crosscutting themes emerge. The first of these is the extent to which there has evolved a normative system that can be seen to provide solutions to international disputes *without* inquiry as to which side is "right" or has a "just" cause. In an ideologically polarized age, opposing positions continue to be adopted and differing solutions continue to be proposed for specific disputes precisely on the ground that the position or solution in question is just and right *because* it is motivated by a certain ideology. While this observation would prima facie tend to negate the notion of a procedure for settlement of disputes (particularly superpower disputes) that is neutral to the values of the two contending ideologies, a principal aim of this study is to demonstrate that the international legal system is in certain important respects evolving in a manner that is not deliberately planned or controlled by those operating within the system, and to that extent it is value-neutral. It therefore becomes enlightening and useful to develop an appropriate method of studying the evolution of the normative system mentioned above—a method which, in keeping with the observed procedure of dispute settlement, is itself empirical and value-neutral.

This study also proposes to contrast, by using the same method, the superpowers' opposing ideological approaches to law in its relation to the contemporary world's most fundamental problems: "coexistence," "nonaggression," "indirect aggression," and "peace." An overall normative pattern can be synthesized from behavior in a number of crisis situations in which one or the other power, or both, have felt their political and security interests to have been threatened and have taken extraterritorial measures to neutralize the threat. The comparison of the opposing approaches is presented not only to pierce the veil of legalistic labels and to expose the ideological and policy considerations that motivate superpower conduct, but also to study how two competing and ideologically polarized worlds can coexist under a normative system whose development neither of them directly or deliberately controls. It is also instructive to explore the extent to which general acts of codification can promote legal development in the light of the fundamentally different world-views of the two powers and the absence of a supreme international law-giving authority.

These links are best shown under an empirical approach. This type of approach provides interesting insights into the nature and inclusiveness of that "nonregulated" or unwritten regime that is evolving more or less spontaneously and autonomously through crisis management. It will, for example, show that conduct which may appear erratic or "lawless" at the most inclusive level of international society is, in fact, normatively patterned when studied at the regional, hemispheric, or other subgroup level. It is, therefore, also a principal aim of this study to catalog in detail, norm by norm, the substantive content of the autonomous regime operating at the "bloc" or hemispheric level and to identify its unique characteristics. The normative content of this regime will, in turn, show how it is neutral to the value-systems of the two opposing ideologies and yet is accepted by both.

While the international legal system will be seen to be evolving independently of the free will or control of the actors in question, this is not the only way in which it is evolving. Deliberate control over its evolution has been attempted by the powers. It will be seen that the two powers have actively negotiated with a view to arriving at definitely agreed-upon rules of conduct. Included in these negotiations have been such topics as "peaceful coexistence" and the problems of defining "aggression" and the "peaceful uses" of international ocean space, of outer space, and of celestial bodies. These attempts will be critically reviewed from the standpoint of the substantive results of the negotiations—i.e., the specific normative content of the codified rules—and from the standpoint of their potential for effective regulation of state conduct in the light of the previously suggested unwritten, autonomous regime.

It will also be seen that the empirical approach chosen to study this regime can perform certain auxiliary functions in assessing the potential of written codes generally, in assisting the interpretation of specific ones, and in making realistic projections as to particular normative trends of the future.

CHAPTER I

In Search of a Code of Coexistence

The absence of a supreme international law-giving authority has often been used as a reason for denying the existence of an international "law." For the same reason, it has been contended that specific codes of law governing relations between states are futile exercises, being honored more in their breach than in their observance, and will remain so, in the absence of international enforcing mechanisms.

Such charges are even more strongly made when they concern the very narrow field of relations involving the two superpowers. For it is indeed military power that seems in large measure to ensure their pre-eminence in world politics. Military power and "self-help" in international relations generally are seen as evidence of a lack of respect for and enforcement of international law. It is further obvious that each superpower refuses to acknowledge the leadership of the other over itself, and that the two are locked in an ideological war which makes agreement on many crucial issues of bilateral coexistence difficult if not impossible.

This chapter defines the ideological context in which the debate on both sides over a code of peaceful coexistence between East and West has evolved. An attempt will be made to assess the implications of the ideological barriers for the legal regulation of superpower conduct under the present system of international organization. Particular attention will be paid to the usefulness of "codes" in the light of the East-West experience in defining peaceful coexistence. The central theme of the study, namely, investigation of the possibility of regulating conduct through a modality other than a formal "code," will thereby be introduced.

1

THE CHANGING SOVIET CONCEPT OF PEACEFUL COEXISTENCE

The Soviet concept of coexistence has been evolving ever since the revolution of 1917. Since the concept has been well documented, no elaborate description of it is given here. The focus rather will be on the reasons explaining why the concept has changed and shifted over the past sixty years and why it continues to be in a state of flux. This is done not only with a view to highlighting the ideological and policy considerations which have been molding Soviet legal theory, but also with a view to arriving at a preliminary assessment of the viability of general "codes" of behavior between East and West in the light of the West's own philosophy of coexistence with the East.

In the period immediately after the revolution of 1917, the Soviet belief in the inevitability of world revolution demanded from Soviet legal theoreticians nothing more than a purely "transitional" theory of coexistence. This theory was to prevail up to the time of the demise of capitalism and its replacement by socialism the world over. The spread of socialism has been the central goal of Soviet foreign policy, and it has often been presented as an objective "law" of social evolution to justify or legitimize Soviet action in maintaining and consolidating socialism at home and abroad. It has also been the basic foreign policy dictate that legal theory has been dedicated to serve and legitimize.[1] It has therefore changed in focus and emphasis in accordance with the changes and fluctuations in the international political conditions affecting Soviet foreign policy.

Although a transitional theory was provided by a noted Soviet jurist, Yevgeni Korovin,[2] he was forced to publicly disavow it after the death of Lenin and the emergence of Stalin, under whom there was an important shift in Soviet foreign policy. The shift consisted chiefly of Stalin's attempt to de-emphasize the Trotskyist doctrine of "permanent" revolution.[3] The task of the working class of Russia in 1924 was seen to be not that of instigating world revolution but that of consolidating socialism within only one country—Russia. The uniqueness of the Soviet state and its legal personality was emphasized, as was the need of that state to construct socialism within its boundaries.[4]

The proponent of the new theory was E. B. Pashukanis, who, in contrast to Korovin, declared international law to be a *permanent* set of legal norms. These norms were, however, only weapons in the continuous struggle of the two world classes. From the socialist point of view, therefore, international law was only a weapon to advance the goals of Soviet foreign policy.[5]

The next major shifts in Soviet foreign policy came in the late

1930s. By then it was becoming clear that the period of "transition" was in fact going to be an indefinite period of continued coexistence of the two systems.[6] Karl Radek,[7] Andrei Vyshinskii,[8] and S. Krylov[9] were the main architects of the new theory, which rejected the idea of law as a changing and shifting weapon of political expediency. The new theory stressed the dual function of international law as regulating the "struggle *and* cooperation" between states.[10] It also emphasized treaties as the chief source of international law. This not only enhanced the importance of the state but also presented international law as a binding set of norms.[11]

The contemporary Soviet concept of peaceful coexistence emphasizes interstate agreement as the only means of creating the norms of general international law.[12] Vyshinskii's theory is denounced as being based on "the capitalist system of social relationships." A refinement introduced by G. Tunkin is that modern international law is seen to have been influenced by the will "of the entire Soviet people" (in whose name the Soviet state acts), while on the capitalist side, only the ruling classes participate in the creation of international law. It is said that because of this uniquely socialist contribution, no definition of general international law can adequately describe the specific nature of the socialist principles of international law. This is a higher system of law, governing relations between socialist states, while the general international law of peaceful coexistence governs the relations between states of different political and economic systems.[13] The principle of peaceful coexistence itself has been given the status of a fundamental principle of general international law by all contemporary Soviet writers, such as Tunkin, Lukashuk, Krylov, Karpov, and Zadorozhny.[14]

2

PEACEFUL COEXISTENCE AND MARXIST THEORY

This stand of Soviet international lawyers gives rise to many questions fundamental to Marxist theory: If law reflects a class character which distinguishes socialist from western law, what kind of class character does international law possess? Since the world is divided between socialist and bourgeois states and since international law is based on the consent of states, can there be a "general" international law? Should not Marxist logic compel the conclusion that, in view of the two opposing systems, there should be two types of international law? Or, to restate Lipson's formulation of the question, "how can two different 'bases' yield the same superstructure of international law?" [15] Another question that can be asked is whether peaceful coexistence can exist as a general norm of international law in view of the axiom of Marxian dialectics that progress is made only through conflict. Yet another question is whether the professed Soviet adherence to the norm is consistent with the Soviet belief in world revolution and the ultimate overthrow of capitalism by socialism. In this regard the principal challenge is: How can the Soviet Union remain the champion of "peace" without repudiating its ideological commitment to a foreign policy that is dedicated to the cause of socialism at home and abroad?

A. INTERNATIONAL LAW AND CLASS STRUGGLE

While Marxist theory does not deny the class character of international law, it also holds that the absence of a common international *Weltanschauung* does not preclude the existence of "general" international law—i.e., law that binds the states of both systems. Indeed, it is even possible to draw the inference that Marxist theory holds that the class conception of international law provides a necessary theoretical foundation for the existence of general international law. This may be deduced from any socialist definition of international law. Thus, a typical socialist definition of present-day general international law is the following formulation:

> International law can be defined as the aggregate of rules governing relations between States in the process of their conflict and cooperation, designed to safeguard their peaceful coexistence, expressing the will of the ruling classes of these States and defended in case of need by coercion applied by States individually or collectively.[16]

A further illustration is that central element of Marxist theory that views the origin and development of law as being in step with what are regarded as objective laws of class-divided human society, evolving from one socioeconomic formation to another. These laws apply to each human society at the municipal level as well as to human society at the global level. At the municipal level the relationship between base and superstructure is a class phenomenon, and changes in the base (and therefore in the superstructure) are due to class struggle. Law as part of the superstructure is viewed as one instrument by which the ruling class preserves its position. Thus, in a class-divided society law is always regarded as a conservative factor resisting change, serving as a tool for the suppression of class conflicts so as to minimize the threat to the base. In this sense class conflict is actually a precondition for the existence of law in noncommunist society. In such societies, generally applicable rules of law do exist, regardless of conflicting ideologies. Thus, under socialist theory the absence of a single unifying common ideology is no bar to the existence of law at the municipal level. In communist society, on the other hand, class differences are by definition "nonantagonistic," hence the theory that such a society can eventually dispense with law altogether.

At the international level, the development of international law is also regarded by socialist theory as determined by the laws of development of class-divided human society. However, no attempt is made to explain the theoretical consequences for international law arising from the fact that in municipal society there is a supreme authority whereas in international law there is no such authority. From this basic difference between the two levels of society follows the conclusion that the source of international law cannot be the same as that of municipal law, accepting for purposes of argument the Marxist thesis of law (i.e., municipal law) as a coercive regime imposed by the most powerful class on the weaker classes. Secondly, even if the source of international law can be identified, that source must be generically different from the source of municipal law. If that is the case, then the methodology of Marxist legal theory must be regarded as deficient in the study of one of the most fundamental areas of international law, for the latter does not quite "fit" into the traditional Marxist scheme of law.

Nevertheless, socialist theory maintains that the genesis of all law—including international law—lies in class conflict, the distinctive characteristic of international law being that it develops through interstate agreement "expressing the will of the ruling classes of these states" (to use Korovin's words)[17] or the "co-ordinated wills" of the ruling classes of states (to use Tunkin's phrase).[18] This, however, does not signify any lessening of the world class struggle.

The class struggle is not only to be peaceful but, under socialist theory, it is to be a long and patient struggle in which what are believed to be the objective laws of history will assure the eventual triumph of socialism the world over.[19] Before this mission is accomplished, the law of peaceful coexistence is regarded as "one of the possibilities of ensuring the most painless transition of society from capitalism to socialism."[20]

B. WORLD REVOLUTION

Although contemporary Soviet writers attribute the policy of peaceful coexistence to Lenin, the latter's position on peaceful coexistence and world revolution was not as consistent as Soviet writers claim it to be. Lenin himself never used the actual phrase "peaceful coexistence"—*mirnoe sosushchestvovaniye*—but rather he made numerous declarations which flatly contradict the idea of peace and nonintervention abroad:

> [T]he existence of the Soviet Republic side by side with imperialist states for a prolonged period is inconceivable. Ultimately either one or the other shall be victorious. And when this end comes, a number of terrible conflicts between the Soviet Republic and bourgeois states are inevitable.[21]

On other occasions, when Lenin's position was not clearly in favor of the doctrine of the inevitability of war and worldwide revolution, his stand was highly ambiguous. In such instances it tended prima facie to reject war, but upon closer examination the rejection appears to have been intended only as long as socialist power was weaker than the forces it opposed.

Lenin's position in the 1918 controversy over the signing of the Brest-Litovsk treaty between Russia and Germany serves as a good example. The Moscow regional bureau of the Communist Party disagreed with the Central Committee over the conclusion of the treaty on the ground that it was the Party's "primary task . . . to spread the ideas of the socialist revolution to all countries and resolutely to promote the workers' dictatorship" and that "[i]n the interests of the world revolution, we [i.e., the Muscovites] consider it expedient to accept the possibility of losing Soviet power."[22]

Attacking this stand, Lenin argued in favor of the treaty, since fighting Germany would, in his opinion, have meant certain defeat for Russia and the liquidation of Soviet power.[23] Considering the argument that "the interests of world revolution require that it should be *given a push*, and that such a push can be given only by war, never by peace," he declared it to be at variance with Marxism, which, in his opinion, viewed internal class antagonisms as the only legitimate cause of revolution within a state.[24] He further declared that "the interests of the world revolution demand that Soviet power . . . should *help* that revolution, but that it should choose a *form* of help which is commensurate with its own strength."[25] A few months later he condemned as "left-wing childishness" a recently published document of the "left communist" group entitled "Theses on the Present Situation," which suggested that the "collapse of the imperialist system must begin" in the "coming spring and summer." Lenin argued against any such specific timetables, since "the balance of forces" was against socialism.[26] Two years later he reiterated this stand.[27]

On the economic front, Lenin was of the view that the only way to rehabilitate Russia's war-ravaged economy was by cooperation with nonsocialist countries through the granting of concessions to them to develop the natural resources of Russia and to receive machinery and technical aid from abroad.[28] He had declared as early as 1918 that "[a] socialist republic surrounded by imperialist powers could not . . . conclude any economic treaties and could not exist at all, without flying to the moon."[29]

The earliest record of the use by Lenin of a term equivalent to "peaceful coexistence" was in 1920. When questioned by a news correspondent about Soviet intentions in Asia, he replied: "They are the same as in Europe: peaceful coexistence [*mirnoe sozhitel'stvo*] with all peoples."[30]

It must at the same time be noted that if Lenin did intend to pursue a policy of peace, coexistence, and even cooperation with the West, he was motivated firstly by a belief in the inevitable collapse of capitalism and secondly by the belief that the "balance of forces" was clearly not in favor of Russia. Coexistence in this sense meant little more than a temporary agreement not to fight. Thus, Lenin said in 1920: "As soon as we are strong enough to defeat capitalism as a whole, we shall immediately take it by the scruff of the neck."[31]

Soviet writers beginning with Stalin have, however, refused to interpret Lenin as believing peaceful coexistence to be only a tactical short-term policy and as regarding war between the two systems to be inevitable.[32] The emphasis is instead placed on the numerous dicta of Lenin on peace, economic development, and cooperation and on what are held to be the laws of social development, which assert that socialism in every country will arise through internal revolt only.[33]

C. SCOPE OF APPLICABILITY

It has been claimed since the early days of the 1917 revolution that the scope of applicability of the principles of peaceful coexistence is confined to relations between states with different political and social systems. This appears to mean that the concept of peaceful coexistence does not apply to relations among nonsocialist states or to relations among socialist states.[34] More specifically, the concept does not regulate internal class struggle within a state and does not apply to movements within states fighting against colonial rule. "Class struggle within a state," says Tunkin, "is an internal affair and cannot be regulated by international law."[35] It is also necessary to quote the following passage by Lenin:

> To recognise the defense of the fatherland means recognising the legitimacy and justice of war. Legitimacy and justice from what point of view? Only from the point of view of the socialist proletariat and its struggle for its emancipation. We do not recognise any other point of view. If war is waged by the exploiting class, such a war is a criminal war, and "defencism" in *such* a war is a base betrayal of socialism. If war is waged by the proletariat after it has defeated the bourgeoisie in its own country and is waged with the object of strengthening and developing socialism, such a war is legitimate and "holy."[36]

If this is so, why should class struggle at the international level be regulated by international law? If one accepts, for purposes of argument, the Marxist scheme of the evolution of society in historical stages, and if, again for purposes of argument, one accepts that the last and ultimate stage is socialism, why does socialist theory not leave the international class struggle unfettered so as to "facilitate" the transition to socialism in the same way that class struggle at the municipal level is left uncontrolled by law? Four possible answers may be identified. The first goes back to the Leninist concern with the "balance of forces" argument. It is clear that the world balance of forces has never been so decisively in favor of socialism as to ensure a quick and certain world-wide victory. In the immediate postrevolutionary period, Russia was too weak economically and too war-weary to push for world revolution, as Lenin himself openly admitted. The same reason operated in the post–World War II period as during the period between the two world wars. While the contemporary world balance of forces shows a considerable increase in socialist military strength, it still is not sufficient to guarantee world victory. The current nuclear stalemate can in fact be seen to be a stabilizing factor in the division of world power, since the nuclear deterrent effectively rules out war as an instrument of national policy.[37]

Second, the duality of the Leninist position on world revolution provides another way out.[38] Again reliance is placed on that aspect of the policy which forbids cross-frontier interventions to promote world revolution. Khrushchev, writing on peaceful coexistence in 1959, adopted this approach. Using the word "socialism" as synonymous with "freedom," he declared: "Romain Rolland was right when he said that 'freedom is not brought in from abroad in baggage trains like Bourbons.' It is ridiculous to think that revolutions are made to order." [39]

The third reason why, in contrast to unfettered internal class struggle, the struggle at the international level is to be controlled by international law is that the municipal law of a nonsocialist state is regarded as imposed on society by its ruling class, and as such it is coercive in character: "Law is the regulation of the relations between the classes of human society corresponding to the interests of the ruling class and sustained by its organised force." [40] This definition, emphasizing the coercive element of law, obviously envisages enforcement by some supreme authority representing the ruling class at the national level. Contemporary socialist definitions of international law do not, however, envisage such a supreme law-making and law-enforcing source. One socialist definition states that international law is enforced "by coercion applied by States individually or collectively." [41] It is in this sense that, as seen above, the nature of the source of international law does not seem to fit the Marxist scheme. While the early international law of the pre-1917 era regarded (as is municipal law) as serving the interests of only the capitalist classes and as being essentially coercive, post-1917 international law is regarded as being based on the principle of the sovereign equality of capitalist and socialist states, as not being imposed by one class on another class, and as having undergone changes (since 1917) to accommodate socialist ideals.[42] The changes are said to be in three areas: (1) Relations among socialist states are governed by the principles of socialist internationalism. (2) Relations between colonial and colonized states are governed by "the principle of self-determination of nations and peoples,"[43] which also includes the fight against "national oppression and inequality."[44] (3) Relations between capitalist and socialist states are governed by the principles of peaceful coexistence.

To find reasons to justify the application of contemporary international law to the class struggle between the socialist and capitalist states, socialist theory up to now has been shown to look, first, to the "balance of forces" argument put forward by Lenin; second, to Lenin's attitude toward the strategy for world revolution; and third, to the Marxist-Leninist concept of municipal law as the coercive instrument of the ruling class and of international law as a dynamic, changing law that is consensual and is based on the sovereign equality of all states.[45] A fourth possible answer lies in a reliance on what are believed to be the objective laws of social development that eventually lead every human society to live under a socialist government. This hope is held for world society as a whole; it is asserted that, given the operation of such laws within nations, world socialism must necessarily follow.

3

THE SOVIET CONCEPT OF COEXISTENCE AFTER HELSINKI

With the signing of the Final Act of the Conference on Security and Cooperation in Europe at Helsinki in 1975, the Soviet concept of peaceful coexistence has undergone further refinement, a refinement which Soviet writers have striven hard to portray as consistent with past interpretations of the concept, particularly as it relates to "just" wars and world revolution. The Soviet Union had long sought recognition of its post–World War II position in Europe through a pan-European conference with the major Western nations of Europe and the United States. Although commentators have differed in their assessment of the extent to which the Soviet Union succeeded in this goal in 1975,[46] one of the agreements resulting from the conference did recognize the "inviolability" of the existing frontiers of all European states.[47] This agreement is the first of four parts or "baskets" of the Final Act. The relevant part here is Basket 1, entitled "Questions Relating to Security in Europe," which contains a Declaration of Principles Guiding Relations Between Participating States.[48]

The Final Act as a whole (including the Declaration) contains a number of provisions which are of relevance on a uniquely bilateral plane between the United States and the Soviet Union, in addition to those that apply multilaterally among the participating states generally. It is in the Basket 1 Declaration of Principles that provisions of special relevance to the concept of peaceful coexistence are found. The Soviet Union identifies the provisions of Basket 1 itself with "peaceful coexistence." In 1973 the Soviet leadership declared its desire to create "in Europe . . . a lasting system of security and cooperation, which would become a living and attractive example of peaceful coexistence."[49] Accordingly, the provisions of Basket 1 will be the focus here.

In view of the flexibility of meaning of the concept of peaceful coexistence as interpreted by the Soviet Union—i.e., since the concept appears to comprise two regimes, one governing relations between socialist and capitalist states and the other governing relations among socialist states—and in view of the declared identity between peaceful coexistence and the Helsinki provisions, the Helsinki Declaration of Principles presented a unique challenge for the Soviet Union. The challenge was that of interpreting the principles in a manner that was consistent with both meanings of the concept.

The declaration contains a number of express prohibitions—namely, against violation by one participating state of the sovereignty of another participating state; against the threat or use of force; against the "assaulting" of existing frontiers; and against violation of territorial integrity. It also calls for respect for human rights and fundamental freedoms and nonintervention by one participating state in the internal or external affairs of another participating state.[50] To many Western international lawyers these provisions would make any post-Helsinki application by the Soviet Union of the "Brezhnev Doctrine" contrary not only to the spirit of the Final Act but also to its letter.[51] The Soviet Union had, however, even before the Final Act was signed, laid the theoretical foundations for a different interpretation. A carefully orchestrated campaign extolling the virtues of detente and cooperation in Europe presented the Helsinki conference and its Final Act as itself an example of peaceful coexistence in action.[52] Detente was said to be creating "favorable opportunities for an ideological offensive by the forces of Socialism," during which the struggle would further show "the irreconcilability of the class positions of the proletariat and the bourgeoisie, and the conflict between the two social systems."[53] At the same time, peaceful coexistence, the fundamental law governing relations between states with different political and economic systems, was also presented as one of the forms of the international class struggle.[54] Thus, peaceful coexistence and detente represent a two-pronged strategy designed to achieve one goal, the worldwide spread of socialism. For these reasons, peaceful coexistence and detente are, from the Soviet viewpoint, "irreversible."[55]

The irreversibility of detente also necessarily implies the nonabandonment of ideological warfare. The strategy is not oriented toward the preservation of the status quo; rather, it is designed to change the status quo in favor of socialism and also to prevent it from changing in a direction unfavorable to socialism.[56] The strategy is therefore offensive as well as defensive: offensive in the sense that it promotes ideological struggle, with support, where necessary, for local "national-liberation" wars (while avoiding an *international* war);[57] and defensive in the sense that any change within the established socialist camp is regarded as a threat to the collective "gains" of socialism, to be suppressed with force if necessary.[58]

The pliability of the concept of peaceful coexistence is further utilized to emphasize that it is a law governing relations between *states* with different social systems.[59] Similarly, detente applies only to relations between states, not to relations between classes or the political parties which represent them.[60] Thus, the law of peaceful coexistence between antagonistic systems does not apply to relations among the socialist states, and, likewise, agreements of cooperation and detente (such as the Helsinki Final Act) are agreements only among governments, not among "peoples" or "classes."[61] Relations among different classes are inherently antagonistic, and there can be no detente in the class struggle. As Brezhnev declared before the 25th Congress of the Communist Party of the Soviet Union in February 1976:

> [D]etente and peaceful co-existence refer to interstate relations
> . . . . Detente does not in the slightest abolish or alter, the laws of class
> struggle . . . . We make no secret of the fact that we see detente as the
> way to create more favourable conditions for peaceful socialist and com-
> munist construction.[62]

In the same vein, agreements, such as those expressed in Helsinki, in which boundaries are declared to be "inviolable" refer only to *state* boundaries, for there can be no permanent boundaries between "classes." Inter*class* solidarity is, on the other hand, permanent, and support for revolutionary wars is a manifestation of such solidarity and is in aid of a "just" cause. Such solidarity within the socialist camp is elevated to the status of a collective duty, and any "threat" to socialism is to be countered with collective force, if necessary.[63]

4

WESTERN NOTIONS OF PEACEFUL COEXISTENCE

It is perhaps apposite to begin this discussion with the views of George Kennan, a former United States ambassador to the Soviet Union and advocate of an official American policy of "containing" communism within its immediate postwar boundaries.[64] In his opinion, Soviet foreign conduct, right from the days of Lenin and later Stalin, has always been inconsistent with peaceful coexistence as defined by the Soviet Union itself.[65] For example, he points to Lenin's sympathy for international revolution as an early illustration that contemporary Soviet declarations in favor of peace do not inevitably flow, as has been often asserted, from the nature of the social and political system of the Soviet Union.

Kennan rejects as impracticable Khrushchev's call in 1959 for "unrestricted international trade,"[66] since in his opinion the very nature of a Soviet-type economy places severe limitations on East-West trade— e.g., the state monopoly of foreign trade, the denial of residence privileges to private foreign businessmen, etc.[67] He does not altogether exclude trade between the two systems, however, but merely emphasizes its limitations.

Commenting on Soviet allegations about the expansionist nature of capitalism, Kennan points out that there is no such thing as pure "capitalism" in the modern world, and that in Western societies ownership of the means of production is not a question of any great concern. What is of concern, rather is

> the right of people to choose and alter their own social and political systems as they like, to select those who shall govern them within the framework of those systems, and to enjoy, within that same framework, the civil liberties which relieve them of the fear of arbitrary injustice, permit them to practice freedom of the mind. . . .[68]

After asserting that these rights are best guaranteed by a Western-type democracy, Kennan enunciates what has often been called the "live and let live" formula:

> [W]hile the social and political system now dominant in Russia is one that may not commend itself to us, its existence and prevalence there is not our responsibility; it is not our business to change it; it constitutes in itself no reason why a relationship of peaceful coexistence should not prevail.[69]

The factors which complicate the question of coexistence are, in Kennan's opinion, the extension of Soviet power in Eastern Europe in the years 1944 and 1945 and the manner in which it so expanded. He asserts that, since it expanded through direct and indirect intervention by the Soviet Union, the Soviet Union cannot demand peaceful coexistence with the West without the latter's being able to question this "major alteration in the world strategic and political balance."[70] He further points out the inconsistency between peaceful coexistence and several aspects of postwar Soviet foreign policy: e.g., the "political attack" by the Soviet Union on Western Europe in 1947 and 1948, the Berlin blockade, the Hungarian intervention, and finally "the launching of the Korean War."[71]

These instances, as Kennan rightly points out, show that the word "peace" cannot be meaningful in an abstract sense; the word has meaning only in what may be called a "situational" sense. Peace is not the mere absence of overt hostilities; sheer physical might coupled with the threat of its use in the future may deter overt hostilities and may at the same time foster or protect a repressive status quo. On the other hand, indirect intervention may again support a similar situation without there necessarily being any open hostilities.

In Western eyes, the installation of communist regimes in Eastern Europe by the Soviet Union through direct and indirect assistance to certain minority groups or parties in the countries of the region is therefore incompatible with peace, as, of course, was also the case with the even more overt forms of intervention in Hungary and later in Czechoslovakia. Lerner in fact argues that the belief inherent in communist doctrine is not peaceful coexistence but world revolution, and that the former doctrine is proclaimed only when revolution abroad is impracticable and would be discarded if there were an opportunity to expand abroad.[72] Expansion in Eastern Europe is regarded as proof of the validity of this contention, as is the establishment by Lenin of the Communist International in March 1919.[73]

Regardless of all this, however, in 1960 Kennan counseled "political realism" and declared that Eastern Europe represents "a heavy commitment of the Soviet Government, which the latter cannot reasonably be asked to alter in any abrupt or drastic manner dangerous to its own political security."[74] Similarly, the Committee on Peaceful Coexistence of the American Branch of the International Law Association declared in its 1958 report that

> events in the wake of the Hungarian revolution of 1956 indicate that Americans will restrain their military forces in the interest of peace. They may hope for a change of policy in subjugated areas, but they will not fight for it. They will denounce the intervention of others, but they will not initiate a liberating military venture on behalf of the popular American view of democratic government.[75]

In contrast to the early days of the Truman Doctrine, when the Soviet economic system per se was seen as a threat to the United States system and the demand was made that the whole world adopt the latter,[76] contemporary scholarly treatment in the United States of the concept of peaceful coexistence suggests that the conflict between the two powers is viewed no longer in terms of economic systems but rather in terms of political philosophy.[77] The socialist system is seen as a denial of free political choice of leadership and of the social and economic policies of the state. The concept of the "just" war within a state, as well as the belief in the world mission of socialism, is found to be particularly offending in the West. Related to this is the Western emphasis on the termination of colonial rule through peaceful means, with due note being taken of what are believed to be "the significant contributions to human welfare that colonialism in some instances has made." [78]

In a style reminiscent of the socialist claim of having made an original contribution to international law through the principle of self-determination, American scholars appear to draw inspiration for the same principle from one of their own leaders, Woodrow Wilson, and affirm the principle while at the same time making it clear that they "would not advocate elimination of colonial conditions in a sudden cataclysmic upheaval which would rupture the peace." [79] Here appears another major philosophical disagreement between East and West. Marxist doctrine holds a war of national liberation to be "just" and "progressive" because the dialectics of history are understood in terms of conflict and struggle between classes, including violent struggle, which is often regarded as an inevitable byproduct of social progress. Yet another disagreement is that while Western scholars appear to accept the right of a nation to nationalize foreign property as an incident of the right of self-determination, they insist on fairness, nondiscrimination, and prompt and full compensation. [80]

As seen previously, under socialist doctrine the interclass law of peaceful coexistence does not apply to relations among socialist countries; a separate body of law known as socialist internationalism is the applicable law here. In contrast to this view, the Western view is that international law is universal and nonsectarian, so that there is no such thing as Moselm, Hindu, Jewish, Christian, socialist, or capitalist international law. [81]

Another principle advocated in the West has been the freedom to travel (including the right of dissenters to emigrate) and to gather and disseminate ideas and information in all parts of the world. Although this has been thought to be a desirable goal, it has never been declared by the West to be a "principle of peaceful coexistence" in the same way as certain other controversial principles such as those of "just" war, self-determination, universality of international organizations, etc., have been publicly asserted to be principles of peaceful coexistence by Soviet writers such as Tunkin and Zadorozhny. One may observe that one reason that Western scholars have refrained from making such sweeping declarations is, as Lipson said at the 50th Conference of the International Law Association in Brussels, in order to prevent peaceful coexistence from being "degraded from an ideal to a slogan." [82]

On the issue of the free exchange of ideas, Lipson observes: "I think that the freer interchange of ideas is of great importance to a better world; but that does not qualify it as a principle of peaceful coexistence." To emphasize the point he adds: "The world probably would be a better place if we could find a cure for cancer; but the need to cure cancer does not thereby become a principle of peaceful coexistence." [83] In this way, Lipson raises a fundamental jurisprudential question: whether as a matter of legal science, an enumerative legal definition of peaceful coexistence can serve as an intelligible guide to action. He points to the lawyer's dilemma that, on the one hand, if he makes only pious statements that nobody would dispute he sounds "vacuous," while on the other hand if he goes beyond that he runs the risk of making statements that are not accepted by all states, thus stirring up controversy and struggle between states over the acceptance of certain norms. Further consideration will be given to this question in the next section of this chapter.

Another principle advocated by Western scholars is the unrestricted right of innocent passage through the air and across the seas. This has been thought to be an essential concomitant of "the right to travel, to observe scientific and social facts, to improve the condition of life and culture, to gather news, and to conduct the business of the world with an eye to the improvement of commerce and the preservation of peace." [84] Consistent with the above-mentioned desire to avoid unilateral additions to the list of the principles of peaceful coexistence, United States scholars recognize that this "open sky doctrine" needs "progressive development," and they acknowledge that for the moment bilateral agreements are the best way to proceed: "American scholars find reason for anticipation of general acceptance of the concept [of open skies] *but the progression is not yet complete.*" [85] The same moderation is displayed by the Committee on Peaceful Coexistence in its 1958 definition of the concept:

> Peaceful coexistence, is, then, for American scholars, a concept requiring vigorous efforts to bring all peoples of the world closer together so that there may be an evolution of an informed, educated world public prepared to formulate policies designed to further the economic and political development of all peoples. It is a concept opposed to forceful measures designed to impose the will of a strong power or group of powers upon a power or group of powers believed to be less strong. [86]

In this sense, the concept poses the idea of active participation by states in creating conditions of lasting peace and not merely, as Hazard puts it, "an armed truce." [87] Yet the caution among American lawyers about making unilateral "legal" declarations under the rubric of peaceful co-existence, as do their counterparts in the East, appears to have led one Western jurist to declare that "[i]t would be difficult . . . to agree . . . that peaceful co-existence is or may become a legal institution. It is rather a goal, like permanent peace is a goal, a chiefly political one." [88]

Another Western jurist, Myres McDougal, takes an even stronger position. McDougal's theory of international law views what he calls the "world public order" as being made up of diverse subsystems of (national) public order contending "for completion of control and dominance in the world arena," each such system representing values that it sees as the closest approximations to "the goals of human dignity." [89] He argues:

> [T]he belief in a universal international law . . . is today largely an illusion. The universalism, to the extent that it exists, is a universalism in words only: in their specific interpretations in particular instances of concrete controversy representatives of the different contending systems of public order ascribe very different meanings to the universalistic words in promotion of very different values. [90]

While McDougal's idea of constant struggle and competition between systems, and his concept of law as nothing but a servant of national policy or value standpoints (rather in the style of Pashukanis), would not be entirely unwelcome to scholars of Marxist persuasion, the assertion that international law is "largely an illusion" would certainly be unacceptable. It was seen above that the Soviet stand on peaceful coexistence is that it is a fundamental principle of general international law and as such binding on all states. So strong is the Soviet enthusiasm for the principle that it has now been declared to be a statement about contemporary international law *as a whole*.

McDougal also urges that the chief task of scholars of international law engaged in developing the law of peaceful coexistence is that of "identifying and recommending, from all the many contending systems of international law, the principles and procedures, whatever their origin, which most effectively promote human dignity." [91] While in theory this seems a laudable goal, premised on the belief of participation by all systems in the international legal process, it is impossible to reconcile this proposal of McDougal's with another statement of his own in which he declares that certain public order systems are "totalitarian orders" which, by "monopolizing power . . . in effect monopolize all values in high degree." [92] The obvious implication is that such systems cannot contribute to his public order of human dignity and therefore cannot participate in its creation. The major difficulty with this line of argument is that its proposer never articulates *whose* value position is to be used to make judgments when all value systems are supposed to compete equally. That is, it seems to negate the very system of pluralism that it appears to advocate. Another possible difficulty is the absence of universally acceptable criteria for the selection of those values which promote human dignity, not to mention the difficulty of defining what "human dignity" itself means. [93]

The same problems arise from the following statement of McDougal about studying and promoting peaceful coexistence in a world order of human dignity:

> The scholar who would be effective will rather seek to clarify the common interests of all mankind in an international law of human dignity, to appraise the conditions under which such interests must be sought, and to recommend the principles and procedures most appropriate for securing and enhancing such interests. [94]

That furthering the "common interests of mankind" is a desirable goal is probably an indisputable proposition for all scholars, regardless of their political or ideological predilections. Yet such pious statements of the obvious run the risks, as suggested above, of reducing peaceful coexistence to a mere slogan and of being, to use Lipson's term, "vacuous."

5

PROBLEMS OF NORM-CREATION AND NORM-IDENTIFICATION

Two conflicting ideological views of peaceful coexistence as a legal concept were described above. It is apparent that the differences are indeed fundamental; there is disagreement not only over the procedure for reaching a definition but also over the philosophical approach and substantive content of the principles. The enthusiasm of the socialist side for a general code of peaceful coexistence is not shared by the West. Conversely, the "class conception" of international law, its total subordination to the goals of foreign policy (particularly that of spreading world socialism), and its restrictive application only to relations between "socialist" and "capitalist" states, are all ideologically alien to the West. On the other hand, many principles advocated by the Western side are not acceptable to the socialist side. The widely differing approaches and interpretations by East and West to the Helsinki Final Act, and at the so-called "review" conferences in Belgrade and Madrid, are further illustrations of the gap.

What, then, are the possibilities that two such antagonistic sides will ever arrive at a legal code through agreement? Can they arrive at canons of conduct in a manner other than deliberate agreement? If they can, then regardless of the content of the rules regulating state conduct, how can the source or manner of creation of such rules be identified? Without necessarily reopening the Hart-Fuller debate on law and morals, it may be observed that even these two contending municipal schools of thought accept procedural rules of law-making as one of the preconditions for law. Thus Hart, defending the positivist school (which the Soviet Union has relied on heavily in the past), asserts that legislators cannot make law "unless they comply with fundamental accepted rules specifying the essential law-making procedures." [95] Fuller agrees, but argues that, in addition, before a legal order so created can enjoy the fidelity of the general populace, the law-making procedures must themselves be accepted by it as "necessary, right, and good." [96]

Under the present system of international organization, and particularly in the absence of an international law-making authority, one may ask whether there are any rule-making procedures for international law which are accepted by states (especially by the two powers) as "necessary, right, and good," or whether there is even a mature enough international system whose law is always clearly identifiable because it complies with "fundamental accepted rules specifying the essential law-making procedures." The Fullerian question can be reformulated to ask whether all international law, and particularly that governing relations between the two powers, is consciously planned and deliberately created through procedures explicitly accepted as right and just

by the powers. Are there other ways, not necessarily planned or deliberately controlled, in which legal evolution may occur, and if so, what
method can be used to study and chart it? In other words, are there
ways whereby law emerges without reference to whether the law or the
procedure for its creation is right or just? This section introduces
an approach which, in the following two chapters, will lead to the
identification of an entire subsystem of unwritten and unplanned rules
governing relations between the two powers and the blocs they lead.
The approach is here introduced still within the context of an East-West
perspective of the problems of codifying the principles of peaceful
coexistence.

The vagueness inherent in all "general" definitions of peaceful coexistence as a concept, and their inability to provide reliable guidelines
for state conduct, have shifted attention to the substantive content of
the principles of peaceful coexistence. However, there has arisen a
division, largely along East-West lines, even on how to evolve a common method of defining the content of the concept. The difference of
approach appears to center on the Soviet preference for a general list or
"declaration of principles," in contrast to the preference of the major
Western powers (the United States, Canada, and the United Kingdom)
for prior careful research into specific areas and identification of those
that are "ripe for codification" and those that are fit for "progressive
development." [97] Tunkin, for example, suggests that if the core of international law is made up of general principles, there would be nothing methodologically wrong in an attempt to codify the "existing" general principles of peaceful coexistence, to which could be added what
Tunkin calls those principles "which are in a state of formation," or
"provisions *de lege ferenda*." [98] Zadorozhny's enumerative definition of
eighteen principles appears to be the most recent comprehensive Soviet
definition,[99] but it too freely mixes traditional and controversial principles, quite apart from the Western objection to the inclusion of abstract formulations of even the more traditional principles of, e.g.,
nonaggression, nonintervention, etc.

Thus, Western disagreement with the Soviet approach seems to be
operative at two levels: (a) at the level of traditional rules, because of
the vagueness and ambiguities inherent in abstract rules not derived
from concrete cases; and (b) at the level of nontraditional rules, where
the degree of agreement is even lower and state practice more diverse

(e.g., on questions involving freedom to travel and to emigrate, the free expression, dissemination, and exchange of ideas, the "open sky" doctrine, etc.), and where very often there are fundamental ideological differences, as in the Soviet formulations of self-determination and "just" wars. It is therefore not without justification that Lipson observed in 1965 that "Soviet international law remains in large measure a fighting international law rather than a thinking international law." [100]

Yet one may ask whether this "fighting" element, the attempt to push and jostle what are basically Marxist concepts into the realm of "general international law," is consistent with the classic Marxist view of law as a passive reflection of reality. If law is an ex post facto creation within the superstructure, and if the superstructure itself is merely a reflection of economic reality, is not the Soviet attempt to introduce a priori principles of the above-mentioned type inconsistent with an important tenet of Marxist theory of social science? It is easy to imagine the standard Soviet response: The question itself is a "bourgeois distortion" based on an inability to comprehend the "dialectical interconnection between base and superstructure" which, if properly understood, would show that the superstructure is not completely static and that class struggle in fact *starts* with new ideas about new institutions, all within the superstructure. Yet this argument overlooks the fact that the Marxist dialectic permits only incremental (i.e., nonradical) change in the superstructure during the process of its interaction with the base; fundamental change is not possible without a complete transformation of the basic economic relations. Thus, radically "new" international principles purporting to reflect a socialist reality cannot be introduced as international "law" without a socialistic transformation of the basic world economic reality—a change which has not occurred on a worldwide scale.

In spite of this jurisprudential difficulty, the Soviet Union has continued to advocate definition of the general principles of peaceful coexistence; furthermore, it has even proceeded to introduce socialist-oriented principles in its enumerative definition of the "general" principles of peaceful coexistence. Because of the sustained Soviet emphasis on the concept of peaceful coexistence as being of socialist origin and as signifying prolonged ideological struggle up to the triumph of world socialism, Western scholars have, to the chagrin of their Soviet counterparts, often preferred a more "neutral" term, such as "peaceful cooperation" or "Principles Governing Friendly Relations and Cooperation among States." [101] When, in the early 1960s, many of the newly independent and developing countries demanded a reassessment of some of the fundamental assumptions of traditional international law, the Eastern bloc advocated that the review take place under the rubric of "peaceful coexistence." [102] Western reaction to what was seen as a Soviet propaganda ploy, as well as philosophical differences between the code-oriented civil-law countries (including the USSR) and the common-law countries, led to a compromise title for the new principles. The review, which began in 1963,[103] culminated in 1970 with the adoption by the UN General Assembly of the rather cumbersomely titled "Declaration on Principles of International Law Concerning Friendly Relations and Co-operation Among States in Accordance with the Charter of the United Nations." [104]

The drafting history of the declaration shows that, even though it had been intended to be a general statement of law governing relations among all states, great-power rivalry tended to treat it as if it were to govern only relations between the major power blocs.[105] Indeed, some of the major disagreements on basic principles, such as peaceful settlement, renunciation of the use of force, nonintervention, and sovereign equality, were essentially along East-West lines.[106] The final product was, not surprisingly, rather a bland declaration of general principles susceptible of different interpretations.[107]

Western jurists, preferring a problem-oriented, case-by-case approach, have advocated the examination of specific categories or principles instead of general declarations of principle. Thus Baxter and Franck (United States) suggest that the following areas be studied before a definition is attempted:

(a) Machinery for peaceful change of existing rules of international law.

(b) The existence of a common international law and of general principles of law binding upon all nations and the relationship of international law to national law.

(c) The legal consequences of the accession of new states to independence.

(d) State responsibility for the use of its territory to the injury of other states.

(e) Direct and indirect aggression.
(f) The content of the rule of nonintervention.
(g) Peaceful settlement of disputes.[108]

Similarly, Bowett (United Kingdom) suggests study of each area and urges exploration of every conceivable hypothetical situation in which the rules in question can come into play.[109] This proposal has some merit, but its drawback is the inability of the human mind to foresee all the possible ranges and forms of future disputes in a complex international society.

A valuable complement to Bowett's approach is that suggested by Lipson (United States). Lipson advocates the case method of "reducing general principles to concrete reality."[110] This appears to involve a search for principles that impose limits on a state's extraterritorial competence, as well as a search for limits to the applicability of the principles in question. Thus, for example, the U.S. involvement in the Bay of Pigs invasion of Cuba and the Soviet intervention in Hungary in 1956 would indicate the limits to the applicability of the rules of nonintervention and noninterference in the internal affairs of other states. Unfortunately, the body of case law in this area is not as rich as it is in most branches of case law at the municipal level, and, of course, there is no single compulsory "law-making" judicial tribunal whose decisions are final, binding, and authoritative. Instead of a central adjudicative authority evolving a body of abstract rules from concrete fact situations, there is an amorphous body of sporadic and unilateral state interventions carried out in times of national or political emergency, with scant attention paid to legal niceties. In other words, to borrow Lipson's phrase, there is no *jurisprudence constante* to speak of arising from case law in this area. However, as will be seen in chapter III, norms can emerge in the *absence* of international courts, and the sporadic instances of unilateral state interventions outside national boundaries, discussed in the next two chapters, will be seen to follow a distinctly normative pattern.

In these circumstances, it is suggested that all three sources be used wherever possible to arrive at a satisfactory *modus vivendi* among all nations. These three sources are (a) declarations of "general" principles supported by the majority of writers in the field and the largest number of states; (b) scholarly research on peaceful coexistence area by area, together with a full examination of every conceivable hypothetical conflict situation that might arise and of the opinions and decisions of writers or governments formulated at international conferences held to discuss "peaceful coexistence" or "friendly relations and cooperation among states";[111] and (c) case law as evolved through decisions taken by international organizations and by national and international courts or tribunals in crisis situations, and even the unilateral acts of governments, if accepted or acquiesced in by other governments over long periods, and acts which, though they were unilateral in origin, have become generally recognized as legitimate by other states and have been repeated since then with a reasonable degree of regularity by all states.

The combination of the three sources may introduce a certain "political balance," so that neither East nor West would feel it had won any kind of political victory over the other by having its method adopted. But the primary reason for the proposal is that each source by itself has only a limited potential for offering clear rules to guide state conduct in concrete situations. Thus, the positivist approach involves the search for clear-cut abstract rules written into a binding code or some authoritative statute—a condition which the present-day law of peaceful coexistence does not satisfy. Furthermore, even if such a code materializes at some future date, its usefulness would remain limited because of the vagueness and ambiguity inherent in all abstract rules.[112] The second approach—detailing different hypothetical situations, identifying their respective causes, and suggesting rules for their resolution—can, at best, rely on only an informed guess as to the future course of international conflict. As experience at the national level has shown, no amount of human ingenuity can foresee every possible type of human conflict or all the possible sets and combinations of circumstances that may influence state conduct in particular directions. For this reason, the case method (the third approach) is of obvious relevance. Yet this source also has its limitations: There is a near-total absence of even the most rudimentary institutional infrastructure that is essential for the development of case law on peaceful coexistence. Case law develops through authoritative decisionmaking by an agency entrusted with a specialized and socially accepted judicial function and backed by other agencies having the power to enforce these decisions. The narrower the jurisdictional competence of the judicial organ, the less is its potential for exercising effective control on behavior. Thus, although there is an institution known as the International Court of Justice, it is partly an advisory organ, and its jurisdiction is not compulsory for all states in all disputes. States therefore remain free to exclude any number of disputes from the jurisdiction of the court, and no state, least of all a superpower, has declared or is likely to declare in advance its acceptance of the court's compulsory jurisdiction on such politically sensitive questions as whether or not it has committed aggression or has interfered in the internal affairs of another state.

It may with reason be argued that there are no compelling reasons why national-parochial definitions of "case law" as a product of authoritative decision making should be imposed on international law; that on a time continuum the international legal system can be seen, when compared with most national legal systems, to have only just been born; and that case law *can* develop in the absence of specialized law-making and law-enforcing organs, as indeed must have happened before the more sophisticated forms of political organization of society emerged at the national level. Presumably, however, this was possible only because of the emergence of de facto authority of leadership, whether defined in Marxist terms such as class rule and economic power or in non-Marxist terms such as social status, physical power, personal charm, etc.

Modern anthropological studies of preindustrial societies confirm that the leadership principle is central to social organization.[113] One noted authority in this field defines law as

> principles of institutionalised social control, abstracted from decisions passed by a legal *authority* (judge, headman, father, tribunal, or council of elders), principles that are intended to be applied universally (to all "same" problems in the future), that involve two parties locked in an "obligatio" relationship, and that are provided with a sanction of physical or nonphysical nature.[114]

This definition is not offered here in order to test whether or not international law meets these four attributes of law, or to assert that these are the only attributes of law, or even to decide whether or not international law is "law"; it is cited simply to show that a modern legal anthropologist, who developed the definition by way of the case method,[115] regards the presence of de facto or de jure authority as a precondition to the emergence of case law.

Since international society has no functional equivalent of a "judge, headman, father, tribunal or council of elders," it is in this sense "leaderless," and the effectiveness of such international decision-making bodies as do exist today is severely restricted by the principle of consensual jurisdiction, by weak law-enforcing mechanisms, and by the principles of sovereignty, equality, and the universality of international organizations—the cumulative effect of which has tended to leave states free to throttle *in limine litis* the discussion of issues or the taking of decisions inimical to their interests. Thus, under the principle of sovereignty no sovereign body can be made a party to a suit without its consent (hence the principle of consensual jurisdiction);[116] under that same principle no sovereign body can be compelled to participate in an international organization, and so on. It becomes obvious that some of the very principles traditionally listed under "peaceful coexistence" act in ways which prevent their own further development (through the case method) and the development of the law of peaceful coexistence itself generally.[117]

Because of these difficulties, if the case method is to be of any help at all, one has to fall back on the method suggested by Lipson in 1962: the study of "trouble cases," in which the actions of one power or another are analyzed with a view first to identifying particular causes of conflict and second to abstracting rules therefrom to govern specific fact situations. However, the words "cases" and "case method" in legal parlance generally convey the idea of cases before law courts, and the case method in the strict sense involves the study of the legal decisions of an institution (comprised of one or more persons) that has a publicly recognized judicial function. This applies to industrial as well as preindustrial societies, the difference being only in the degree of formality in the judicial administration of law in the two types of society.[118] Therefore, the term "trouble situations" will be substituted for the term "trouble cases," and the term "case method" will not be used at all. Lipson does not use the term "trouble cases," and while he does use the term "case method" he clearly refers to it in what may be described as a situational sense:

If we are told, for instance, that the United States' support of the anti-Castro revolt in Cuba is to be justified under international law, then that very fact gives us a clearer idea of what the speaker means by the principle of non-intervention. If the Indian embrace of Goa, or the Israeli advance in Sinai, is acceptable under international law, then we have a better idea of the content being given to the principle of the settlement of international disputes by pacific means. If the Soviet suppression of the Hungarian Revolution of 1956 is supported under international law, then we can understand better the meaning ascribed to the principle of non-interference in the internal affairs of other states. If the events on the Chinese-Indian border are accepted as being lawful under international law, then we may better understand the meaning of Panch Shilah. If the annexation of the Baltic States is described as having been in accordance with international law as proceeding from a free plebiscite of the local population, then we understand better the meaning given to the principle of self-determination.[119]

This situational approach to international law is analogous to that of the behaviorist school at the national level. The latter views law at the national level as rules abstracted from the actual behavior of the people who are the subjects of law—what Ehrlich called the "living law." Since this kind of behavior is the product of the actors' *own* conceptions of what they should or should not do, the abstracted rules cannot be decisions passed by a legal authority.

Similarly, the abstraction of international rules from the actual behavior of states in trouble situations is the product not of systemic legal decision making, but of autoevaluation by the subjects of international law themselves. This process shall be referred to as "crisis management." The problem that presents itself for further scholarly examination is whether it is possible and/or desirable to abstract a coherent and consistent pattern of rules from the era of the cold war and after, when peaceful coexistence was viewed almost exclusively through a bipolar prism. It would seem that even the gradual replacement of a bipolar world by a polycentric one does not for that reason alone render the attempt undesirable, because the original bipolar hostilities still prevail and are likely to prevail for a long time, and also because the problems selected for the present study are essentially bipolar in nature. This subsidiary question aside, the major problem is the extent to which it is possible to abstract rules from observing and analyzing superpower conduct in trouble situations and crisis management.

The following two chapters will analyze superpower conduct in crisis management—i.e., conduct during crisis situations involving the interests of one or both powers in which action is taken spontaneously and unilaterally rather than through any systemic decision making. The analysis begins with two early crisis situations of the postwar era in which the powers committed themselves to extraterritorial interventions. These interventions will be analyzed with a view to detecting patterns and uniformities in behavior which would signal the development of an entire subsystem of regular and expected patterns of behavior (or norms) that amounts to an unwritten "code" of coexistence.

CHAPTER II

Early Patterns of Crisis Management

1

COEXISTENCE AT THE DAWN OF THE ATOMIC AGE

In September 1949, four years after the first American use of the atomic bomb against Japan, the Soviet Union achieved an atomic explosion. While both powers were by then embroiled in an arms race, they were also concerned about the spread of nuclear weapons and the need for international controls. Since the powers failed to agree on controls, each side sought security in new and better weapons, and President Truman's order in 1950 that the hydrogen bomb be developed should be understood in this light.

With the American nuclear monopoly broken, notable personalities such as Albert Einstein and Walter Lippmann condemned not only the arms race but also the policy of containment,[1] and called for more diplomacy instead of the threats and warnings that were associated with what has since come to be known as the Truman Doctrine.[2] The containment policy had been weakened: The *ultima ratio* of the policy was no longer plausible, because even if nuclear weapons were actually used to prevent communist expansion, they could be used against the United States in retaliation, with unacceptable consequences. In addition, since the containment policy precluded diplomacy and dialogue, it excluded the possibility of negotiations to control the arms race and the proliferation of nuclear weapons, thereby increasing the potential of each side to inflict serious destruction on the other. The policy also excluded negotiations to resolve or minimize conflicts *generally*, so that each step was taken with some possible future conflict in view. Thus, each side strove for coexistence from a "position of strength," so that "a sort of nervous balance of power [could] be maintained." From the point of view of the United States, the best that could be hoped for was " 'a terribly precarious yet lasting truce . . . a hair-raising calculated risk' to be alleviated 'in the very long run' by a change in the Soviet regime."[3]

Before there was an opportunity to develop a more affirmative policy of diplomacy and negotiation, events in Korea caused the United States to reaffirm the Truman Doctrine.

2

THE KOREAN CONFLICT AND THE TRUMAN DOCTRINE

In response to the action of the United States in bringing the North Korean attack on South Korea to the notice of the UN, the Security Council passed a resolution on June 25, 1950, condemning the attack and calling on all members of the UN to assist the organization in implementing the resolution.[4] On June 27, the Security Council passed a resolution calling on member states to give "such assistance to the Republic of Korea as may be necessary to repel the armed attack."[5] These resolutions escaped a Soviet veto only because the Soviet Union was at the time boycotting the council in protest against the latter's refusal to seat the delegate of the People's Republic of China. In real terms, this was not of much consequence for, as will be seen below, the United States would have acted independently of the UN. In fact, President Truman had given the order for U.S. cover and support for South Korea well before the authorizing resolution was passed.[6] The U.S. action was taken for several reasons. The United States was convinced that the attack was ordered by Moscow,[7] and it feared that if the North Korean attack succeeded, the whole of Indochina would fall under Communist control, with similar consequences for Malaya, the Philippines, and even Japan. The Truman administration was coming under increasing domestic criticism for failing to enforce the Truman Doctrine against the People's Republic of China. U.S. intervention in Korea appeared to be the only way to save the complete failure of the doctrine in Asia.[8]

It must, however, be noted that the fact that the United States sought UN support is perhaps an indication of the lessons learned from the failures of the League of Nations in Ethiopia, Spain, the Rhineland, etc. One of the main reasons for the demise of the League was its inability to check aggression and unilateral acts of intervention by its own members. Thus, integration of the Korean operation into the collective security system of the UN Charter would set a good precedent for the fledgling organization, as well as giving the operation the look of collective action rather than unilateral intervention. The mainspring of the American resolve to fight in Korea was, however, not the desire to strengthen the machinery of collective security, but the fear of the spread of Soviet-inspired communism, which, after China's entry into the war, was called "international communism" by John Foster Dulles.[9] This fear was so strong that in November 1950 President Truman called for worldwide mobilization against communism and declared that if military action against China were authorized by the UN, General MacArthur, the U.S. commander of the UN forces in Korea, might be empowered to use the atomic bomb at his discretion.[10]

Although the spread of communism was "contained," the U.S. action in Korea was more an outgrowth of the Truman Doctrine *stricto sensu* than an implementation of the containment theory as put forward by George Kennan. As indicated above, the action was prompted by the fear that failure to act would result in a chain reaction of falling dominoes elsewhere in the world. Moscow was assumed to be "testing" the will of anticommunist countries in preparation for world conquest, recalling the fact that Hitler was able to advance after his initial acts of aggression were unopposed.[11] Kennan's formulation of the containment doctrine did not impute to the Russians any Hitler-like ambition for world conquest. Rather, patience and caution were the key elements of his concept of Soviet conduct; he suggested that the Russians would not engage in overt forms of aggression which involved the risk of a general war.[12] On the other hand, the original formulation of the Truman Doctrine was premised on considerations almost identical to those on which the Korean action was grounded: that Soviet policy was inherently expansive and aggressive, and, if unchecked, would have important geopolitical consequences. It promised prompt United States intervention in any part of the world where the Soviet Union tried to extend its system of government. Truman's call for world mobilization against communism during the Korean war was reminiscent of an earlier call for a worldwide alliance against communism.[13]

Although several motives have been suggested for what was presumed to be a Soviet-inspired attack on South Korea, the "will-testing" explanation—i.e., the theory behind the original formulation of the Truman Doctrine—fits the assumptions underlying the United States action in Korea more closely than do any of the other explanations. These other explanations are: (1) The Korean move was merely a "diversionary" move prior to a major Soviet attack elsewhere. If that were so, the United States would probably not have taken any action. (2) The Soviet Union was "probing for soft spots"—a theory probably derived from Kennan's concept of Soviet conduct. (3) Korea was only the first of a series of "demonstrations" of Soviet strength and American weakness. (4) The attack was a strategic move to put Japan, in Dulles' words, "between the upper [Sakhalin] and lower [Korean] jaws of the Russian bear" and so to prevent it from becoming a full ally of the West.[14]

It is, of course, impossible to "prove" that one or another explanation is the one that truly explains any great-power act. Each action depends heavily on the context (political, military, economic, or other) in which it took place. It also depends on the subjective evaluation by each side of the impact of its own actions upon the other and on the rival side's perception of the other's intentions. If either side miscalculates anywhere along the line, conflicts may develop in areas or directions undesired by both sides. In the Korean episode, a rational evaluation of the conflict would depend on the following:

(a) whether the Soviet Union had actually ordered the North Korean attack on the South;

(b) whether the attack was so perceived by the United States;

(c) if so, what the U.S. estimate was of the probable consequences of the attack;

(d) what measures were, in its judgment, best suited to counter the perceived threat;

(e) evaluation by the United States of the impact these measures would have on the Soviet Union; and

(f) the actual impact of U.S. actions on the Soviet Union and its perception of U.S. intentions.

The inquiry under (a) is relevant because it provides the key to the answer to (f). The nature of the impact of the U.S. countermeasures on the Soviet Union may well have depended on whether or not the Soviet Union had actually ordered the attack. It is not unreasonable to speculate that the U.S. measures may have evoked one set of responses from the Soviet Union if it had not ordered the attack and another set of responses if it had. Although Soviet conduct during the Korean War provided no evidence toward a definitive conclusion either way, correct evaluation by the side taking countermeasures of the acts and intentions of the other side is of obvious importance in all great-power conflicts.

The answer to (b) is clear: it was assumed throughout the crisis that the Soviet Union was the perpetrator of the attack. The U.S. estimate of the consequences (c) was, of course, that the dominoes would fall, so that the measure thought to be best suited to prevent this was the immediate use of armed force (d). The political and military difficulties of making landings on enemy territory to reverse a *fait accompli* would have been disproportionately greater than those involved in going to the defense of the existing order. It must have been thought that such measures would communicate to the Soviet Union the determination of the United States to resist the spread of communism with force even in areas that were only peripheral to its interests (e). All these considerations lead to the conclusion that the underlying assumptions of United States action in Korea were more consistent with the philosophy of the original Truman Doctrine than with its subsequent variants. UN support was therefore not crucial from the point of view of the United States.

3

THE INTERVENTION IN HUNGARY

The Hungarian crisis occurred during the de-Stalinization period in Hungary, which began in February 1956. In October 1956, a revolt broke out in protest against the regimes of Premier Rakosi and later of Gero, both members of the former Stalinist administration. On October 23, Gero called in Soviet troops to suppress the revolt. By popular demand Gero was replaced by the widely respected Imre Nagy, in the hope that he would be able to prevent the revolt from spreading much further.[15]

Nagy abolished the one-party system and announced that free elections would be held. This precipitated a crisis with Moscow, and the Soviet troop withdrawals were halted because it was feared that if the elections brought an unfriendly government into power, the Soviet Union would be deprived of a valuable buffer territory which insulated it from the West.

The crisis accelerated when the Roman Catholic church declared itself against communism. Then Nagy declared the presence of the Soviet troops a violation of the Warsaw Treaty, which he shortly afterward denounced, following that up with a declaration of neutrality. This now raised before the Soviet Union the specter of falling dominoes in Eastern Europe—fears that other East European states would go Hungary's way. This fear was felt not only by the Soviet Union but by the Communist parties of these states as well.[16] The cumulative effect of these events and fears led to crushing of the revolt by Soviet troops in November 1956.

While in the West this was widely condemned and treated as evidence of the aggressive nature of communism, the Soviet Union argued that the action was necessary to counter rightist reaction. In fact, a Soviet declaration of October 30, 1956, had already rationalized the initial use of Soviet troops by acknowledging that the original demands of the Hungarian people were "legitimate," adding:

> However, this just and progressive movement of the working people was soon joined by the forces of black reaction and [the] counter-revolution, who sought to take advantage of the dissatisfaction of part of the working people in order to undermine the foundations of the people's democratic system in Hungary and restore the old landowner-capitalist regime.[17]

As in the appraisal of United States motives in Korea, it should be possible to analyze Soviet motives in Hungary by applying the same six guidelines mentioned before, concerning the actual cause of the conflict, the perceived cause of the conflict and its anticipated consequences, the appropriateness of the measures and the evaluation of world reaction to them, and the actual impact of the measures. As to the first, it is, of course, clear that the cause of the original revolt was internal dissatisfaction with the existing regime, rather than any desire to restore "the old landowner-capitalist regime." That this soon became apparent to the Soviet Union and caused some embarrassment can be gleaned from several indicators. When Gero first called in the troops, he had consulted only the Soviet general, Tikhonov, and *not* Moscow. The day after Gero called in the troops, Suslov and Mikoyan, members of the Soviet Presidium, arrived in Moscow. Mikoyan was "beside himself with anger" at Tikhonov and Gero for having called in the troops.[18] Gero was then dismissed by Suslov and Mikoyan, sent off to seclusion in Russia, and supplanted by a man who had considerable popular support. What followed was a hasty announcement of troop withdrawals and, under the October 30 declaration, a formal public assurance, not only to Hungary but to all Warsaw Pact members, of Soviet good intentions. This assurance was coupled with a promise to respect sovereignty by stationing troops only after prior consultation and consent.[19] All of these moves indicate that the Soviet leadership had to act quickly and decisively to reverse its mistake.

As to the second question, the foregoing shows that no threat to the socialist order was perceived to exist at that time. The questions about the actual and the perceived causes of the revolt are more difficult to answer with respect to the second and final operation to crush the revolt. The actual cause appeared to be the original dissatisfaction with the regime. This accelerated into a much more widespread revolt, which culminated in the country's influential clergy showing anticommunist sympathies and in Nagy's steps, which finally led to Soviet intervention. Thus, it seems not unreasonable to conclude that by the time the second decision to intervene was taken, the Soviet Union did perceive a threat to the socialist order of Hungary.

As to the third question, the Soviet estimate of the probable consequences of a successful revolt was of course the loss of a strategic buffer zone and the possible creation of a second "window to the West" after West Berlin, as well as a chain reaction of falling Communist dominoes throughout Eastern Europe. In view of this, the fourth question, as to the measures considered the most appropriate to deal with the situation, was answered by armed intervention. Again, the first intervention was probably not considered an appropriate measure for the above-mentioned reasons, and other measures were quickly taken which must have been regarded as more appropriate (i.e., the dismissal of Gero, his replacement by a leader of popular choice, the withdrawal of troops, the symbolic written guarantee of respect for sovereignty contained in the October 30 declaration, etc.). Thus, evaluation of the "appropriateness" of the particular countermeasures taken does appear to be an important element in extraterritorial interventions by both powers—even if such evaluation is at a purely subjective level.

The fifth and sixth questions involve the expected and the actual impact of the measures taken on the rival power. To the extent that the

Hungarian crisis was very much an internal crisis and did not involve any direct superpower confrontation, the need for careful impact prediction, and indeed the likelihood of an unacceptably adverse reaction from the United States, were correspondingly diminished. This is discussed more fully in the next section.

4

IMPACT PREDICTION AND PROPORTIONALITY OF FORCE

Both the Korean and the Hungarian cases compel the conclusion that only such action will be taken by either power in a crisis situation as will be tolerated by the other power. This implies that no action will be taken which threatens the interests, goals, or security of the rival power and that no action will be taken which would spark another war. If, as in the Korean case, countermeasures are taken against what is believed to be a definite move to expand influence on the part of the rival power, they must, in the view of the state taking them, be effective enough to neutralize the move. At the same time, however, the countermeasures should not go beyond what is necessary to achieve the aim of neutralization, for overreaction would increase the risk of war. Thus, in the Korean case, only conventional force was used; the use of nuclear weapons would have heightened the risk of a general war or, at least, would have created disproportionate damage.

On the question of the proportionality of the countermeasure, one may observe that the United States, after repelling the North Korean attack, actually attacked North Korea to reduce the possibilities of new acts of aggression. The result was the entry of China into the war and a general increase in the risk of a world conflict. The war began as a war between North and South Korea; it then became a war between North Korea and the United States, and by the end of 1950 it had become one between the United States and China. The potential of a fourth stage— a war between the United States and Russia—had become very real. Since the attack on North Korea was not prosecuted to its avowed end, it would seem reasonable to conclude that the United States soon realized that the attack was beyond the proportionate force required to repel the original attack on the South. Truman's dismissal of MacArthur would seem to confirm this. It was also seen above how the risks of a

belated effort to reverse a *fait accompli* were thought to be disproportionately greater than quick and decisive measures in defense of the
status quo.

The U.S. effort to integrate the Korean operation into the collective
security system of the UN Charter was undertaken out of concern for
the impact that a unilateral U.S. intervention would have had on the
future of the collective security system (and therefore on the existence
of the UN organization itself) and also on the world at large, particularly the Soviet Union. At the same time, the principle of proportionality operated both as a restraining influence on the severity of
measures taken as well as a means of communicating to the attacker (or
presumed attacker) that the United States would meet forcible Communist expansion with equal and effective force.

It is possible to detect a similar correlation between impact and proportionality in the Hungarian case. In that case, the proportionality of
measures was concerned not so much with the neutralization of any
threat perceived to be emanating directly from the West, but with the
neutralization of a purely internal crisis in an area that was (unlike
Korea) well within the sphere of influence of the intervening power. It
therefore does not seem very surprising that in Hungary the intervening
state moved first, whereas in Korea the intervening state moved only in
response to an attack. Because Hungary fell within the Soviet sphere,
the intervening state seemed to have greater freedom of action than it
would otherwise have had, while at the same time there was a much
smaller risk of an impact on the West so adverse as to increase the prob-
ability of war. This explains the haste of the ill-considered first intervention, which, as suggested above, involved measures that were
rather out of proportion to the actual threat. Furthermore, when the
first withdrawal was announced, the United States, while welcoming it,
declared that it had no intention of interfering with the security of the
Soviet Union.[20] Thus, by the time the second intervention was ordered,
the usual restraints on the severity of measures were almost inoperative
and, likewise, the possibility that the measures would have an adverse
impact on the United States was minimal because (a) the United States
had already issued a declaration of noninterference, (b) the West as a
whole was at that time preoccupied with the Suez crisis, and (c) Hungary was in a pre-established sphere of influence.

The fact that there was no seriously adverse reaction from the West answers the sixth and final question by showing that the Soviet Union could not have been very far wrong in predicting the actual impact of its action in Hungary.

Just as Hungary was an example of Soviet intervention in an area outside U.S. influence, the U.S. interventions in Jordan and Lebanon in 1958, in pursuit of the so-called "Eisenhower Doctrine," [21] were examples of U.S. action in areas outside Soviet influence. Furthermore, again as in Hungary, the crises in Jordan and Lebanon were internal crises and did not involve any direct great-power confrontation. [22] To that extent the problem of impact prediction for the United States in 1958 was simplified. Since the Soviet Union or communism in general was not the cause of the unrest, [23] the U.S. estimate of the probable consequences of the unrest (if left unchecked) may have been either a subsequent Soviet intervention to fill the power vacuum in a troubled situation, [24] or the ascendance to power of pro-Nasser and pro-Soviet regimes. Thus, limited troop landings were considered to be sufficient to neutralize these threats. Since the operations were not primarily directed at any threat from the Soviet Union, and since they were limited in terms of troop numbers and duration and were in an area outside immediate Soviet spheres of influence, no elaborate evaluation of their possible impact on the Soviet Union was necessary.

5

CONCLUSION

The coexistence of the two ideological powers became de facto and permanent as of the time in the 1950s that the two sides became able to maintain rough nuclear parity. During the early period of "cold war" coexistence, patterns of relationships emerged not through negotiation but through crises involving extraterritorial intervention. Conduct in these crises has shown how each side perceives threats to its security, what measures it will take to protect and safeguard that security, and what considerations would be regarded as relevant in each case.

During the discussion of the first such crisis, a series of six guidelines was developed to identify the policy considerations underpinning United States action in Korea. These guidelines were also used to evaluate Soviet action in Hungary, and they will be used again in chapter III, in which other extraterritorial interventions by the two powers are discussed. This will be done in an effort to discover whether such actions are simply acts of lawlessness in a normatively unordered international society torn apart by ideological rivalry, or whether they can be made to fall into some ordered pattern which teaches the observer something about the international system or about the dynamics of superpower relations. It will be seen that the six guidelines facilitate the task of identifying the kinds of policy considerations which have influenced and will continue to influence the evolution of a more or less autonomous subsystem of international law governing relations between the two blocs—autonomous in the sense that it has evolved in a manner independent of the free will or control of the two blocs.

Application of the six guidelines to the two crises just discussed leads to the following general conclusions:

(1) The principle of nonintervention becomes inapplicable if any event in any part of the world threatens either the existing superpower balance or their vested interests.

(2) In the event of such a threat, the threatened state has a "right" to intervene in another country with armed force that is proportional to the threat.

(3) The degree of force must not go beyond the minimum necessary to neutralize the threat and must not threaten the interests, goals, and security of the rival party.

These are the principles marking the beginning of a larger and more comprehensive subsystem of norms governing relations between the two rival blocs. For the moment it suffices to note that the trouble situations in Hungary and Korea ought to be interpreted not as totally negating the principles of nonintervention but as merely illustrating the limits to its applicability in concrete fact situations; normal state behavior does affirm the principle of nonintervention, as shown by the fact that, despite its weaknesses, the international order is not one of total anarchy. There are very few "absolute" rights or principles of law, and time and again the complex processes of human interaction have shown that trouble situations—i.e., situations of human conflict—are a necessary condition to the further development of law, whether by the addition of new rules, by the modification or abrogation of existing ones, by creation of exceptions thereto, or by the definition of the limits to their applicability in the light of specific fact situations.

The right of self-defense at the national as well as the international level is a clear example of a rule developed to mark the limits to the applicability of other rules. As a general rule one subject of law should not kill, injure, or otherwise disturb another subject, yet this prohibition ceases to be applicable if the former's survival or safety is threatened by the latter. The Korean and Hungarian situations may therefore be regarded as having developed an exception to the general rule of nonintervention in interbloc affairs in a way analogous to the development of the right of self-defense as an exception to the general rules prohibiting murder, assault, etc.

So far, two principal ways of international norm creation have been identified. These present two different methodologies for the study of international law—namely, the study of abstract rules embodied in written codes or in custom as a proper manifestation of international law, and the study of international law as an aggregate of the actual behavior of states in specific trouble situations. In view of the absence of or defects in international law-making and law-enforcing mechanisms, it is submitted that the latter or behaviorist approach is best suited to the study of the nature of international law and the links between the various policy considerations and particular patterns of state conduct. A proper understanding of the reasons and causes of state conduct will reveal the extent to which attempts to "prescribe" particular modes of state conduct will succeed.

Thus, either the Soviet advocacy of an all-out attempt to "codify" the law of peaceful coexistence or the Western preference for a step-by-step approach to codification should, if pursued, be preceded by a careful study of actual state behavior in general, and in trouble situations in particular, such as is attempted in the next two chapters. Such a study will reveal that norms can emerge in the absence of specialized law-making and law-enforcing machinery, even though the normative process in question may not necessarily be the product of the free will of the actors themselves. For example, the three principles were derived from the Korean and Hungarian crises even though no prior agreements or codes were drawn up to authorize the interventions in question; furthermore, it seems unlikely that even if there had been such a code it would have deterred the interventions.

This is not to say that codes do not have a role to play in the regulation of state conduct, nor is it intended to give the impression that codes can be nothing but passive reflections of actual practice. Codes can perform a creative function in regulating conduct, and they can help to consolidate stable patterns of expectations. At the same time, however, the international lawyer should be aware that the absence of international law-making and law-enforcing institutions makes fidelity to law at the international level a much more delicate question than at the municipal level. In view of this limitation, overzealous advocacy of idealistic codes may only disturb established patterns and create uncertainty.

It can already be seen that the behaviorist approach strongly signals the possibility of legal development in a manner independent of the free will of the actors. It also implies that law can emerge in the absence of a supreme international law-making authority; that even in the absence of a supreme authority the actors cannot completely control their law; that deliberate codification is not the only way to legal development; that codes, though useful, are of limited value; and that failure to codify does not imply the impossibility of legal regulation.

CHAPTER III

The Concept of Aggression and the Emergence of Interbloc Norms

The previous chapters suggested that one of the three sources to be drawn on for the progressive definition of the laws of peaceful coexistence is scholarly study of the conduct of states in particular trouble situations where the disputed "norm" of international law acquires operative significance. This would be done with a view toward identifying the causes of conflict and extrapolating from the behavior patterns of states (under normal and trouble situations) certain generalized rules of conduct.

This chapter is a modest contribution in that direction. In keeping with the essential object of this study, the examination must perforce be restricted to problems of superpower rather than worldwide coexistence. The focus here will be on one of the most fundamental principles of contemporary superpower coexistence: the principle of nonagression. This principle has been chosen (a) because of its obvious importance as the foundation of the present international legal order; (b) because of the manner in which the doctrinal and definitional problems of aggression expose the potential as well as the actual causes of conflict between the two powers; (c) because it represents an area of problems which also gives insight into the operative significance of other important principles, such as sovereignty, noninterference, and self-defense; and (d) because the principle of nonaggression acquired a unique status in contemporary international law when the UN General Assembly finally approved a definition of aggression in April 1974, after more than fifty difficult years of international discussions on the subject.[1]

These and other aspects of the concept of aggression will be examined with the situational approach described in chapter I—i.e., an examination will be made of actual situations of conflict in which force was used by one or the other power. The use of this approach will lead to the identification of the nature and substantive content of an unwritten but complex "subsystem" of international law, which will be seen to be evolving spontaneously and without any prior attempts to deliberately create or codify its rules. The principles of this unwritten regime of law will be synthesized from observed conduct by utilizing the six guidelines for analyzing conduct in crisis situations proposed in chapter II, where two early cold-war crisis situations—Korea and Hungary—were discussed.

It needs to be emphasized that detecting the presence of this unwritten law and assessing its full significance are possible only under the behaviorist approach suggested in the previous two chapters. Furthermore, it is in the light of this law that the value and the potential usefulness of existing and future codes of aggression can be best assessed, as will be seen below in the section which critically appraises the 1974 definition of aggression.

The differences between the powers over defining aggression are basically the same as those over defining peaceful coexistence. Soviet enthusiasm for a code on aggression is again not shared by the West; and as with peaceful coexistence, the West has preferred contextual consideration in each case instead of a general code. Furthermore, as seen in the controversy over peaceful coexistence, there are strong differences between the powers over the meaning and substantive content of the provisions that could be included in a code prohibiting aggression. Notable examples (elaborated upon in the section which immediately follows) are disagreements over the meaning of "self-determination," "national liberation," "self-defense," and "just wars." Another important area of disagreement is over the meaning of "indirect aggression."

One may therefore again ask: How valuable are codes in the light of such fundamentally contradictory approaches? To what extent does the 1974 definition of aggression succeed in reconciling the opposing viewpoints? Do the conflicting views negate all possibilities of agreement on unsettled issues, or do they negate all possibilities of legal regulation—in a manner *other* than direct agreement—of those issues which cannot be settled by direct agreement? These questions are approached by making a detailed inquiry into disagreements of a doctrinal nature and by examining how these differences have come to be resolved in a number of crisis situations involving the use of force by the two powers beyond their national frontiers.

This examination will point out the deficiencies of the 1974 definition. The approach used earlier to study instances of conflict resolution and crisis management will permit the drawing of certain general conclusions as to the advantages and disadvantages of the position which holds abstract (usually codified) rules as the sole manifestation of international law. It will also show how specific questions of self-defense and indirect aggression have been settled in concrete cases without exclusive reliance on abstract rules or codes drawn up through direct agreement.

1

DOCTRINAL PROBLEMS

One major reason for the failure of so many previous efforts to define aggression and indirect aggression has been the desire of each superpower to retain freedom of action to counteract its rival when the latter is indulging in what are perceived to be expansionist activities. The desire to maintain this freedom to counteract manifests itself more strongly in the United States than in the Soviet Union, for reasons that will become clear shortly.

Another reason for the failure has been, of course, the radically different outlook on law of each system, which leads to different interpretations of what can be or should be permitted or prohibited by a renunciation of aggression, indirect aggression, and subversion. Since these differences in interpretation are the result of opposing doctrines, this section will provide a general outline of the differences in the doctrinal approach of each power. Special attention will be given to the socialist doctrine of war (particularly revolutionary war), and comparisons will be made where possible between the Soviet and American positions on this and the related question of indirect aggression.

A. THE JUST WAR DOCTRINE IN SOCIALIST LEGAL THEORY

Until recently, Soviet formulations of peaceful coexistence, particularly in the 1950s, did not contain any explicit prohibition against war as such.[2] This was to accommodate Soviet doctrine on the "justness" of certain wars. However, contemporary Soviet formulations of peaceful coexistence contain both a prohibition against aggression and an express provision concerning "the principle of self-defense and the lawfulness of national liberation wars."[3] The concept of "just war" that they contain includes war waged in self-defense or for national liberation: "A just war is a non-predatory, liberatory war. Its aim is the defence of a people against external attacks and attempts to enslave it. Just wars include defensive wars and wars of national liberation."[4]

Under socialist doctrine, war is merely the continuation of policy. Policy, in turn, is the concentrated expression of economics.[5] All war therefore has economic motivations, the basic motivation under capitalism being the search for markets and sources of raw materials. War for this purpose is "aggression" and unjust, and this would clearly include wars for colonization. A revolutionary war—aimed not at national liberation from foreign domination or foreign aggression but at overthrowing an indigenous capitalist elite—would not be an unjust war under socialist doctrine. However, its justification would be found not so much in the concept of just and unjust war, but among one of the component principles of the flexible law of peaceful coexistence— e.g., the principle of self-determination of peoples and the right of each people to choose its own form of government. Although such a war would be "just," that recognition falls short of permitting direct assistance by, say, a socialist state to the rebellious forces within a capitalist state. Recent expressions of Soviet attitudes toward the law of peaceful coexistence, as seen in chapter I, seem to emphasize that the confrontation between the two major systems of the world is a nonviolent struggle:

> But when we say that in competition with capitalism the socialist system will win, this does not signify by any means that we shall achieve that victory by interfering in the internal affairs of non-socialist countries. Our confidence in the victory of communism is based on a knowledge of the laws governing the development of human society.[6]

The socialist conception of unjust war or aggression appears to have at least two aspects: a foreign element and an expression of the policy (i.e., the foreign policy) of a class-divided society.[7] Thus, Ozhegov's *Dictionary of the Russian Language* defines aggression as "an armed attack by one or several imperialist countries against other countries with a view to the occupation of their territories, their forcible subjugation and the exploitation of their peoples."[8] An earlier definition of an unjust war, by Lenin, was as follows: "Unjust war is a predatory war. It aims at the seizure and enslavement of foreign lands and peoples. Unjust wars include aggressive, imperialist wars . . . struggling for the division of the spoils—that is, to see who can oppress or plunder most." [9] Thus, the Soviet doctrine of aggression may be conceptualized as follows:

Just war	Revolutionary armed struggle
	Defensive armed struggle
Unjust war	Imperialist war
(aggression)	Interventionist war

The foregoing distinction is based on the premise that, since a socialist state is by definition not imperialist, it cannot commit imperialist aggression.

One Soviet writer has asserted that socialist countries will, in the fight against colonialism, "uphold the peoples' right to use *any* means in their struggle against the colonial yoke, including uprisings, liberation wars and revolutions." [10] No attempt is made to lay down criteria for the verification of whether a movement for national liberation is in fact representative of the "people," despite the fact that the "right" is said to belong to the people. Thus, an anticolonial struggle is by definition "just" under socialist doctrine, and any assistance (direct or indirect) given for this purpose is regarded as for a "just" cause. [11]

Any assistance by any state, and particularly by a nonsocialist state, given for the purpose of suppressing the liberation struggle is regarded as "the export of counter-revolution" and illegal. [12] Colonialism per se is regarded as a form of direct aggression. [13] Further, not only is socialist assistance for wars of national liberation defended as being for a "just" cause, but assistance by African states—e.g., "establishing training facilities for insurgents" or the grant of "political, moral and material aid" to them—is also characterized under socialist doctrine as "legitimate collective self-defence against the colonialists' collective aggression." [14] The Soviet-Cuban intervention in Angola in 1976 was therefore in Soviet eyes aid for a "just" cause because, first, it was given to a liberation movement that had been waging an anticolonialist war of "self-defense," and, second, because of its leadership's well-known commitment to socialist ideals (which under this interpretation are inherently "just").

B. INDIRECT AGGRESSION

On the other hand, Western perceptions of aggression depend on the West's own evaluation of Communist intentions, capabilities, and strategies in different parts of the world. The early Western opposition to a definition of aggression should be understood in this light. The absence of a rigid controlling definition would leave the West and the United States their much-desired freedom to counteract such Communist activities as were thought to be expansionist. This is because Communist foreign strategy very often is such that, even when nonmilitary in character, it is nevertheless perceived as expansionist in essence, and armed assistance or intervention is seen by the West as the only effective way of counteracting such expansion.

Communist access to or influence upon the domestic politics of a foreign territory may be by means of friendly relations with or even control of a local Communist party, support for guerrilla tactics, infiltration of guerrilla movements, encouragement of revolution abroad by inflammatory radio broadcasts, or support for "proxy" wars. In these circumstances, a volatile situation in the state seen as the victim of such "indirect Communist aggression" may well be considered by the West to threaten its own security zone and the provision of military supplies and/or personnel may be seen as the only means of neutralizing the situation.[15] Falk observes: "[I]t might be argued that Sino-Soviet patterns of coercive influence are so elusive and minor (although highly effective) as to escape the definition whereas Western patterns are necessarily explicit and major and would be caught within the definitional web."[16] This difficulty illustrates not only that the need to define indirect aggression is more urgent and more difficult than that of defining aggression, but also that it is symptomatic of the wide ideological disparities which arise out of the coexistence of two opposing legal systems.

These disparities usually lead to widely differing perspectives between the superpowers on questions of support for rival domestic factions fighting for internal power or against a foreign or colonial administration. In such situations, there is usually no clear-cut act of intervention into or invasion of the territory in question. Influence in the internal affairs of the territory is gained through more subtle means, often described as "indirect aggression." It is on questions involving indirect aggression that the extent of disagreement is the greatest. This is confirmed by the rather conspicuous absence of an enumerative definition of indirect aggression in the UN definition of 1974. By way of contrast, in questions involving "direct" aggression, i.e., the use of force by one nation against another, there is a greater degree of consensus on the definitional aspect of the term,[17] although the gap between their respective juridico-doctrinal underpinnings remains as wide as ever, as will be seen below.

Thus, it has been argued that it is both more difficult and more necessary to define *indirect aggression* and *subversion* than direct aggression.[18] As will be seen in due course, the UN definition has not made the task of defining indirect aggression any less urgent, for the original disagreements still prevail. For example, the Soviet Union and other socialist nations tend to interpret as indirect aggression any nonsocialist or Western military aid to foreign governments considered by socialist standards to be "nonprogressive" or "reactionary." This is because, as Falk points out, "[t]he Soviet interpretation of history precludes an automatic assumption that the incumbent regime is legitimate and thus entitled to support."[19]

In another category of examples, what the West would identify as indirect aggression, the East would call a "just war of national liberation"; what the West would regard as legitimate assistance to a lawfully constituted government, the opposite side would regard as imperialism and indirect aggression against "a people" who have the right, under the socialist approach, of self-defense. If the authority is a colonial one, its existence is *ex hypothesi* aggressive by socialist doctrine. It may, however, be noted that the concept of colonialism as a form of aggression was first given prominence in the case of the annexation of Goa, in which India justified her use of force against the Portuguese colony on the ground that Portugal's presence in Goa constituted an aggression, begun 450 years before but still continuing, against which India was said to have a right to retaliate in self-defense.[20]

The foregoing shows that the objective facts of indirect aggression in each case give rise to inherently contradictory interpretations, whereas there appears to be at least a measure of consensus on the concept of aggression as implying a prohibition of the explicit use of force across state boundaries. In this regard, it should be noted that the secretary general of the UN in a 1952 report made a useful start: "The characteristic of indirect aggression appears to be that the aggressor State, without itself committing hostile acts as a State, operates through third parties who are either foreigners or nationals seemingly acting on their own initiative."[21] The report indicated that intervention in the affairs of another state, subversive action, incitement to civil war, maintenance of a fifth column, and ideological aggression or propaganda were the major ways to commit indirect aggression.

However, political differences between the two superpowers along the lines outlined above have prevented agreement on a definition of indirect aggression. Falk suggests that, apart from political differences, there is what he calls "a nonpolitical aspect of intellectual history that leads the United States and the Soviet Union to oppose one another" on the question of definition. He contrasts the Russian attitude, in favor of definition since the time of Tsar Alexander and the Congress of Vienna, with the attitude of the "British and Americans [who], nurtured in the nominalism of the common law tradition, dislike what they regard as the pretense of generalization."[22]

Falk suggests that another reason for U.S. opposition to the definitional approach is its desire to preserve its role in world politics. "It suggests that we [i.e., the United States] need to keep available the discretion to use force to prevent detrimental shifts in alliance or affinity, *whether or not* these shifts are attributable to Communist influence."[23] The shifts in alliance which Falk appears to contemplate are those adversely affecting "American national interest," whose protection requires military action by the United States "to preserve a certain position of power in the world." He cites as examples American activities in the Middle East (Iran and Lebanon), illustrating in his opinion "coercive participation that could not be reasonably justified by the theory of counter-preventive or therapeutic intervention." He comments, finally: "It is not only that we cannot find rules that would reliably govern our rivals but that we do not want to find *ourselves* bound by such rules."[24] As will be seen in the next section, this statement has become true of Soviet conduct as well.

2

CASE STUDIES IN INTRABLOC INTERVENTION

Law cannot develop at the same pace and in the same manner in a politically organized society as in one without a central political administration. Chapter I demonstrated that international society as presently constituted is far from being centrally organized within any single and all-embracing political framework. It has no specialized law-making or law-enforcing organs and is in fact "leaderless." [25] Contemporary anthropologists have found that in unstructured and leaderless societies, norms can crystallize through behavior patterns that are based on mutual tolerance and also mutual benefit—i.e., through the principle of reciprocity, to use the expression of one noted anthropologist. [26] Another anthropologist has developed a concept of law in which one central element is the attribute of "the intention of universal application," signifying the principle that the same rule is to be applied to all similar cases. [27]

Although this attribute of law was identified in a society in which an informal leadership pattern had already emerged, [28] it applies to law in every society, regardless of leadership. If such studies are conducted in politically underdeveloped societies and if the presence of only a loose or informal leadership among their subjects is indicative of the lack of sophisticated political organization, then their conclusions are a fortiori applicable to international society. This would apply particularly to the conduct of the two "subjects" under study here, because neither acknowledges the leadership of a higher authority over itself, nor does either acknowledge the political leadership of the one over the other. [29] In this sense, both have been competing in an international leaderless arena. [30]

While "intention of universal application" is not the only attribute of law for purposes of this study, it is the attribute focused on at this stage. This section will show that one of the ways in which norms have emerged in international society as presently constituted is through the principle of mutual tolerance and reciprocity between the two systems. The foundation of this reciprocity has been the assumption that like cases are to be treated alike. It will also be seen that the six guidelines suggested in chapter II for analyzing superpower conduct in crisis situations show that the substantive content of the norms extrapolated through such analysis is the same as that of norms abstracted from reciprocal behavior patterns in the corresponding trouble situations. This suggests that the six guidelines provide a basically sound method of analyzing superpower conduct. The fact that any norm, either abstracted through the behaviorist approach or deduced through formal ex post facto analyses of superpower conduct in specific trouble situations, is found to be unjust or unacceptable from a moral or ethical point of view points to defects in the existing institutions for regulating the behavior of states, rather than to defects in the particular methodological tool of analysis used. This point is elaborated upon in the concluding section of this chapter.

Examination and comparison of the doctrinal justifications advanced by each power on the several occasions on which each has intervened extraterritorially show that, while both powers have achieved positions of power and military strength that no third state can effectively challenge, the present loose system of international organization has been powerless to check the extraterritorial use of these positions of strength for purely national or ideological reasons. By examining the trouble situations in which force has been used extraterritorially, one can abstract from the behavior of the two powers those norms which appear to have been accepted and through which appears to run the single unifying thread of reciprocity. It will further become apparent that one of the main reasons for the mutual acceptance of these norms is, in fact, the element of reciprocity, which, in its own right, introduces a certain measure of predictability and, indeed, a reasonably stable pattern of mutual expectations in the crucial areas of superpower coexistence.

A. GUATEMALA AND HUNGARY

The concept of indirect aggression, although not formally articulated by the Soviet Union until the 1950s, was nevertheless a concept which it found to be as serious as direct aggression in the late 1930s, during the crucial negotiations between itself, France, and Great Britain, when the aim was to create an alliance against German aggression. The Soviet Union sought a guarantee of the independence of the Baltic states as a counterpart to the projected commitment of the USSR to come to the assistance of the Allies in the event of Nazi aggression against Poland, Romania, Switzerland, Belgium, or the Netherlands. The Soviet proposal was for mutual assistance in case of German "aggression, direct or indirect . . . against any European State." This commitment was to be applicable in the event of "an internal coup d'état *or a reversal of policy* in the interests of the aggressor" causing the state in question to lose its independence or neutrality.[31]

A Soviet draft of 1953 contained the following provisions on indirect aggression:

> 2. That State shall be declared to have committed an act of indirect aggression which:
>   (a) Encourages subversive activity against another State (acts of terrorism, diversion, *etc.*);
>   (b) Promotes the outbreak of civil war within another State;
>   (c) Promotes an internal upheaval in another State or a reversal of policy in favour of the aggressor.[32]

It is pertinent to observe that the USSR viewed a mere "reversal of policy" or "subversive activity" in the form of "diversion" as being sufficient to constitute indirect aggression. No objective criteria were proposed, nor was the allocation of competence to determine the question defined. The Soviet proposal of 1939 to the Allies on the prevention of Nazi aggression implied that the question of whether or not there was a reversal of policy was to be a decision by the parties to the agreement, not by the European state that was the victim of such aggression. Similarly, in the aftermath of the Czechoslovakian intervention in 1968, the Soviet Union proclaimed that it was not Czechoslovakia but the socialist community as a whole that had the competence to determine the nature of the alleged capitalist threat in that country and the gravity of the danger of "a re-orientation of her foreign policy." [33]

In a situation where one state is the dominant partner within a group, this would, in practice, mean that the interpretation of the dominant state would be important if not decisive. In fact, in such situations the dominant partner's decision can be presented as the "unanimous" decision of the group as a whole. In the Soviet bloc, for example, a decision of the USSR to intervene would be formally presented as a unanimous decision for collective action, and public criticism of the decision from any country within the bloc would not be tolerated.

In other situations, the dominant partner's unilateral decision may take the place of the group decision if it has the necessary military means to intervene. In this situation, it makes little difference whether the decision is presented as a unilateral one or as a collective one. The USSR did not claim a unilateral competence to determine the nature of the alleged aggression in Czechoslovakia, but presented its decision as a "collective" one. However, in a parallel situation three years earlier, the United States publicly asserted a unilateral competence not only to make a decision but also to intervene in any state within the Western hemisphere to prevent a Communist government from taking power.[34] This marked the culmination of a trend in U.S. foreign policy beginning at about the same time as the formulation of the first Russian draft on indirect aggression in 1953. A brief outline of the American doctrine follows.

The doctrine originated in 1954 with what the *New York Times* subsequently described as "the CIA-engineered revolution against the Communist-oriented President of Guatemala, Jacobo Arbenz Guzman." [35] The intervention consisted of an invasion by a U.S.-supported army from bases in Nicaragua and Honduras, led by Colonel Castillo Armas. The Guatemalan government appealed to the UN Security Council to take action under Articles 34, 35, and 39 of the charter and determine the source of the aggression. According to the United States, the aggression had been perpetrated by "international communism," using Guatemala as its "tool." The Guatemalan government also complained that American-made planes had bombed a port and military bases in Guatemala.[36] However, the U.S. representative, Mr. Lodge, with the support of other members of the Organization of American States, successfully prevented the Security Council from investigating the matter. The United States argued that the situation then prevailing in Guatemala was "precisely the kind of problem which, in the first instance, should be dealt with on an urgent basis by an appropriate agency of the Organization of American States." [37] The United States also argued that in appropriate circumstances, the charter should not be invoked if parallel regional arrangements existed to deal with a problem. Lodge argued that it was only because a satisfactory balance had been struck between universalism and regionalism by Articles 51 and 52 of the charter that the U.S. Senate had approved the charter. Had the inter-American system been abrogated, he contended, the charter would have been unacceptable to the U.S.[38]

In the face of Soviet objections to the matter being dealt with at the regional level, the U.S. representative made a declaration which re-ciprocal practice over the next two decades was to stamp with almost a jural quality: "I say to the representative of the Soviet Union, stay out of this hemisphere and do not try to start your plans and your conspira-cies over here." [39]

Earlier in 1954, the United States had proposed for adoption by the Tenth Inter-American Conference, held in Caracas, a "Declaration of Solidarity for the Preservation of the Political Integrity of the American States Against International Communist Intervention." The declara-tion, adopted with a few modifications, stated *inter alia* that "interna-tional communism, by its anti-democratic nature and its interventionist tendency, is incompatible with the concept of American freedom," and member states resolved to "adopt within their respective territories the measures necessary to eradicate and prevent subversive activities." [40] It further said:

> The aggressive character of the international communist movement con-tinues to constitute, in the context of world affairs, a special and imme-diate threat to the national institutions and the peace and security of the American states, and to the right of each state to develop its cultural, political and economic life freely and naturally without intervention in its internal or external affairs by other States.[41]

The final clause of the declaration was an amendment introduced by the United States:

> This declaration of foreign policy made by the American Republics in relation to dangers originating outside this Hemisphere is designed to protect and not to impair the inalienable right of each American State freely to choose its own form of government and economic system and to live its own social and cultural life.[42]

But the main provision of the declaration was that

> the domination or control of the political institutions of any American State by the international communist movement, extending to this Hemisphere the political system of an extracontinental power, would constitute a threat to the sovereignty and political independence of the American States, endangering the peace of America, and would call for a *meeting of consultation to consider the adoption of measures* in accor-dance with existing treaties.[43]

This was the first joint declaration by states in the Western hemisphere to the effect that communism was an ideology alien to that region and that these states had an individual and collective duty to guard against encroachments upon their system by the rival system. The declaration came close to characterizing communism (within the Western hemisphere) as a form of aggression: it referred to communism as inherently "interventionist," as a "threat to the sovereignty and political independence of the American States," as "endangering the peace of America," and, finally, as possessing an "aggressive character."

If communism was a form of aggression, then any action taken individually or collectively by the American states to prevent its appearance among them would be an exercise of the right of self-defense. As mentioned above, the U.S. representative in the Security Council specifically invoked Articles 51 and 52 of the UN Charter guaranteeing the right of states to individual, collective, and regional self-defense.[44] In this way, it has been observed, the U.S.-initiated declaration

> asserted a new principle in postwar international relations: A regional organization may designate a particular socio-political ideology as exclusively indigenous to the region and may act collectively in self-defense of ideological conformity. It should not have been presumed that such a principle could be insisted upon by *our* regional organization without also being insisted upon by *theirs*.[45]

The first test of the application of the Caracas declaration came, of course, only a few months later over the Guatemala affair. In June 1954, the U.S. Senate passed a resolution declaring:

> Whereas for many years it has been the joint policy of the United States and the other states in the Western Hemisphere to act vigorously to prevent external interference in the affairs of the nations of the Western Hemisphere; and
>
> Whereas in the recent past there has come to light strong evidence of intervention by the international Communist movement in the State of Guatemala, whereby government institutions have been infiltrated by Communist agents, weapons of war have been secretly shipped into that country, and the pattern of Communist conquest has become manifest; and
>
> Whereas on Sunday, June 20, 1954, the Soviet Government vetoed in the United Nations Security Council a resolution to refer the matter of the recent outbreak of hostilities in Guatemala to the Organization of American States: Therefore be it

Resolved by the Senate (the House of Representatives concurring),
That it is the sense of Congress that the United States should reaffirm its
support of the Caracas Declaration of Solidarity of March 28, 1954,
which is designed to prevent interference in Western Hemisphere affairs
by the international Communist movement, and take all necessary
and proper steps to support the Organization of American States in taking appropriate action to prevent any interference by the international
Communist movement in the affairs of the states of the Western
Hemisphere.[46]

Less than two years later, the USSR intervention in Hungary brought
a parallel assertion of bloc solidarity in East Europe. The Soviet equivalent of the Caracas declaration was the "Declaration on the Principles
Underlying the Development and Further Consolidation of Friendship
and Cooperation Between the Soviet Union and Other Socialist Countries," issued in October 1956 in the aftermath of the intervention.[47]
Just as the Caracas declaration had affirmed "the inalienable right of
each American State freely to choose its own form of government and
economic system and to live its own social and cultural life," the Soviet
declaration affirmed "the immutable foundation of the complete sovereignty of every socialist State" and the principles of "equality, respect
for territorial integrity, State independence . . . and non-interference in
each other's internal affairs." Furthermore, just as the concurrent resolution of the U.S. Congress found "intervention by the international
Communist movement in the State of Guatemala" to be such that "the
pattern of Communist conquest ha[d] become manifest," the Soviet
declaration alleged the existence of "the forces of black reaction and
the counter-revolution." There is yet another parallel: both powers insisted that the course of action they supported to settle the crisis in each
case was pursuant to the request of the legitimate government of the
country concerned. U.S. representative Lodge had argued in the Security Council that the government of Guatemala, having itself re-
quested assistance from the OAS, could not bypass the organization
and appeal to the United Nations,[48] while the Soviet Union alleged that
it had introduced its army into Budapest at "the request of the Hungarian Peoples' Government . . . to help the Hungarian Peoples' army
and the Hungarian authorities restore order in that city."[49]

The only difference in the approach of the powers in the above two
cases is that the Soviet Union openly admitted that it was the *Soviet*

army that had intervened in Hungary, and, although the October declaration mentioned the Warsaw Treaty, no attempt was made to portray
the intervention as an integrated or collective one carried out under that
treaty. The United States, on the other hand, categorically denied com-
plicity in the Guatemalan intervention, and all the action taken by it
was covert and through indirect channels. Yet in each case, it must be
noted, each power sought justification of its position not merely in
terms of a narrow concept of national interest, but in terms of the general interest of regional or hemispheric security: the Soviet declaration
of October referred to "the great commonwealth of socialist nations,"
while the Caracas declaration referred to the "solidarity" of the "Western Hemisphere" as a whole.

B. CUBA, THE DOMINICAN REPUBLIC, AND CZECHOSLOVAKIA

For purposes of this study, the most convenient starting point for a discussion of the Cuban crisis is the abortive U.S.-supported Bay of Pigs
invasion.[50] Cuba's attempt to bring the matter before the UN[51] met with
the same argument from the United States as had Guatemala's attempt
in 1954: The dispute could be properly dealt with only at the regional
level, in accordance with the Inter-American Treaty of Reciprocal Assistance of 1947 and the Charter of the OAS of 1948.[52] Ambassador
Lodge went on to assert that the Monroe Doctrine had in fact become
part of the Rio Treaty of 1947, so that all parties had an obligation to
take "common action to prevent the establishment of a regime dominated by international communism in the Western Hemisphere."[53]
Again, the principle of hemispheric solidarity was affirmed in 1960 at
an OAS foreign ministers' conference:

> [A]ll member states of the regional organization are under obligation to
> submit to the discipline of the inter-American system, voluntarily and
> freely agreed upon, and . . . the soundest guarantee of their sovereignty
> and their political independence stems from compliance with the provi-
> sions of the Charter of the Organization of American States.[54]

Two years later, in 1962, in Punta del Este, Uruguay, at a meeting of
the Organ of Consultation of the OAS, called at the initiative of the
U.S., it was decided that "adherence by any member of the Organiza-

tion of American States to Marxism-Leninism is incompatible with the inter-American system and the alignment of such a government with the communist bloc breaks the unity and solidarity of the hemisphere." It was also decided that "the present Government of Cuba, which has officially identified itself as a Marxist-Leninist government, is incompatible with the principles and objectives of the inter-American system." [55]

At the ninth meeting of the Organ of Consultation, held later the same year, it was decided that all OAS members should break diplomatic and consular links with Cuba and should suspend all trade (except in foodstuffs, medicines, etc.). The Organ of Consultation also declared that the OAS, as a regional system, had the right to employ coercive measures against any member—thus overriding Article 53 of the UN Charter, which provides that no enforcement measures shall be taken through regional arrangements without the authorization of the Security Council.

With regard to the alleged primacy of the obligation to settle the dispute within the OAS framework, reference may be made to Article 103 of the UN Charter, which provides that "[i]n the event of a conflict between the obligations of the Members of the United Nations under the present Charter and their obligations under any other international agreement, their obligations under the present Charter shall prevail." The U.S. representative did assure the Security Council that "there is no question, of course, of replacing the United Nations," but, he said, it should be called upon to act only as a "last resort." [56] The Soviet delegate, on the other hand, emphasized the "primary" responsibility of the Security Council. [57]

While the states of the Western hemisphere were grappling with the uncertainties created by the appearance of a communist government in their own midst, there was another event which suddenly and drastically altered the already disturbed pattern of reciprocal interbloc expectations. This was the installation of nuclear missiles by the Soviet Union on Cuban soil. President Kennedy, in an address to the nation on Oct. 22, 1962, declared that the missile sites constituted "an explicit threat to the peace and security of all the Americas, in flagrant and deliberate defiance of the Rio Pact of 1947, the traditions of this nation and hemisphere, the Joint Resolution of the 87th Congress, the Charter of the United Nations, and my own public warnings to the Soviets."[58] The joint resolution referred to by the president had been adopted by both houses of Congress in September 1962 and provided in part:

> Whereas the international communist movement has increasingly extended into Cuba its political, economic, and military sphere of influence: Now, therefore, be it
>
> *Resolved by the Senate and House of Representatives of the United States of America in Congress assembled*, That the United States is determined—
>
> (a) to prevent by whatever means may be necessary, including the use of arms, the Marxist-Leninist regime in Cuba from extending, by force or the threat of force, its aggressive or subversive activities to any part of this hemisphere;
>
> (b) to prevent in Cuba the creation or use of an externally supported military capability endangering the security of the United States; and
>
> (c) to work with the Organization of American States and with freedom-loving Cubans to support the aspirations of the Cuban people for self-determination.[59]

The president, in his October speech, also touched on the sudden nature of the Soviet move, which he saw as an attempt to change the status quo:

> But this secret, swift, and extraordinary build-up of Communist missiles—in an area well known to have a special and historical relationship to the United States and the nations of the Western Hemisphere, in violation of Soviet assurances, and in defiance of American and hemispheric policy—this sudden, clandestine decision to station strategic weapons for the first time outside of Soviet soil—is a deliberately provocative and unjustified change in the *status quo* which cannot be accepted by this country.[60]

After announcing a quarantine of Cuba, the president said that an immediate meeting of the Organ of Consultation of the OAS was being called "to consider this threat to hemispheric security and to invoke articles 6 and 8 of the Rio Treaty in support of all necessary action. The United Nations Charter allows for regional security arrangements. . . ."[61] The quarantine was ratified by the adoption of a U.S.-drafted resolution at a meeting of the OAS Organ of Consultation the next day.[62]

There was considerable debate within American legal and academic circles as to the legal basis of the Cuban quarantine. In November 1962, Abram Chayes, the legal advisor to the State Department, developed several legal grounds. The first of these rested on the "inherent right of individual or collective self-defense if an armed attack occurs," under Article 51 of the UN Charter. Chayes asserted that "[t]he quarantine action was designed to deal with an imminent threat to our security," implying that this alone was justified self-defense under Article 51.[63] Chayes, however, did not specifically invoke Article 51; in fact, after this rather elliptical reference to self-defense, he pointed out that even President Kennedy in his October 22 address did not invoke Article 51 or the right of self-defense.

It may, however, be reasonable to argue that in certain circumstances, the qualitative threat posed by the mere installation of nuclear missiles within range of the target state *should* give rise to the right of self-defense and that Article 51 is accordingly now ripe for amendment. It may further be argued that the failure of the member states of the UN to agree to an amendment of the article cannot mean that each member, at the time that it signed the charter, intended to render itself helpless while another state prepared to strike a first, and possibly lethal, blow against it. Such threats were not foreseeable in 1945. On the other hand, it has been pointed out that Soviet weaponry was sophisticated enough by 1962 to launch nuclear attacks on any part of the Western hemisphere *from Soviet soil* or from Soviet submarines. Thus, as Franck and Weisband observe, "It was never made clear how the installation of more Soviet-controlled missiles in Cuba added substantially to the aggregate threat." [64]

Other arguments have been invoked to justify the quarantine: for example, that the right of self-defense is described by Article 51 as an "inherent" right, and that this right antedates the charter, so that nothing contained in the charter—not even the restriction in Article 2(4) or, for that matter, in Article 51 itself—can limit that traditional right. The charter thus merely acknowledges this inherent right of all states, so that the above argument of Chayes in support of the quarantine did not have to rely on the charter, since the ultimate ground for the action was not the charter but that inherent right of self-defense which logically and chronologically preceded the charter. Thus, an "armed attack" is not a condition precedent for the right to become available. It may further be noted that, in any case, the reference to "armed attack" in Article 51 does not necessarily mean that the right under that article becomes available "if and only if an armed attack occurs." [65]

It is therefore not surprising that during the drafting of the Declaration on Principles of International Law Concerning Friendly Relations and Co-operation Among States in Accordance with the Charter of the United Nations,[66] the Soviet Union insisted on a highly restrictive interpretation of the right of self-defense.[67] During debate on self-defense as an exception to the prohibition on the use of force, the Soviet Union had argued in 1964, in response to the U.S. argument of self-defense just two years before, that the right was to be limited to situations in which an armed attack had occurred, in accordance with Article 51 of the charter, to the exclusion of every other kind of act, including provocation or anticipatory self-defense.[68]

Another possible justification for U.S. action concerning Cuba has been the argument that the quarantine was a "regional" measure under Article 52 of the UN Charter, that this marks the second exception to the general rule in Article 2(4),[69] and that the "authorization" of the Security Council required for regional measures under Article 53 should not be read as meaning "prior authorization" or even as "prior express authorization." A related argument, advanced by Chayes, was that the quarantine was instituted by an organization created precisely for peacekeeping purposes and whose political process is such that there is a reasonable assurance that its action will not be rashly taken. He contended that, if UN action in Korea and the Congo rested on this basis, the Cuban quarantine could also be justified along similar lines.[70] Finally, Chayes argued for a flexible approach to decision making in international law; he rightly pointed out that, because of the "withering away" of the powers of the Security Council, alternative peacekeeping institutions had to be relied on. He also observed that in international law "the membrane that separates law from politics is thin and permeable." He went on to remark that "[t]he consequence of having a system with this kind of 'play in the joints' is that we must live without the certainty, provided by more formal systems, that we have done well." [71] He acknowledged, then, that each decision or action taken at the international level "must await the riper judgment of history." [72] This position, avant-garde though it may seem coming from a State Department lawyer at a time when he was charged with the task of defending the U.S. action, confirms the proposition that law in an unstructured society cannot always provide certainty and predictability in the form of a coherent pattern of normative guidelines to govern and to predict behavior.

Other ingenious arguments were devised ex post facto in American legal circles to justify the quarantine,[73] while others argued that the quarantine was illegal under international law.[74] It is not the concern of this study, however, to classify certain actions as "legal" and to brand others as "illegal." When some arguments in favor of the quarantine were criticized, it was not with a view to suggesting that the action was "illegal" but rather, first, to point to the problem that seems to afflict all ex post facto rationalizations, namely, the apparent inability of existing law to provide a clear and unambiguous answer to the matter in question; and second, these criticisms were intended to suggest that the uncertainty is in fact aggravated by the peculiar nature of an unstructured international society. Even an ardent supporter of the quarantine acknowledged the difficulty: "It cannot be surprising that no settled law was ready at hand to deal with the situation created by the clandestine Soviet introduction of strategic missiles into Cuba in 1962. That situation was unprecedented."[75] Chayes himself asserted that "[t]he confrontation was not in the courtroom and, in a world destructible by man, a legal position was obviously not the sole ingredient of effective action. We were armed, necessarily, with something more substantial than a lawyer's brief."[76] Such a statement can only indicate the absence of controlling legal principle at the time. Finally, it is necessary to quote the following statement of the secretary of state at the time, Dean Acheson:

> I must conclude that the propriety of the Cuban quarantine is not a legal issue. The power, position and prestige of the United States had been challenged by another state; and the law simply does not deal with such questions of ultimate power.[77]

While the Cuban quarantine was the first overt use of force by the U.S. for the preservation of hemispheric solidarity, it, of course, did not amount to an outright invasion of territory, as had happened in Hungary in 1956. In 1965, however, during the Dominican crisis, the United States took overt action by landing approximately 25,000 troops in that country to protect U.S. as well as hemispheric interests. The justification for the intervention initially rested on the danger to

American lives as a result of the revolution that had overthrown the rightist military regime of the Dominican Republic on Apr. 24, 1965. President Johnson announced that the authorities in the Dominican Republic had "reported that the assistance of military personnel [was] . . . needed for that purpose [i.e., to safeguard the lives of U.S. citizens]." [78] A few days later, the president advanced additional grounds for his action, namely, "to preserve law and order" and because "people trained outside the Dominican Republic [were] seeking to gain control. Thus the legitimate aspirations of the Dominican people and most of their leaders for progress, democracy, and social justice [were] threatened and so [were] the principles of the inter-American system." [79] On May 2, the president elaborated by saying that the threat came primarily from certain leaders trained in Cuba who had tried to seize control of the revolution.[80] He then declared that "[t]he American nations cannot, must not, and will not permit the establishment of another Communist government in the Western Hemisphere." [81]

Thus came to be formulated what has since come to be known as the "Johnson Doctrine," under which the president asserted the unilateral right of the United States to intervene militarily in any state within the hemisphere which, in its opinion, was about to have a Communist government. Franck and Weisband have observed that the president "drew no distinctions among communist accession by external invasion, internal coup, or democratic election, nor among communist influence upon, infiltration into, or control of, a revolutionary movement." [82]

As for the legal basis for the action, the State Department emphasized that the urgency of the matter justified disregard of the legal procedures for formal OAS authorization prior to the action: "The United States refused to observe merely the form of legalistic procedures to the detriment of fundamental rights of a nation." [83] The State Department nevertheless did invoke the regional peacekeeping argument: "The propriety of a regional agency 'dealing with such matters relating to the maintenance of international peace and security as are appropriate for regional action' is expressly recognized by Article 52 of the Charter of the United Nations." [84] The department then articulated the U.S. view on a question that has eluded agreement between states for so long—indirect aggression:

> Participation in the Inter-American system, to be meaningful, must take into account the modern day reality that an attempt by a conspira-

torial group inspired from the outside to seize control by force can be an assault upon the independence and integrity of a state. The rights and obligations of all members of the OAS must be viewed in light of this reality.[85]

In another defense, Leonard C. Meeker, Chayes' successor as State Department legal advisor, also invoked the regional security concept, arguing that the action fell within the Punta del Este resolution of 1962 and that it was taken to ensure the necessary conditions for future OAS action.[86] Again emphasizing the urgency of the action and criticizing what he called "fundamentalist" legal arguments (such as those insisting on prior OAS authorization), Meeker declared: "It will surprise no one . . . if I say that international law which cannot deal with facts such as these, and in a way that has some hope of setting a troubled nation on the path of peace and reconstruction, is not the kind of law I believe in."[87] Referring to the Cuban missile crisis, Meeker observed:

> We recognize that, regardless of any fundamentalist view of international law, the situation then existing required us to take action to remove the threat and at the same time to avoid nuclear war. In the tradition of the common law we did not pursue some particular legal analysis or code, but instead sought a practical and satisfactory solution to a pressing problem.[88]

Meeker sought to draw an analogy between the urgency of the quarantine action and the urgency of the Dominican action, while at the same time introducing a newer and more flexible form of "play in the joints" within the international legal system than that advocated by his predecessor, Chayes, in 1962.[89]

While this hemispheric intervention had certain unique characteristics distinguishing it from previous U.S.-OAS interventions (e.g., the assertion of unilateral competence, the further refinement of the concept of indirect aggression, the overt landing of troops in another country, and the frank acknowledgment of the inadequacy of existing law to keep abreast of new political imperatives, it is possible to detect certain parallels between this action of the United States and that taken by its rival, the USSR, in Hungary almost a decade before the Dominican crisis. In both cases there was an outright invasion of the territory of another country. Both powers tried to justify their actions on the ground *inter alia* that they were pursuant to the request of the government of the receiving country. The facts in neither case were as clear and straightforward as alleged by the intervening state. One may add that in situations of internal political crisis, with different factions fighting for power, it would not be difficult to procure a request from one of them for intervention by a sympathetic big power. Both powers admitted that in each case, the revolution began as a legitimate expression of the people's grievances, but that it was later led "astray" by undesirable elements.

Thus, the Soviet Union declared that in Hungary the people were "legitimately raising the question of the need to abolish the serious shortcomings in economic development, of further raising the standard of living and of eradicating bureaucratic distortions in the State machine." It then went on to add:

> However, this just and progressive movement of the working people was soon joined by the forces of black reaction and the counter-revolution, who sought to take advantage of the dissatisfaction of part of the working people in order to undermine the foundations of the people's democratic system in Hungary and restore the old landowner-capitalist regime.[90]

Similarly, President Johnson declared for the United States that in the Dominican Republic "[t]he revolutionary movement took a tragic turn. Communist leaders, many of them trained in Cuba, seeing a chance to increase disorder, to gain a foothold, joined the revolution. They took increasing control. And what began as a popular democratic revolution, committed to democracy and social justice, very shortly moved and was taken over and really seized and placed into the hands of a band of Communist conspirators."[91]

The Soviet equivalent of the Johnson Doctrine emerged less than three years later, during the crisis in Czechoslovakia. Following the invasion of that country on Aug. 20–21, 1968, by the Warsaw Pact countries, the Soviet Union put forward several rather inept ex post facto justifications. The first Soviet announcement claimed that it had acted together with other "fraternal socialist countries" in accordance with a request by "party and state leaders of the Czechoslovak Socialist Republic" for "immediate assistance, including assistance with armed forces." It further declared:

> This decision is in complete accord with the right of states to individual and collective self-defense, as stipulated in the allied treaties concluded

between the fraternal socialist countries. It also complies with the vital interests of our countries in defending peace in Europe against the forces of militarism, aggression and revanchism.

A promise was then made that

[t]hey [the troops] will be immediately withdrawn from the C.S.R. as soon as the threat to socialism's achievements that has developed in Czechoslovakia, a threat to the security of countries in the socialist commonwealth, is eliminated and the legal authorities find that the further stay of these military units is no longer necessary.[92]

The "threat" to socialism was described as follows:

Subversive activities are being conducted by the same anti-socialist elements that in recent months have spoken out day after day against the principles of socialism in the C.S.R., against the Czechoslovak Communist Party and against friendship with the Soviet Union and other socialist countries. Behind all this counterrevolutionary activity the directing hand of imperialist circles can be perceived.[93]

In fact, the Soviet perception of indirect aggression in Czechoslovakia had been publicly declared about a month before the intervention. It appeared to be influenced by the belief that the enemy could no longer risk the consequences of a direct or what was called a "frontal" attack. The alternative form of aggression (i.e., indirect aggression) was held to include "ideological and political means combined with secret subversive measures to 'shake' socialist society, undermine the unity of the socialist countries, and thereby weaken their ability to resist direct aggression."[94] In the Soviet view, indirect aggression also involved what was called "a 'differentiated' approach to individual countries, a combination of external political and ideological sabotage with subversive activities by their agents in attempts to weaken the unity of the socialist commonwealth."[95] These statements are as vague as the corresponding American view of indirect aggression put forth by President Johnson in his statement of May 2, 1964, on the Dominican affair, and in the legal defense of it which the State Department issued thereafter. Perhaps the vagueness was in both cases intentional, so as to preserve maximum freedom of action (or counteraction). Yet the broad sweep of the language in the Soviet formulation seems to go beyond the somewhat narrower wording of the State Department's legal argument, which characterized indirect aggression as "an attempt by a conspiratorial group inspired from the outside to seize control by force."[96] However, while this referred to seizure of control "by force," President Johnson's statement, as seen above, did not contain any such limitation.

In the weeks following the Czechoslovak invasion, not only was the argument of regional self-defense repeatedly invoked, but—in a style reminiscent of previous American accusations of "international communism" engaged in the infiltration of the Western hemisphere—the Soviet Union charged that "world imperialism" was the cause of the crisis and that "[a] situation ha[d] been created where saboteurs and spies, sent in from Western countries by imperialist intelligence services, [had] been flooding Czechoslovakia. Imperialist agents [had] had a chance to transport weapons into Czechoslovakia secretly."[97] In the same way that President Johnson had blamed the troubles in the Dominican Republic on "a band of communist conspirators," so the Soviet Union alleged that the Czech crisis had been caused by "the conspiratorial activities of the counter-revolutionaries in the C.S.R."[98]

Other parallels between the Czechoslovak and Dominican crises can be detected. In each case, officials in the target state denied the intervening power's claim that it was acting on the basis of a "request" from the government of the target state. The "request" from the Dominican Republic emanated from a pro-U.S. faction of the junta, while Juan Bosch, the president-designate of the Dominican revolutionary party, insisted that the "constitutional forces are not communists and are not under communist influence. They are in control of the situation."[99] Similarly, the Czech foreign minister, Dr. Hajek, declared before the Security Council that the invasion "did not take place upon the request or demand of the Czechoslovak Government nor of any other constitutional organs of this Republic,"[100] and that "[t]he Government had the situation firmly in hand."[101]

Another parallel was what Franck and Weisband have referred to as the transformation of a politically undesirable group within the target state into the "vicarious instrument" of the rival bloc. Thus, the U.S. alleged that a "group inspired from the outside" was present during the Dominican crisis. Once a group was "inspired" by a foreign ideology, further evidence of overt action was not deemed necessary for the exercise of collective self-defense.[102] Similarly, the liberalization experiment of the Dubcek regime made it in Soviet eyes the vicarious instrument of the West.

The early signs of the evolution of what has since come to be known as the Brezhnev Doctrine culminated with the publication in *Pravda* of an article on sovereignty and the international obligations of socialist countries.[103] This article seemed to raise once again the traditional cold-war, bipolar perspective of "the division of the world into two antithetical social systems."[104] "Every person," Lenin is quoted as saying, "must take this, our, side or the other side. All attempts to avoid taking sides end in failure and disgrace."[105] The argument was that even "liberalizing" trends in a socialist state, such as those which led to the Czech crisis, would necessarily lead to the restoration of capitalism.[106]

The *Pravda* article also restated the concept of regional solidarity in terms of the maxim of the Marxist dialectic that "every phenomenon [must] be examined in terms of both its specific nature and its overall connection with other phenomena and processes." Thus, every Communist party had a dual duty, one to its own people and one to the entire communist movement of the socialist bloc. General Secretary Brezhnev himself later reasserted the concept of regional intervention for the preservation of "the security of the socialist commonwealth as a whole."[107] While betrayal of bloc solidarity was theoretically a matter for collective determination, it is obvious that in situations in which one nation is the clear leader of the bloc, its interpretation of what constituted an infringement would be crucial for the outcome, if not decisive.

The article further asserted the disturbing proposition that, while every socialist nation had the right to self-determination, it was not competent to decide when or in what ways the exercise of that right was detrimental to its own interests; *that* was a matter for community decision.[108] It also declared that when a threat to socialist solidarity was perceived, the community had an international "duty" to neutralize it "by using any means that are necessary."[109] Finally, it dismissed, in a style reminiscent of the U.S. State Department's rejection of "fundamentalist" legal arguments during the Cuban and Dominican crises, the "legalistic considerations" of "those who speak of the 'illegality' of the allied socialist countries' actions in Czechoslovakia," and it declared that the socialist states could not "remain idle in the name of abstract sovereignty while the country was endangered by antisocialist degeneration."[110]

The point concerning de facto leadership within the bloc appears to be the most important one. This is because without it the action would, of course, not have been possible, and also because the successful assertion of bloc leadership in such an extreme form reveals something more than the mere location of the center of power in that region: It is an example of the emergent law of interbloc reciprocity, in which one nation has emerged with overwhelming power within each of the two rival blocs, and to that extent it has been easier for the two powers to come to a tolerable *modus vivendi* than had there been, within each bloc, several equally powerful states vying for leadership *inter se*. This reciprocal acceptance of de facto bloc leadership has introduced the desired minimum of certainty in interbloc expectations. It has further simplified the task of impact prediction when extraterritorial force is used in a crisis situation. The Czechoslovak operation would not have been mounted had its impact on rival bloc leadership been uncertain or unpredictable, or, if predictable, it had pointed to a high risk of war with the West. In fact, the impact of the invasion on the West *was* predictable and, as subsequent events showed, it was accurately assessed.

As to the probable consequences, the Soviet Union saw the reformist tendencies of the Dubcek regime as involving a threat to its own leadership of the socialist region, as well as signaling a reorientation of Czechoslovak policy in favor of West Germany, which, it was feared, would in turn weaken the military and strategic position of the Warsaw Pact vis-à-vis NATO.[111] It was pointed out in chapter II that if either party miscalculates the impact of its actions on either the world at large or, more specifically, on the rival bloc, a dispute may take a course unforeseen by one or both parties. The Cuban missile crisis showed a clear miscalculation of this kind by the Soviet Union.[112] There was, apparently, no such grave miscalculation by it over Czechoslovakia. It can thus be seen that reciprocity fosters impact predictability in trouble situations (when it is most needed).

As the Hungarian and Korean crises showed,[113] there is also a link between impact and proportionality of force. By way of reminder, the superpowers' conduct in these two crises implied that the severity of countermeasures tends to be proportional to the nature of the perceived threat, the location of the threat, and, most important, the probable consequences if no action were taken to neutralize the threat and the impact that the action would have on potential adversaries. It must again be emphasized that none of these considerations can be compartmentalized into neat, watertight categories. For example, the nature of the threat is, quite obviously, better understood if its probable consequences are first calculated, and the probable impact of actions on potential adversaries cannot be calculated without a sober evaluation of what measures are necessary to deal with the threat, how severe the measures are to be, the location of the area, the presence or absence of rival interests in that area, etc. Thus, the crisis over the Cuban missiles centered not on the disruption of the overall East-West power balance but on the disruption of that balance in an area so close to the United States and within the Western hemisphere. On the other hand, during the Hungarian crisis, as was argued elsewhere, the fact that the target area fell within an existing sphere of influence permitted greater freedom of action for the intervening state. The same applied to the American intervention in the Dominican Republic and to the Soviet intervention in Czechoslovakia. The risks of adverse impact on the rival power were correspondingly minimal in each case.[114]

By thus analyzing the behavior of the powers in trouble situations and the doctrinal justifications advanced in each instance, it is possible to extrapolate a number of abstract rules that seem to be accepted by the two powers on the basis of reciprocity and that provide the minimum conditions necessary for superpower coexistence.

C. THE EMERGING LAW OF INTERBLOC RECIPROCITY

The following rules for the conduct of the superpowers and the member states of their blocs may be abstracted through the behaviorist approach to the trouble situations examined above:[115]

(1) Bloc or regional solidarity is to be respected, as is the principle of mutual noninterference in bloc affairs.

(2) A breach of bloc solidarity, whether perceived as threatened or caused by external intervention or by a local group acting with or without external help, is a matter for bloc determination. In real terms this, of course, requires recognition that it is the *leader* of the bloc that decides whether or not there has been or is likely to be a deviation from bloc solidarity, and if so, whether the threat requires countermeasures. The Hungarian and Dominican interventions show that the intervening power asserts a unilateral competence to determine threats to regional or hemispheric solidarity. The Hungarian intervention and the Cuban

quarantine suggest that the natural extension of this competence is the further competence to take unilateral countermeasures whenever necessary. Thus, in 1956, the USSR did not even bother to seriously portray its intervention in Hungary as a collective action. Similarly, the Cuban quarantine was initiated before any OAS meeting was convened, and NATO allies were informed only afterward, while the UN was informed even later. The same kind of after-the-fact approval was sought from the OAS in the Dominican intervention. Finally, the competence to determine the existence of the threat and to decide whether to take countermeasures necessarily includes a competence to determine the nature, quality, and severity of the countermeasures.

(3) The severity of the countermeasures is proportional to the nature of the threat and the potential impact on rival parties. The Korean, Hungarian, and Cuban crises all illustrate this. The Cuban incident shows how miscalculation by one party of the impact of its actions on its rival may suddenly and unexpectedly create a crisis. The quarantine also serves as a good illustration of the principle of proportionality vis-à-vis the perceived threat. There was available to the United States a wide range of options against Cuba, with varying degrees of severity, from direct air strikes against the missile sites to outright invasion.[116] Attorney General Robert Kennedy wrote: "We were not going to misjudge, or miscalculate, or challenge the other side needlessly, or precipitously push our adversaries into a course of action that was not intended or anticipated."[117]

Although the Soviet Union had miscalculated the impact of its action on its rival, the United States was still concerned with the impact of its counteraction. As stated previously, the problem of impact prediction cannot be considered without taking into account the severity or proportionality of force used. Leonard Meeker, at the time the State Department's deputy legal adviser, declared in 1963 that "[t]he quarantine, though involving ultimately a resort to force if such should be necessary to stop ships that might be carrying offensive weapons, was a limited measure, carefully proportioned to the needs of the situation."[118]

Various military, diplomatic, economic or ideological strategies may thus be used, and with varying degrees of emphasis, depending on the nature of the dispute. As McDougal has observed, these strategies can be seen to be operating as an unorganized or informal sanctioning machinery "with each participant [state] reacting unilaterally to other participants in a process of reciprocity and counter-reciprocity, including, with varying degrees of explicitness, both offers of rewards and inducements and threats of reprisals and retaliations."[119]

No mathematical formula can be provided for the precise linkages between the various policy considerations regarding the choice of strategy, impact prediction, and proportionality. Each case depends on its particular facts and circumstances. Thus, in the Cuban case, no direct force was used to challenge the Soviet Union, yet a firm intention to use force was obvious. At the same time, it provided time for the Soviet Union to withdraw, and, of course, it also provided an opportunity for resolving the dispute peacefully through bilateral negotiations.

(4) Regionalism has precedence over the UN Charter provisions. In all the interventions that have been discussed, both powers vigorously argued that the matter was best settled at the regional level, mainly because of the inability of existing law to cope with new political imperatives and because of the impotence of the Security Council in such matters. The powers on separate occasions took enforcement action on a regional basis, in disregard of Articles 53 and 103 of the charter,[120]— for example, the OAS sanctions against Cuba. A corollary to the primacy of collective regional peacekeeping over all other international obligations is the denial of competence to individual nations to decide for themselves in what ways they may be threatening regional solidarity. Thus, the range of permitted leeway within the norms of bloc solidarity is a matter of bloc rather than individual competence. This idea appeared to be behind President Ford's justification of U.S. assistance to forces opposed to the government of President Allende of Chile: "The effort that was made in this case was to help and assist the preservation of opposition newspapers and electronic media and to preserve opposition political parties. I think this is in the best interest of the people of Chile, and certainly in our best interest."[121] President Ford also reaffirmed that in matters seen to endanger national security, legal provisions may not be strictly controlling when the state against which the action is directed is not competent to decide for itself what is in its best interest. This is illustrated in the following exchange between the president and the press:

> *Q.* Under what international law do we have a right to attempt to destabilize the constitutionally elected government of another country, and does the Soviet Union have a similar right to try to destabilize the Government of Canada, for example, or the United States?
> *President Ford:* I am not going to pass judgment on whether it is per-

mitted or authorized under international law. It is a recognized fact that, historically as well as presently, such actions are taken in the best interest of the countries involved.[122]

(5) Whenever bloc intervention takes place for the preservation of intrabloc solidarity, there is to be no active resistance from the rival bloc. This, however, is contingent upon careful impact prediction and proper respect for the principle of proportionality, as explained above. At the risk of repetition, it should be noted that particular caution is required with action in overlapping zones of influence; the need to neutralize the threat requires a careful balance against rival interests. The Cuban missile crisis was the clearest illustration of conflict in a zone of overlapping interests. Korea was another.

(6) The members of each bloc have the right of individual and collective self-defense against indirect aggression for the preservation of the ideological purity of their region. What is "indirect aggression" is in each case to be left to the subjective evaluation of the intervening state. It is the latter aspect of the rule that has generated so much debate and disagreement between the two powers. In all its interventions, the Soviet Union has alleged, with an almost ritualistic monotony, that its action was caused by the "imperialists" or the "counterrevolutionaries" or the "enemies of the working class," etc. On the other hand, the United States has blamed its interventions on "international communism" or "groups inspired by an alien [communist] ideology" or "bands of communist conspirators," etc. Each side has regarded as aggression the influence of the rival ideology within its bloc. A particularly poignant example of the excesses that can be committed when such evaluations are made at purely subjective levels was the Czechoslovakian invasion. Not only was there no danger of a capitalist takeover, but members of the Dubcek government repeatedly affirmed that the situation was under control. However, in accordance with the rules of bloc intervention, that government had no competence to determine threats to its own security.

The difficulty with allowing individual states to assert unilateral competence to make factual determinations was also illustrated during the Dominican crisis. It appears that even the U.S. ambassador to the UN, Adlai Stevenson, disagreed with the president's perception of the facts and was opposed to the intervention. He did not believe that the movement to restore Juan Bosch was dominated by Communists. Therefore, according to his biographer, Richard J. Walton, in order to defend U.S. action, Stevenson had to use "his considerable lawyer's skill to obfuscate the situation" by "[arguing] endlessly that the question was not really a UN matter, but one for the OAS." [123] In doing so, Walton alleges, "Stevenson . . . had to repeat endlessly statements he knew not to be true and justifications he believed indefensible." [124]

Nevertheless, the clear conclusion from the cases of extraterritorial superpower intervention is that "[a] superpower's allowed perimeter of self-interest and self-defense includes the whole of its 'region.' Within that region a superpower's perceptions are fact and its self-interest is law." [125]

Within that context, however, one can observe a certain asymmetry between the Johnson and Brezhnev doctrines, involving a difference between what they would keep out of their respective spheres of influence. While the Brezhnev Doctrine would exclude everything but a small range of conformist Communist regimes, its American counterpart would keep out only a narrow range of communist doctrines.

(7) Another interbloc norm concerns the preservation of the status quo through the renunciation of nuclear war and the maintenance of a rough equivalence in conventional and nuclear weapons. At the heart of considerations about proportionality of forcible countermeasures and impact prediction lies the awareness of each side that neither can risk an open military war with the other because the risks and losses arising from even a conventional war would be tremendous, and those arising from a nuclear war would be simply unacceptable. This is what McWhinney would describe as the principle of "nuclear age Due Process," [126] and its rationale stems not only from an effective mutual deterrence factor, but also from the fear that even a conventional war could easily escalate into a nuclear war.

The reader need hardly be reminded that the installation of nuclear missiles by the Soviet Union in Cuba in 1962 was seen by the United States as upsetting the nuclear balance and giving an advantage to one side. During the ensuing negotiations, the Soviet Union made the removal of the missiles conditional upon the removal of NATO missiles from Turkey and Italy as well as a U.S. guarantee against any future attack on Cuba. [127] In return for the removal of the Cuban missiles, President Kennedy offered the lifting of the quarantine and a pledge of nonaggression against Cuba,[128] but he made no mention of the missiles in Turkey. In accepting the U.S. proposal, Khrushchev also refrained from insisting on the prior removal of the missiles from Turkey. This could only suggest that the bases in Turkey and elsewhere in Europe were already part of the political and military status quo, which, as Lipson points out, had after all already been tacitly accepted by the Soviet Union. Yet while this status quo had to be respected, the installation of missiles in Cuba had the effect of creating a sudden and unilateral military advantage, thus *disrupting* the status quo. They therefore had to be removed. Thus, to extend an analogy used by Lipson, the patient (Cuba) was cured of pneumonia (the missile installations) but continued to suffer from a cold (its Communist government).[129] Since the latter malady had been contracted during the cold-war era, and since one previous attempt to cure it had failed, it had become part of the status quo and had to be tolerated.

(8) Individual member states of the existing blocs cannot voluntarily withdraw their membership or escape bloc jurisdiction over internal or external policies of theirs that are deemed to affect bloc solidarity. For example, the Soviet Union has exerted sustained pressure on Poland over the latter's labor crises. Not only has the Soviet Union charged "counter-revolution, supported by foreign imperialist centers of subversion," but it has publicly reminded Poland of its "enormous responsibility for the common interests of the socialist commonwealth."[130] This appears to indicate that Soviet bloc solidarity, in the name of socialist internationalism, is far from dead and buried, despite the specific and fairly detailed provisions of the Helsinki Final Act. This is consonant with the fact that, as indicated in chapter I, the Soviet concept of peaceful coexistence after the Helsinki Act has increasingly emphasized relations between states having *different* political and economic systems, as well as a strategy for preventing any change in the status quo to the detriment of socialism.[131] Another ground for bloc jurisdiction over Poland could well be the Treaty of Friendship, Cooperation, and Mutual Assistance between the USSR and the Polish People's Republic, concluded on Apr. 8, 1965. This treaty has been declared to be "based on the principles of socialist internationalism."[132]

Just as in the case of Soviet tolerance of U.S. missiles in Turkey and U.S. tolerance of Soviet actions in Czechoslovakia, there are indications that a post-Helsinki application of the Brezhnev Doctrine in Poland would not provoke any serious U.S. reaction that would be unexpected by or unacceptable to the Soviet Union. Even the Reagan administration, which has vigorously asserted the doctine of "linkage" between its relations with the Soviet Union and Soviet conduct abroad, appears to have ruled out a military response to a Soviet invasion of Poland. Former Secretary of State Haig declared that while the "price and consequences [of an invasion] would be grave and long lasting," he "would not envisage a military reaction [from the United States] to such an outcome." [133]

While U.S. policies have continued to be generally supportive of greater autonomy in Eastern Europe, such policies have not actively challenged the status quo in that area. The so-called "Sonnenfeldt doctrine" must be examined against this background. Former State Department counselor Helmut C. Sonnenfeldt, being of the opinion that the relationship between the USSR and Eastern Europe was based solely on force and was therefore "unnatural," has urged that U.S. policy "strive for an evolution that makes the relationship . . . an organic one" and also seek for Eastern Europe "a more autonomous existence within the context of a strong Soviet geopolitical influence." Similarly, as this book went to press, the Reagan Administration commenced large-scale land and sea exercises with Honduras and El Salvador, and, in October 1983, landed troops in Grenada. While it was not possible to analyze these events, it can be predicted that the Soviet Union will show a parallel acceptance of a U.S. geopolitical presence in the Caribbean and Central America by not effectively challenging these operations. [134]

3

CASE STUDIES IN EXTRAHEMISPHERIC INTERVENTION

The foregoing rules appear to be clearly discernible with regard to superpower conduct in pre-existing zones of influence, and they may be said to provide a fair degree of certainty and predictability of future superpower conduct in those areas. The questions that now arise are: To what extent can these norms assist in understanding superpower conduct in zones outside their immediate regional or hemispheric interests? What norms would govern an extrahemispheric intervention (i.e., in zones outside the superpowers' traditional spheres of influence)? There are no easy answers to these questions. Norms to guide conduct in areas outside established spheres of influence appear to be still in the process of crystallization. This process is again best studied via the trouble-situation method.

A. ANGOLA AND ZAIRE

The first clear example of a trouble situation involving an overt superpower intervention in an area outside its traditional sphere of influence was the Soviet-Cuban intervention in Angola in 1976, which was prima facie a unilateral extension of the principle of intrabloc intervention. Its subsequent reassertion in Afghanistan suggests that the concept of spheres of interest is expanding rather than contracting. The six guidelines proposed in chapter II concerning the actual and perceived causes of the crisis, the probable consequences, the countermeasures thought necessary, impact prediction, and assessment of actual impact may be employed here to evaluate the Soviet-Cuban action.

Angola had long ago begun emerging as a potential zone of Soviet interest and influence because of strong ideological affinities between Moscow and the leadership of one of the major nationalist movements, the Popular Movement for the Liberation of Angola, or MPLA, to which the USSR had given military and other assistance for over a decade during its fight against Portuguese rule. After the collapse of that rule and the outbreak of civil war, a threat was seen to this long-term political commitment, and the perceived cause of this threat was Western (British, U.S., and South African) and Chinese assistance to the two rival parties, including the actual entry of South African troops into southern Angola.[135]

Brezhnev sought to justify the intervention on the ground that, "barely constituted, this progressive state [Angola] became an object of foreign intervention, the handiwork of imperialism and the South African racists . . ."[136] It was further charged that "[t]he USA began intensively to implant its agents in the country and to encourage the establishment of splinter and pseudo-patriotic outfits . . ." and that U.S. funds were being used to recruit foreign mercenaries to fight against the MPLA.[137] Again, Soviet aid was said to have been given "at the request of the legitimate government of the People's Republic of Angola and in complete accord with the well-known decisions on decolonisation taken by the United Nations and the Organisation of African Unity." [138]

Among the probable consequences forecast by Moscow must have been the loss of a promising zone of influence in a vast, rich, and strategically located country just south of Zaire, a staunch U.S. ally. This was, of course, a rather speculative danger, which would arise only in the future; it is difficult to see that there was any tangible threat to *existing* Soviet interests. This, however, is to be expected, since Angola was not within a pre-established Soviet sphere of influence. Nevertheless, a decision was taken to intervene militarily—a move that on the face of it ignored the well-known rules of bloc intervention and reciprocity. Yet the Soviet action may not appear to be so surprising if the link between proportionality and impact prediction in this case is explored. One factor that may shed some light on the move is the element of impact prediction. Considerable reliance must have been placed on the hope for a favorable impact of the action within the Organization of African Unity (OAU) and the UN. [139] One ground for such hope was undoubtedly that more states had by that time recognized the MPLA than the other two movements. The possibilities of adverse reaction from these two potential adversaries having been assessed as minimal, the other main party whose reaction had to be taken into account was the United States. The latter had no pre-established vital interests in that area; furthermore, it had only recently emerged from the trauma of Vietnam, and public and congressional opinion was firmly against another foreign interventionary war. The Senate, in fact, voted to bar funds for U.S. involvement. [140]

Weighing all these considerations and balancing the possible risks and advantages, a rather drastic form of intervention was chosen by the Soviet Union. As events turned out, its assessments were substantially accurate, for not only was its action widely supported within the OAU, but the South African troops withdrew, the MPLA took firm control, and the United States did no more than issue verbal condemnations. [141] One commentator has suggested that the decision to use Cuban instead of Soviet troops may have been influenced by a fear on the part of the USSR that the United States might have reacted more firmly if Soviet troops had been used.[142] However, one effect of a Soviet foothold in Angola was to spur the Ford, Carter, and Reagan administrations to develop a more active foreign policy in Africa.[143] Not only did this result in a renewed and successful attempt to resolve the Rhodesian question, but the Reagan administration has been actively pursuing negotiations with South Africa to resolve the Namibian question,[144] and in September 1983 it moved decisively, in cooperation with France, to end what was seen to be a Soviet-Libyan inspired rebellion in Chad.

Anxiety over Soviet influence in Angola also apparently made the Carter administration more sensitive to developments in Zaire, a traditional ally of the United States. Troubles in the Shaba province of Zaire resulted in a request for U.S. military assistance from President Mobutu Sese Seko. The request was denied, but $15 million worth of "nonlethal" aid was supplied. This could only have been in accordance with the U.S. government's evaluation of the nature of the perceived threat, the probable consequences, an impact prediction, etc. As to the nature of the threat, U.S. intelligence reports convinced the administration that, contrary to President Mobutu's claims, Angolan, Cuban, and Soviet troops were not directly involved.[145] Also relevant was the fact that another major Western power, France, as well as Belgium, together with a firm French ally, Morocco, were already providing military assistance to the Zairois government. It must therefore have appeared that, in view of the size of the rebellion and the continuing assistance from other friendly governments, the rebellion would eventually peter out—a forecast which events later bore out. The experience with the Angolan problem would have made impact prediction almost exclusively a question of the administration's assessment of congressional reaction to assistance in Zaire. While indications were that military assistance would probably not have been approved, the question was never raised because nonmilitary assistance was thought to be sufficient, in view of the nature of the threat and the relative insignificance of Zaire to U.S. interests.

B. AFGHANISTAN

The rules of impact prediction, proportionality, etc. can also be used to analyze the Soviet intervention in Afghanistan in December 1979. In some respects, this Soviet thrust took the world by surprise. It therefore appeared to have an even more destabilizing potential for the slow and tortuous evolution of the unwritten norms regulating superpower conduct. It could even have strengthened the belief of some that the USSR was nothing more than a "world revolutionary state, denying the possibilities of coexistence, committed to unrelenting ideological warfare, powered by a messianic drive for world mastery." [146] Apart from this, and considering the matter from a purely pragmatic angle, the Soviet Union could, arguably, not have wanted to risk another world political outcry and to commit scarce resources in Afghanistan over and above its risks and commitments in Angola and Ethiopia. Furthermore, in September 1979, there had been a strong U.S. reaction against the Soviet Union over the alleged presence of a Soviet combat brigade in Cuba. [147] In addition to the public condemnations, the United States increased its intelligence surveillance of Cuba, resumed reconnaissance flights over it, and established a permanent Caribbean Contingency Joint Task Force in Key West, Florida, to deal with future Soviet or Cuban threats anywhere in the Caribbean basin. [148]

In retrospect, however, the invasion of Afghanistan was not entirely unpredictable. It was the product of a vast complex of factors and considerations that make the explanation that the USSR was motivated by a "messianic drive for world mastery" too simplistic, if not misleading. Soviet interest in Afghanistan antedates its interest not only in Angola and the horn of Africa, but even in Eastern Europe. Ever since Persia (now Iran) was forced to yield Transcaucasia to Russia after its (Persia's) defeat in the Russo-Persian War of 1826–28, it became the objective of the Russian tsars to extend Russian influence in this region in the direction of Persia, and in Central Asia in the direction of Afghanistan. Both areas became scenes of intense competition between the British and Russian empires throughout the nineteenth century, with Russia insisting that they belonged to its security zone. [149] This view prevailed even after the Revolution of 1917, with the Soviets maintaining contacts with Afghan socialists as well as good relations with the anti-British monarch of Afghanistan, King Amanullah (1919–29). This was backed with financial subsidies in 1919 and other forms of economic as well as military aid. [150]

The intensity of Soviet interest grew dramatically after World War II, with massive Soviet economic and military aid being granted to the Daoud regime, which came to power after a coup in September 1953.[151] After a ten-year rule, Daoud resigned, but he returned to power after another coup in July 1973, whereupon the monarchy was abolished and the Republic of Afghanistan was proclaimed. In April 1978 yet another coup occurred, in which Daoud, a friend and ally of the Soviet Union, was ousted and killed. The new rulers were the Khalq or People's Party, a Marxist group which espoused an openly revolutionary ideology and publicly associated itself with the "international socialist movement."[152] Not surprisingly, the Soviet Union carefully nurtured the new relationship by concluding more than thirty aid agreements with Afghanistan. Finally, in December 1978, the Soviet-Afghan Treaty of Friendship and Cooperation was signed in Moscow.

The Khalq party, however, was torn by internal rivalry between two factions, one led by Taraki and Amin and the other by Karmal. The Taraki-Amin faction, which temporarily had the upper hand in the government, was able to exile most members of the Karmal faction (who sought refuge in Eastern Europe).[153] In the meantime, Soviet support to the revolutionary regime grew in personnel and materiel as the Amin regime met more and more opposition from the local Muslim population, which was historically and culturally unprepared for rapid modernization under a new ideology. In the turmoil, Taraki, Moscow's favored politician, was killed by Amin. By the fall of 1979, the Soviet presence in Afghanistan was already quite substantial, as it became drawn into various efforts to stabilize the situation.

By this time, however, opponents of the revolutionary regime had begun to receive increasing covert assistance from Pakistan and China, and they inflicted heavy casualties on the Soviets. The major Soviet concern became that of preventing any further deterioration, so that Pakistan, Iran, and possibly Saudi Arabia would not have a chance to install a Muslim-governed anticommunist and anti-Soviet Islamic republic in Afghanistan, of the kind that had just appeared in Iran. In this situation, Soviet action was influenced by that country's own perception of the cause of the crisis, its estimate as to the probable consequences of the crisis if left unchecked, the kind of countermeasures thought necessary to remedy the situation, and their impact on rival parties, particularly the United States.

Unlike Angola, Afghanistan has an 800-mile common border with

Russia. Before the crisis, Afghanistan had been a neutral-to-friendly buffer state, and later it even showed promise as a future Soviet satellite within what the Soviets considered to be their geostrategic "arc." Now there was the grim prospect of an Islamic republic, spurred on by the Islamic awakening in Iran, right on the borders of three Soviet Central Asian republics with large Muslim populations, namely, Uzbekistan, Turkmenia, and Tadzhikistan. Not only would this have caused instability on Soviet borders, but it also presented the danger of what one commentator has called the "spillover effects of Islamic fundamentalism." [154] This scenario would further have entailed the loss or abandonment of the already considerable Soviet commitments of resources to the country, not to mention the embarrassment it would have caused for the Soviet Union if it had to explain its inaction to other socialist countries with which it had treaties of friendship.

A quick, sudden, and massive Soviet invasion—of the kind that actually occurred in December 1979—was undoubtedly thought of as the most effective countermeasure that would forestall the above consequences and put an end to the turmoil once and for all. The Soviets would in return regain their strategic foothold in the region, eliminate a buffer state between the USSR and Pakistan, neutralize the Muslim threat on its borders, and possibly even move closer to the warm-water ports and oil wealth of the Gulf states, as well as the vital sea lanes through which oil is shipped to the West, particularly the Strait of Hormuz.

As for impact prediction, the Soviets may well have perceived their action as defensive, designed to protect a recognized and pre-existing interest which had historically grown from strength to strength without any effective outside challenge. To that extent, the problem of impact prediction may have been seen as relatively uncomplicated. The USSR's chief rival, the United States, did not in fact have any vested interests in Afghanistan. Afghanistan had not joined the anti-Soviet alliance of CENTO (Central Treaty Organization), largely because the United States did not see Afghanistan as being within the realm of Western security, even though Iran was a member. What little presence the United States did have in Afghanistan was drastically reduced following the kidnapping and subsequent killing of the U.S. ambassador, Adolph Dubs, in February 1979. After an apparently ill-managed Soviet-directed assault on the kidnappers, all U.S. programs were terminated. In late July, about 100 U.S. diplomatic personnel were evacuated, leaving behind only a skeleton staff at the embassy in Kabul.[155] Furthermore, at the time of the intervention, the United States was preoccupied with the hostage crisis in Iran, just as at the time of the Hungarian intervention in 1956 the West was preoccupied with the Suez crisis. On the other hand, the hostage crisis and the deployment by the United States of several aircraft carriers and other warships in the area may have raised a fear on the part of the Soviet Union of U.S. intervention in Iran.[156]

There was, therefore, a large combination of factors which the USSR must have carefully weighed before finally deciding to intervene. The U.S. reaction to the intervention was intense but ultimately ineffective. An effort to bring about a boycott of the Olympic games being held in Moscow fell short of its desired objective, and the much publicized grain embargo imposed by the Carter administration was lifted by the Reagan administration.[157] The increased economic and military aid to Pakistan, as well as the declaration by the United States that it would consider the sale of offensive weapons to China for the first time, may, in time, prove to be important signals to the USSR, especially if they are backed up by other U.S. measures.

While the Soviet calculation of impact on the United States was not altogether incorrect, calculation of the impact of its intervention on the local population was much wider off the mark. Guerrilla activity has intensified, and the Soviet Union, far from being able to withdraw its troops and leave behind a trusted regime in control, has been forced to commit more troops, even after the invasion was completed.[158] The USSR has sought to legitimize this by reference to the Soviet-Afghan Treaty of 1978 and to a "request" from the "DRA [Democratic Republic of Afghanistan] leadership," the same kind of after-the-fact justifications which were offered to legitimize the original intervention of December 1979.[159]

What emerges from the foregoing is not simply that there are superpower competition and intervention beyond their classical "spheres of influence." It is also apparent that such intervention is a product of complex factors which, when analyzed and categorized, yield certain modes and patterns of superpower behavior that are not as unpredictable as individual acts of intervention may seem when considered in isolation.

It is in zones at the periphery of or outside the traditional spheres of influence that superpower activity will grow in importance. Indeed, on the theory that intrabloc behavior is reasonably settled and tolerable, conduct *outside* the blocs may even surpass intrabloc conduct in importance, as each power gropes its way toward some reasonably predictable order of conduct from the other in these areas. At this stage, one can identify only some of the important variables that may affect such future conduct: a prolonged Soviet preoccupation with Afghanistan; the possible need to cope with increasing Pakistani, Chinese, and perhaps American support to the Muslim rebels; Soviet involvement in the Polish crisis; the emerging U.S.-Chinese rapprochement; Soviet-Cuban commitments in Africa; U.S. commitments in Southern Africa, the Persian Gulf, and the Middle East (especially after the Sadat assassination and the political ferment in the region following the Israeli invasion of Lebanon); as well as the pockets of anti-U.S. nationalism in the Caribbean and Central America. Whether or how these variables will affect a new order of superpower coexistence, only time will tell. The absence of such an order today, however, together with the fundamental philosophical differences between the two sides, will have an important bearing on the 1974 UN General Assembly code on aggression.

4

REFLECTIONS ON THE GENERAL ASSEMBLY DEFINITION

OF 1974

This study has focused on two major categories of difficulties in the legal regulation of international force. These two categories, the definitional and the doctrinal, represent two complementary approaches to the study of law. Previous chapters in this book have discussed why the international lawyer should not be bound to utilize any one approach to the exclusion of all others in studying the evolution and development of international law. It was suggested that no single approach is adequate for a meaningful understanding of the dynamics of conflict and conflict management in international society. Thus, it is not enough merely to examine the body of abstract rules in, say, the UN Charter or the 1974 code on aggression to identify guidelines for effective long-term regulation of international force through law. The code of 1974 by itself offers no panacea. That it is not a perfect definition but rather contains numerous flaws and ambiguities is admitted even by delegates who were closely involved in its drafting. These defects arise out of two conditions: first, that the definition was a product of political compromise, necessitating the inclusion of verbal formulae which, though acceptable to a politician, are a nightmare for a lawyer; and second—a difficulty inherent in all abstract formulations—because of the generality of its content, it cannot always provide clear guidelines in concrete trouble situations, a problem compounded by the tendency to become rigidified and thus irrelevant to current conditions.

For these reasons, this chapter undertook to examine more than just the abstract rules of international law governing aggression. It constructed a Soviet-American perspective of the problems that arose over the articulation of those rules. It adopted a behaviorist approach to the study of the problem, in the belief that this is indispensable for an evaluation of the degree to which the study of abstract rules alone accurately reflects the realities of superpower conduct and of the degree to which this body of rules is capable of maintaining a stable world order. The behaviorist approach led to the abstraction of norms that had an empirical foundation in the actual conduct of the two superpowers in concrete trouble situations. This same approach now leads to the following comments on the 1974 code on aggression:

(1) The definition deals almost entirely with the more overt forms of *armed* aggression.[160] Article 3 enumerates seven acts which would qualify as aggression, but none of them refers either to indirect aggression or to threats of force. The interventions discussed in the previous section showed that most were in response to the more indirect forms of aggression, and the Cuban missiles constituted, in the eyes of the U.S. government, a *threat* to the peace of the region. It will be recalled that during the Dominican crisis the mere existence of a group that was "inspired" by an "alien" ideology was per se deemed an aggression giving rise to the right of self-defense. Soviet views of aggression in Hungary and Czechoslovakia were at least as elastic as the American. That ideological differences make the definition of indirect aggression difficult cannot detract from the fact that the 1974 definition does contain this significant lacuna, whereby such questions are left to auto-interpretation by individual powers.

(2) The definition does not come to grips with the problem of uni-

lateralism—the tendency of bloc leaders to make assertions of their competence to determine threats to regional security, the type of countermeasures to be taken, and, indeed, the ways in which the state against which the measures are taken may be threatening their own security. It is not surprising that the superpowers went along with the idea in Articles 2, 4, and 6 of the definition, which confirm and reconfirm the "primary" responsibility of the Security Council under the UN Charter to maintain international peace and security, since both countries have veto powers over the Council's resolutions. The effect is that only self-restraint by the two powers and concern for the impact of their actions (which may include wariness about world reaction as well as the reaction of the rival power) exercise a moderating influence on unilateralism. Other than such restraints—which are outside the 1974 definition—there are no effective checks on the superpowers' claims of unilateral competence.

(3) The definition makes no reference to the nature, quality, or intensity—in short, the proportionality—of the countermeasures taken during any given crisis. During the drafting stages of Article 3, the Soviet Union strongly opposed any reference to proportionality as an indicator of aggression, and the definition therefore is silent on the subject. Again, the most important checks on severity of force come from outside the definition—e.g., the conventions of impact prediction.

(4) The definition does not resolve (or even attempt to resolve) the inherent tension between regionalism and globalism. Almost all of the superpower interventions or countermeasures to preserve bloc or hemispheric solidarity were ostensibly taken under regional arrangements that were deemed to have primacy over charter obligations. As explained above, such actions were taken in disregard of Articles 53 and 103 of the UN Charter. The intervening states argued that regional arrangements were in fact permitted by the charter. Even one of the extrahemispheric interventions, in Afghanistan, was said to be in accordance with the charter.[161] There is nothing in the 1974 definition that could deter such arguments. Indeed, both the fourth paragraph of the definition's preamble and Article 6, by affirming that nothing contained in the definition affects the scope or meaning of the provisions of the UN Charter, open the way for just such arguments (because Articles 53 and 103 of the charter have been interpreted so loosely), thus again showing that there was no real advance in 1974 in reconciling the re-

gional and global approaches to peacekeeping, so that they might become two complementary rather than antagonistic systems of maintaining world peace.[162]

(5) The language of the definition is highly general and ambiguous and contains certain rather obvious escape clauses. For example, Article 7 permits people fighting for "self-determination, freedom and independence" from "colonial and racist regimes or other forms of alien domination" to seek and receive "support" from other nations. "Alien domination" is undefined, and, as seen previously, "self-determination" has received conflicting interpretations; nor is it clear what kind of "support" is permissible and what is impermissible. The example of Angola illustrates these difficulties, especially since the question of Soviet-Cuban action there arose well *after* the definition had been adopted by the General Assembly, so that the countries involved must be presumed to have been fully aware of the legal implications of their actions in light of the 1974 definition. During the drafting stage, Western nations sought to prevent inclusion of an explicit right to use force. Even now, the U.S. position is that Article 7, when read in conjunction with Article 6, does not legitimize acts of force which would otherwise be illegal.[163] On the other hand, the Soviet Union was opposed to any language that would restrict the freedom of liberation movements.[164] Although a verbal compromise was arrived at, it can still be seen to permit conflicting interpretations.

With regard to escape clauses, it was pointed out by the United States that not all objectionable uses of armed force could be labeled as aggression, because Article 1 made illegal only those acts "set out in this definition."[165] The United States has argued that under Article 2, the first use of armed force by a state is only prima facie evidence of aggression—i.e., that a first strike is not necessarily an act of aggression. Thus, the U.S. position is that if the Security Council remains inactive in a crisis and makes no express finding of aggression, it must be deemed not to have found the prima facie evidence persuasive.[166] By emphasizing also the phrase "other relevant circumstances," the United States has maintained that evidence of purpose or intention may legitimately be taken into account by the Security Council in determining whether an act of aggression had occurred.[167] The phrase "in contravention of the Charter" in Article 2 can be read as limiting the category of acts that are prima facie impermissible, thus further narrowing the scope of the prohibition. This, again, is regardless of the first use of force.

In summary, then, it may be observed that in view of half a century's unrelenting industry, and the application of the considerable intellectual skills and practical experience over that period, the 1974 definition was a comparatively timid product.

Lest these criticisms appear unduly harsh, it should be acknowledged that most of them related to the potential of the definition for coping with the problems of the coexistence of two states, rather than with *worldwide* coexistence. If the definition is not adequate to the former task, it does not follow that it cannot make a useful contribution to the latter. Not every state in the world is a member of an ideological or regional bloc; not every state has the same sort of worldwide security interests or the means to intervene extraterritorially to protect its perceived interests.

Furthermore, progress in the international regulation of the use of force is not to be discouraged simply because it does not also reduce bipolarity. Progress toward one of these goals does not necessarily mean a setback for the other. In any case, the definition can be said to reflect a certain worldwide belief in the international regulation of the use of force. Even the superpowers agree that war ought no longer to be an instrument of national policy, and the examples of prohibited acts constitute an important advance. The study of superpower actions in certain trouble situations serves to illustrate some of the ambiguities in the 1974 definition; it may also be illustrative of future difficulties that could arise in cases not involving the superpowers. Such deficiencies cannot, however, detract from the part the definition has played in the concretization of norms.

The initial opposition to a definition among Western nations, accustomed to seeing the evolution of law through carefully reasoned judicial decisions rather than hasty legislation, was understandable. Yet a code arrived at after fifty years of patient negotiations can hardly be called hasty legislation. The code will receive the support of all nations (including Western nations) insofar as it was arrived at through consensus. Indeed, it is reflective of already accepted custom. There are those who would argue that the code is of little value if its principles would be accepted regardless of whether or not they were committed to writing. If allowed, this argument can be carried to absurd lengths, involving demands that all codes and statute-books be thrown away. The argument further ignores the fact that written norms provide certainty of rights and duties and predictability of behavior. The ultimate argument in favor of definition can, of course, always be encapsulated in the saying, *si ça va sans dire, ça va mieux en le disant.*

Every system of law develops through time, practice, and learning. Louis Sohn has observed that "no civilized system of law is satisfied with a general prohibition of 'acts violating the interests of other persons,' but tries to enumerate the prohibited acts (trespass, larceny, murder) and to define in more precise terms the aggravating and mitigating circumstances resulting in higher or lower punishment." [168] So, the argument goes, the definition of aggression is in fact an indicator of a maturing legal system. Just as the "law against persons" has to be made explicit in the form of such defined wrongs as trespass, larceny, etc., the law against war and aggression needs to be concretized through the definition of such wrongs as aggression, indirect aggression, breach of the peace, threat to the peace, etc. There is no better way to record such progress than in the form of a written code.

5

NORMATIVE ORDER IN AN UNSTRUCTURED WORLD

The behaviorist approach not only led to the abstraction of aggregate norms of conduct but also compelled the examination of the policy considerations motivating behavior and the various linkages between individual policy considerations as well as between policy considerations and state conduct. As McDougal has observed, international decision making is a "dynamic process in which decision-makers, located in many different institutional positions and contexts, are continually creating, interpreting and re-interpreting rules and continually formulating and reformulating, and applying and terminating, policies." [169] It is therefore essential that state conduct be studied in a way that will take full account of all relevant policy considerations. Not all norms abstracted as aggregates of conduct are desirable from certain vantage points. In this sense, the behaviorist approach to law is as value-neutral as it is empirical; it permits the recognition of certain categories of conduct as "norms" even if these are thought to be undesirable from a particular moral or ethical standpoint.

The principal conclusion that the behaviorist approach leads to, however, is that just as weak legal systems are not peculiar to leaderless societies, leadership or a determinate law-making authority is not a prerequisite to the existence of normative patterns of behavior. The entire edifice of reciprocal interbloc rights and duties discussed previously is proof of the latter proposition.

This subsystem of norms is an interesting illustration of what one legal anthropologist has called a "legal level within a multiplicity of legal subsystems in society." Writing on the legal system of China before the Communist regime, Pospisil observed: "What appeared to a traditionalist as a corrupt, confusing, and unpredictable system, characterized by an almost absolute disregard of law, becomes a meaningful configuration of legal systems pertaining to specific groups, arranged into several levels according to the degree of inclusiveness of the type of social groups." [170] The degree of inclusiveness depends on the nature of the subgroup in question. Thus, at the municipal level an individual is first a member of his household or family, but he may also be a member of a club, tribe, lineage, sublineage, and an all-embracing politically organized social unit that incorporates all these subgroups under a centralized political confederation. The study of the law of this political union is just one aspect of the law of the unit in question, and it is incomplete without a study of the functioning subgroups within it: "To disregard such [sub]systems, as is often done in the writings of legal scholars, reflects not a cool scientific introspect but a moral value judgment that has its place in philosophy but not in the sociology or anthropology of law." [171]

Similarly, on the international plane, a state may simultaneously be a member of a trade grouping, a member of a political confederation with other states, a party to a defense treaty with other states organized along political, regional, or ideological bases, and a member of a politically organized community of the states of the world as a whole. In this sense, there are subsystems of law governing relations between states *within* ideological blocs. Another subsystem of law governs relations *between* blocs, one example of which is the law of interbloc reciprocity described earlier. These subsystems coexist with one another as well as with the overall system of world organization under the UN Charter. McDougal, in explaining his "policy-oriented" approach to international law, states that such an approach will not

> demand an impossible "universality" of acceptance for the "validity" of its prescriptions. It will rather make of any proposed prescriptions such inquiries as these: What are the policies embodied in these prescriptions? What has been the degree and area of acceptance of these policies in the past and what are the probable degree and area of acceptance in the future? How relevant are these policies to the particular problem in hand in *its* context? *Policies that have not been, or cannot be made, authoritative on a global scale may yet serve useful purposes in the half world, the hemisphere, the region or lesser areas.*[172]

Ethnographic research also shows that the individual can, by virtue of his membership in more than one legal subgroup, be simultaneously subject to *contradictory* rules.[173] Similarly, a state may be subject to contradictory regimes of law. One can see, for example, that the rules of intervention under the interbloc law are in conflict with the rules of nonintervention of the Final Act of Helsinki[174] and with the law of the UN Charter[175] and the Declarations on Nonintervention[176] and on Friendly Relations.[177] Indeed, the question of a declaration on nonintervention was brought before the General Assembly in 1965 by the Soviet Union in an attempt to embarrass the United States over its intervention in the Dominican Republic.[178] The USSR could not have intended to restrict, through this declaration, its freedom to act within its own bloc, as demonstrated by its subsequent interventions in Czechoslovakia and Afghanistan. The law of interbloc reciprocity would therefore have made it obvious to the Soviet Union that the United States would reserve for itself a parallel power to act within *its* bloc. Thus, if a declaration on nonintervention were to be inoperative at the bloc or hemispheric level, its introduction by the Soviet Union could have been only to embarrass the United States and to bring an item before the General Assembly for its propaganda value, particularly because of its appeal to third-world nations.[179] The fact that the item was sent to the First Committee (dealing with political and security questions) rather than to the Sixth Committee (dealing with legal questions) underscores the essentially political motivations behind the item.[180]

The international lawyer should therefore be aware that the success of the codes he drafts will depend on their degree of inclusiveness of the society or subgroup to which they are addressed. The more inclusive the group, the greater will be the need to balance the interests of competing subgroups within the group. The international lawyer therefore can perform the task of drafting codes only within certain limits. First of all, he must realize that, unlike his counterpart at the municipal level, he must balance the competing and often conflicting policies and ideologies of more than one nation. His recommendations must also take into account the consensual element, without which much of international law would be meaningless. Only by appreciating his operational limits can the lawyer translate policies (including conflicting policies) into rules or codes which have a reasonable prospect of being followed. The best guide for ascertaining the operational limits on his role is the behaviorist approach to the study of norms, for it is this approach which most clearly reveals the policy perspectives of the states in question. (Express verbal pronouncements of policy by governments are, of course, another guide.) It is through this approach that codification can best contribute to international legal development and stability, especially since (a) the international system itself is relatively unstructured, there being no supreme international body competent to hand down and enforce ready-made codes of written law, and (b) the task of securing compliance with written rules is enormously complicated by the existence of philosophies as diametrically opposed as those of East and West are.

The absence of a supreme authority has been responsible for the fragmentary approach to the development of international precedent law. The poverty of this law has in turn resulted in uncertainty, and in sudden crisis situations states have been obliged to acknowledge that there were no clear legal guidelines to govern their actions. Legal justifications have therefore been advanced only after the fact, and in other instances law has been dismissed as irrelevant altogether and states have fallen back upon their own power and ability to guarantee those normative patterns considered essential for their own security. Yet this procedure has been available only to the strongest, and it is no accident that overt manifestations of the extraterritorial use of force are attributable mainly to the two great powers.

It would, however, be erroneous to claim that, for these reasons, there is no international legal "order," or that the contemporary international scene is one of rampant anarchy analogous to some Hobbesian state of nature. Norms *have* arisen; furthermore, they have arisen not from the dictates of some higher unwritten law or "rule of right reason," but from the harsh realities of coexistence, i.e., from the behavior of states in concrete fact situations involving conflicting interests and goals. Behavior in trouble situations was further seen to be not just the fiat of this or that sovereign but the aggregate of complex considerations about the perceived cause of the conflict, its probable consequences, the impact on potential rivals of remedial action taken, etc. In short, predictability and reciprocal expectations are functional to almost every strategy of superpower coexistence, thus refuting the view that relationships among nations are marked only by anarchy and irrationality.[181]

This leads to the conclusion that ideological conflict, which seems to negate the possibility of normative agreement and therefore appears to encourage "lawless" acts (e.g., the extraterritorial interventions, the ex post facto rationalizations, the open admissions of the inability of international law to provide certainty), is in fact the *reason for* the emergence of law. The process of the creation of law is neutral to the value systems of the power blocs whose relations it governs, and so it is accepted by both. This law then serves as a ready guide for the solution of interbloc disputes without inquiry as to which side has the "just" cause—without apportioning blame between the disputants and without the need for some higher authority sitting in judgment over them.

CHAPTER IV

Arms Control through Codified Law

While the international legal system was seen in the previous chapters to be evolving, in certain important ways, independently of the intentions of the actors in question, this is not the only way in which it is evolving.* The nations of the world have also attempted to exert deliberate control over its evolution and sometimes have been able to reach written agreement on legal norms. The definition of aggression discussed in the previous chapter was one such attempt. Another area in which deliberate control has been sought is in preserving the high seas and outer space for nonaggressive or "peaceful" uses. This must be viewed as an extension of the search for rules prohibiting aggression on land to other frontiers of activity. Viewed in a narrower context, however, it touches upon one of the most crucial issues of U.S.-Soviet relations—the arms race. Because of the danger and costliness of this race, keeping the seas and space out of it has been an urgent concern of the two principal actors in the field of weapons development.

Because of the urgency of the problem, there has been an intense international effort, led by the two superpowers, to regulate the military use of the oceans and of outer space through written or "codified" law. One such code, the 1971 Seabed Treaty, was a unique product, arrived at through the exchange of unilateral proposals and counterproposals between the two powers within the framework of the General Assembly of the UN. Unlike the various drafts and negotiating texts produced at the UN Conference on the Law of the Sea, the 1971 treaty was addressed exclusively to the military uses of the seabed. It should not be surprising, therefore, that the two powers took leading roles in its drafting.

This treaty and the Outer Space Treaty signed in 1967 are examples of the continuing effort by the two powers to establish mutual restraints

*This chapter is adapted from a larger study by the present author, *International Law and the Preservation of the Ocean Space and Outer Space as Zones of Peace: Progress and Problems*, 15 CORNELL INT'L L.J. 1 (1982). Permission from the JOURNAL is gratefully acknowledged.

on their activities in the absence of a central law-making body. These treaties established restraints on the emplacement of nuclear and other weapons of mass destruction on the seabed and in outer space. Important though the treaties are, it will be seen that they did not establish any "new" restrictions. Once again, the empirical behavior of the states will be suggested as the most reliable method of establishing the precise reach of the treaty prohibitions; at the same time, the potential of the code as a modality for international law-making will also be assessed. It will be seen that the behaviorist approach gives unique insights into problems of legal regulation beyond those afforded by the agreements themselves. It will further show not only that normative patterns have crystallized independently of formal agreement in these fields, but also that the behavior of states serves as an effective interpretive guide to certain controversial questions arising from codified law. It will also be seen to provide the basis for making projections of the evolution of the sea and space regimes of the foreseeable future.

1

ARMS CONTROL IN THE LAW OF THE SEA

A. THE ECONOMIC AND MILITARY POTENTIAL OF THE SEAS

There are two main reasons for the superpower interest in the high seas: the exploitation of the living and nonliving economic resources of the sea and the seabed, and the use of the sea and the seabed for military purposes. The economic potential of the oceans has up to now been largely untapped; and when it has been tapped—e.g., in the field of fisheries—activity has been almost completely unregulated, creating problems of pollution, overfishing, and the reduction of the quantity and quality of fish stocks.[1] Conservation measures through international regulation could not only reduce or eliminate these problems but could even make it possible for large-scale fish-farming to perform a "blue revolution" of even greater importance than the "green revolution" of recent years.[2] Offshore drilling today provides some 20 percent of the world's total oil production; by the mid-1990s it will account for almost 50 percent.[3] While minerals on land will, at the current rate of consumption, begin to be exhausted by the end of this century, the mineral resources of the seabed are in such great abundance that, once they become commercially exploitable with the requisite technological and legal developments, they will last considerably longer than land minerals.[4] Advances in marine geology will also undoubtedly lead to discoveries of even greater mineral deposits in the seabed. Another growing area of ocean activity is transportation and communications, and underwater storage and even recreational facilities are already being planned.[5] Factories, industries, and oil refineries are being moved to man-made floating platforms or artificial islands.[6] In short, in the years to come, the oceans will open up a vast frontier for a new industrial civilization, which will become more and more dependent on the sea for its survival.

Yet the future importance of the oceans will go beyond the purely economic aspect of man's existence. The sea and seabed are also becoming areas of strategic and military interest, particularly for the United States and the Soviet Union. Both powers are now aware of the fact that technological advances in multiple-warhead missile systems and in observational systems (on land, in the atmosphere, and in outer space) have made land-based strategic weapons systems very vulnerable.[7] Even the deployment of anti-ballistic missile (ABM) systems does not significantly offset the threat posed by MIRV (Multiple Independently targeted Re-entry Vehicle) systems.[8] Thus, moving strategic weapons from land into the protective opaqueness of the sea is currently a highly attractive proposition.[9] Such moves could improve a state's offensive and defensive capability,[10] e.g., through squadrons of submarines, fixed submarine detection systems, and other manned and unmanned underwater weapons systems.[11]

The greater protection gained by the ability to hide under water would ensure at least a "second-strike" capability for the assured destruction of the enemy.[12] The concept of undersea deterrence is based not on the belief that a vessel cannot be destroyed by the enemy,[13] but rather on the principle of the nontargetability of an undersea system at any given time; thus, in the event of attack, enough vessels would survive to strike back.[14] Another advantage to an undersea deterrent system is that its relative invulnerability would provide longer reaction time in a crisis situation.[15] This is especially important in the case of nuclear weapons, the hasty use of which could create untold damage. In the event of a crisis, longer reaction time would permit a sober and more rational assessment of the most prudent measures of retaliation. As seen previously, impact prediction and the proportionality of force (if force is used) in a crisis situation may be of crucial importance to the direction that a particular conflict may take.

The basing of missile systems even on the surface of the sea could make them less vulnerable than land-based systems, especially if they were mounted on very fast vehicles, prototypes of which are already being built in the United States.[16]

The drastic cutback in the space programs of both powers has diverted research in the aerospace industry from outer space to the "inner space" of the oceans. Aerospace firms in the United States have directed their surplus capacity toward the development of prototypes of various kinds of submersibles and equipment for ocean use.[17] The result is that contemporary oceanological research has a military component and thus tends to take place in a shroud of secrecy. The effects of some forms of activity on the ocean environment, e.g., through pollution and the dumping of radioactive waste, therefore remain unknown. An internationalized system of pollution monitoring and pollution control is necessary to any kind of long-term oceanological research. It is also self-evident that such research, particularly that relating to the economic exploitation of the seabed, cannot take place without the preservation of the oceans as a zone of peace. At the same time, the need to reserve the oceans for peaceful uses is becoming more and more urgent in the light of their potential for military use.

The next section presents an overview of efforts by the two powers to restrict the military uses of the world's oceans through codified law.

B. THE 1971 SEABED TREATY

(1) The General Scope of Prohibition

Article I of the 1971 Seabed Treaty provides that "States Parties to this Treaty undertake not to emplant or emplace on the seabed and the ocean floor and in the subsoil thereof . . . any nuclear weapons or any other types of weapons of mass destruction."[18] While the difference between "emplant" and "emplace" is not explained anywhere in the treaty, the references to the "seabed," the "ocean floor," and its "subsoil" suggest fixed installations and apparently exclude from the ban submarines equipped with conventional or nuclear weapons, either while riding at anchor or while lying on the seabed.[19] Perhaps one reason for the exclusion of submarines from the ban is that their deployment provides a peace-through-mutual-deterrence guarantee which should not be tampered with.

Also excluded from the ban would be vehicles carrying weapons of mass destruction and capable of navigating only when in contact with the seabed[20]—e.g., the "on-the-bottom, slowly mobile mines" referred to above. Such vehicles, also known as "creepy-crawlies,"[21] seem to escape the ban by virtue of the fact that they are mobile and not fixed to the seabed, the ocean floor, or the ocean subsoil.[22] It would also follow that such vehicles need not be mobile all the time but can rest on the seabed for indefinite periods of time. The test is whether a vehicle is *capable* of navigation independently of the seabed. If it is, the ban does not apply.

The treaty also bans structures and installations "specifically designed for storing, testing or using" weapons of mass destruction on the ocean floor.[23] Whether or not a particular structure is included in the ban depends on its design and not on its purpose. It is entirely possible that a vehicle may be designed for something other than the storage of weapons of mass destruction but at the same time is *capable* of storing such weapons. If original design is retained as the sole criterion, such vehicles would presumably also escape the ban. Surface-based nuclear missile systems appear to be excluded from the ban as well. By implication, therefore, research in the United States in projects such as SABMIS (Sea-based Antiballistic Missile Intercept System) and BMS (Ballistic Missile Ship System) would still be permitted.

Article II of the treaty provides that the outer limit of the prohibited zone "shall be coterminous with the twelve-mile outer limit of the zone referred to in Part II of the Convention on the Territorial Sea . . ." The treaty thus leaves coastal states free to emplace, or to invite allies to emplace, weapons of mass destruction within their 12-mile coastal zones. This issue will be discussed in greater detail below.[24]

It can be seen, therefore, that the 1971 Seabed Treaty did not prohibit *all* military uses of the seabed, however unpalatable this fact may be to those concerned with excluding the oceans from the arms race. Indeed, the preamble declares that the treaty is only "a step towards the exclusion of the seabed, the ocean floor and the subsoil thereof from the arms race," while in Article V the parties recognize the need for further negotiations to save the oceans from the arms race and pledge continued negotiations in good faith toward this goal.

It has been the American position that only weapons of mass destruction could have enough military significance to warrant the expense of stationing them on the seabed.[25] Hence, the United States preferred a treaty that banned only weapons of that kind. As for conventional military uses of the seabed, the U.S. position is that these are not likely to threaten the territories of states either now or in the near future.[26] Yet if this is the case, there should have been no objection to including conventional weapons in the ban. Most members of the Disarmament Committee felt that by specifically prohibiting only nuclear weapons and other weapons of mass destruction, the Seabed Treaty may have given the impression of legitimizing the use of conventional weapons on the seabed.[27]

(2) The Problem of Verification

While emplacement of nuclear and other weapons of mass destruction is so far a technological monopoly of the two superpowers,[28] the question of verification and enforcement of the ban is one that concerns all parties generally and coastal states in particular. Signatories of the treaty agreed to refrain from doing something that they had no capability of doing, anyway, and something that their national interests did not compel them to do. But verification has become a question of vital national interest for all parties, because emplacement of weapons of mass destruction on the seabed touches the national security of all states, developed and less developed, coastal and inland. Yet the majority of the parties to the treaty do not possess sufficient undersea technology even to allow them to verify the treaty provisions without assistance from the technologically advanced states[29]—which, unfortunately, also happen to be the states most likely to emplace the prohibited weapons.

Verification could therefore become a bipolar issue, with all the attendant dangers of East-West rivalry. Article III of the Seabed Treaty provides that if a party has doubts about the activities of any other party, "the State Party having such doubts shall notify the other States Parties, and the parties concerned shall cooperate on such further procedures for verification as may be agreed upon." The same article also provides that a state may undertake verification by "using its own means, or with the full or partial assistance of any other State Party."

Since only the two superpowers possess the technology for any meaningful verification, and since only these two powers claim to have the sort of worldwide interests which might lead to the emplacement of weapons of mass destruction on the seabed, the process of consultation envisaged by Article III is in real terms reduced to consultation between a less-developed nation and one superpower, in opposition to the other superpower. Even the ultimate right of appeal to the Security Council may prove ineffective, since all five nuclear powers hold the right to veto its action.

Attempts at verification could easily lead to charges of "interference" with legitimate national activity.[30] Article III, paragraph 1, says that the seabed activities of states can be observed "provided that observation does not interfere with such activities." Article III also provides, in paragraph 6, that verification "shall not interfere with activities of other States Parties and shall be conducted with due regard for rights recognized under international law including the freedom of the high seas." Such escape clauses have often served as convenient shields insulating embarrassing state activity from international scrutiny.

The provision that verification must not interfere with the freedom of the high seas could create further difficulties in the future, now that many states have claimed exclusive economic zones of 200 miles. Such question as these could arise: Is observation outside the 12-mile zone but inside the 200-mile line permissible, or is it to be treated as "interference" with sovereign jurisdiction? Are objections from a coastal state to verification attempts within the 200-mile zone to be regarded as an infringement of the freedom of the high seas under paragraph 6 of Article III?[31]

Another source of conflict over verification could be the Geneva Convention on the Continental Shelf. This agreement allows coastal states to establish safety zones up to 500 meters around installations for the exploitation of the natural resources on the seabed, which installations must be respected by ships of all nationalities. If a state suspected of violating the treaty declares the installation in question to be such a facility, it may be able to prevent direct access to it by other states seeking verification. In this way, an undersea facility may be "looked at" but not "looked into." The United States has argued against a blanket right of states to look into undersea facilities. It claims that such a right on the high seas is unnecessary because under the principle of the freedom of the high seas, parties could approach the area of a suspected undersea facility and study surface and underwater engineering activity, surface support platforms for the facility, the type of equipment and material thereon, etc., to decide whether the facility in question violates the treaty.[32] Emplacements of mass-destruction weapons would require sophisticated material and equipment, special engineering facilities on the surface, and other "telltale" signs, so that a direct look into the installation in question would be unnecessary.[33] It is, in any case, noteworthy that the treaty is silent on the question of access to underwater facilities for purposes of verification.

Substantial though the difficulties may be under the scheme of verification envisaged by the treaty, verification by itself is not the major problem in any treaty limiting armaments. The real problem is always whether the parties are willing to accept the obligations imposed by an arms control agreement.

(3) Relationship to the Geneva Conventions

The 1971 Seabed Treaty deliberately skirts the issue of demilitarization (even in the limited sense of prohibiting weapons of mass destruction) of those maritime zones falling into the traditional categories of national waters, territorial sea, contiguous zone, and continental shelf (see figure 1). National waters—i.e., maritime zones landward of the baseline of the territorial sea—are under the complete sovereignty of coastal states under customary international law.[34] The 1971 Seabed Treaty did not attempt to change this situation. As with many provisions of the treaty, restrictions on state sovereignty over national waters exist, but they derive from sources other than the treaty. For example, one possible restriction arises under Articles 4 and 5 of the 1958 Geneva Convention on the Territorial Sea.[35] Another grows out of Article 1 of the Nuclear Test Ban Treaty of 1963, under which each party is obliged to refrain from carrying out nuclear test explosions "at any place under its jurisdiction or control . . . including territorial waters."[36]

As for the territorial sea, it has already been explained that Article II of the 1971 Seabed Treaty leaves coastal states free to emplace weapons of mass destruction within their 12-mile coastal zone. However, Article 14(1) of the territorial-sea convention provides in part that

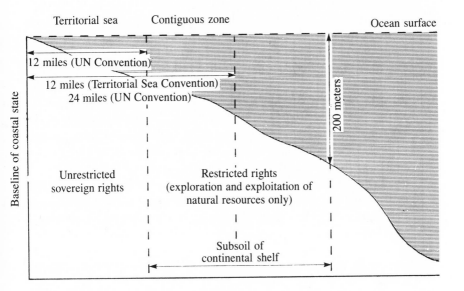

Figure 1. Traditional Categories of Maritime Zones

"ships of all States whether coastal or not, shall enjoy the right of innocent passage through the territorial sea." Under Article 14(5), passage
is innocent so long as it is not "prejudicial to the peace, good order or
security of the coastal state." (The territorial sea is a belt of the sea
adjacent to the coast where the coastal state exercises the same degree
of sovereignty that it is entitled to exercise on its land territory and internal waters. Under the recently concluded UN Convention on the
Law of the Sea, the maximum permissible width of the territorial sea is
12 nautical miles. It should be noted that the United States is not a
party to this convention.) Submarines navigating on the surface, warships, and other foreign military vessels would presumably enjoy the
right of innocent passage, subject to Article 14(4) and the power of the
coastal state under Article 16(3) "to suspend temporarily in specified
areas of its territorial sea the innocent passage of foreign ships if such
suspension is essential for the protection of its security." [37] There can,

however, be no such suspension in respect of territorial-sea straits used for international navigation.[38]

However, none of these restrictions on the rights of states over their national and territorial waters is strong enough to imply a ban on the emplacement of nuclear and mass-destruction weapons in these zones. It would be possible to locate weapons systems on, say, the territorial seabed in such a way that they did not interfere with innocent passage, which after all is allowed only on the surface. Moreover, according to the Geneva Convention on the Territorial Sea, the obligation of states to allow innocent passage exists only within the outer limit of the territorial sea; the obligation does not extend over the *entire* 12-mile contiguous zone referred to in Part II of the convention. The UN Convention on the Law of the Sea (UNCLOS) does not purport to materially change the existing regime of sovereignty; it continues to acknowledge coastal state sovereignty over national waters and the territorial sea.[39] A concomitant power of this sovereignty is the power to exclude foreign military activity in the subjacent seabed and subsoil of both zones.

As for the demilitarization of the continental shelf, the 1971 Seabed Treaty leaves the situation equally unsatisfactory. Under Article 1 of the Geneva Convention on the Continental Shelf, the term "continental shelf" refers in part "to the seabed and subsoil of the submarine area adjacent to the coast but outside the area of the territorial sea, to a depth of 200 meters." Under Article 2, "[t]he coastal State exercises over the continental shelf sovereign rights for the purpose of exploring it and exploiting its natural resources." Under Article 24 of the Convention on the Territorial Seas, however, the coastal state has the right, even in its contiguous zone, to take actions necessary "to prevent infringement of its customs, fiscal, immigration or sanitary regulations within its territory or territorial sea" and to "punish infringement of the above regulations committed within its territory or territorial sea." Yet as figure 1 shows, there may be an overlap between a coastal state's contiguous zone and its continental shelf, and the rights of a coastal state in that portion of its continental shelf falling immediately below its contiguous zone are different from those conferred upon it by Article 24 of the Convention on the Territorial Sea.

Not only does the 1971 Seabed Treaty not indicate whether the above distinction is legally useful or relevant for purposes of determining the areas in which a state may or may not emplace nuclear and other weapons of mass destruction, but in one broad sweep it declares, in Article II, that the prohibited zone "shall be coterminous with the twelve-mile outer limit of the zone referred to in Part II of the Convention on the Territorial Sea . . ." In doing so, it opens the possibility of splitting up continental shelves, leaving the landward portions of these shelves (i.e., those falling immediately below the contiguous zone) exempt from the ban and including in the ban the portions extending beyond the contiguous zone.

The above definition of the prohibited zone has two legal consequences: First, by juxtaposing two zones (the 12-mile coastal zone and the rest of the high seas) and by prohibiting weapons of mass destruction in only one of them, it seems to open the way for the argument that it creates *a contrario* an implied right, freedom, or privilege to emplace such weapons in the other (i.e., the 12-mile coastal) zone. Second, by allowing this interpretation, it appears to lump the area of the contiguous zone and the portion (if any) of the continental shelf falling immediately below it together with the territorial sea, thus creating the erroneous impression that a coastal state has complete sovereignty over the entire 12-mile coastal zone and the seabed below it: for what better evidence of sovereignty can be offered in respect of any given area than a right, purportedly derived from an international legal document, to emplace thereon nuclear and other weapons of mass destruction?

The 1971 Seabed Treaty thus contains numerous omissions and ambiguities. The most remarkable omission is that it fails to address the real threat to peace in the oceans: mobile underwater strategic forces. By banning nuclear installations on the seabed, it is banning something that is no longer of much military significance to the strategic deterrent forces of either of the two superpowers. Since the treaty permits mobile underwater weapons systems, permits the placement on the seabed of installations servicing such free-swimming mass-destruction weapons systems, and fails to restrict the activities of coastal states within their 12-mile zones, it is not likely to contribute significantly to the preservation of the ocean and the ocean environment from the arms race. It can thus be seen that the two great powers, cosponsors of the treaty, were not prepared to propose, much less to accept, a regime of demilitarization in the oceans that would hinder their strategic military programs in the seas, especially given the special attractiveness of the ocean environment and the distinct advantages it offers to underwater weapons.

While existing deployments of underwater weapons systems (especially submarines) may be held to guarantee a certain peace and stability through mutual deterrence, long-term developments could upset this precarious balance. An important factor in the popularity of underwater attack systems—and one which may encourage their further development in ways that could threaten the existing balance—is their relative invulnerability when compared with other (stationary) surface-based systems on land, on the sea surface, or on the seabed. This enhanced invulnerability is due to (a) their mobility, (b) their ability to hide by blending with the ocean environment, (c) their capacity for prolonged submergence, and (d) the fact that most existing detection devices do not have a range commensurate with the vast areas of the ocean.[40]

2

ARMS CONTROL IN THE LAW OF OUTER SPACE

Perhaps because the development of weapons in outer space will be motivated by the same considerations of strategic deterrence as the development of sea-based weapons, there are some remarkable similarities in the codified law on the two subjects. Just as the pertinent treaty law on the oceans did not achieve complete demilitarization,[41] the relevant code law on outer space law also leaves open the possibility of the deployment of weapons in near-earth space.[42] As was done in the treatment of the oceans, an attempt will be made in this part to discuss the military potential of outer space, with a view to drawing certain tentative conclusions as to what kinds of space weapons could develop in the future and how existing weapons and those in the developmental stage have influenced the present law of arms control in outer space. The general conclusion will again be that the prohibitions actually imposed on armaments in space are not a significant setback to the strategic interests of either power.

A. THE POLITICS OF OUTER SPACE

In a remarkable combination of political developments and scientific advances, the space age began at a period in world history when the cold war was at its peak. It is therefore not surprising that the Soviet Union, as the launcher of the world's first earth satellite, sought to exploit its achievement for maximum political gain. Similar political aspects of outer space exploration have colored to varying degrees the space activities of both powers, from the time of the launching of Sputnik I by the USSR in 1957 to the first manned landing on the moon by the United States in 1969 and the first unmanned landing on Mars in 1976 (this last being timed to coincide with America's bicentennial celebrations).

In 1957, the USSR embarked on a concerted publicity campaign designed to convey to the world that the sputnik launching proved that its political system was superior to the West's, that its citizens could expect greater benefits under its system than under any other, and that it possessed scientific, technological, and most importantly military superiority over all other nations.[43] Just five weeks prior to the launching of Sputnik I, the Soviet Union had announced that it had successfully tested an intercontinental ballistic missile (ICBM).[44] Sputnik I was designed to show that it also possessed the rocket booster for launching an ICBM.[45]

Sputnik I was soon followed by Sputnik II and then by Sputnik III, both of them larger and heavier than their precursor.[46] Sputnik II carried a dog into space, and Sputnik III was large enough to accommodate a man. These satellites were injected into orbit with a high degree of precision at predetermined altitudes. Their size and accuracy were used to emphasize that the USSR possessed an ICBM booster capable of producing tremendous thrust, enabling it to carry heavy payloads (i.e., warheads) to any point on the globe,[47] and that the USSR possessed a highly accurate guidance system that would enable it to target its ICBMs with pinpoint accuracy.[48] In 1959, the Soviet Union launched the first of a series of three rockets to the moon, the second of which landed on the moon and the third of which, Lunik III, photographed the far side of the moon and televised the pictures back to earth.[49] Even greater publicity was given to the first manned space flights, beginning with that of Yuri Gagarin in 1961. The Soviet cosmonauts were Party members and were hailed as representatives of the "new Soviet man" and as "true sons of the Communist Party."[50]

In all, the Soviet Union offered as proof of its technical and military strength the following "firsts" in space: the launching of the world's first artificial satellites and of the first rockets to the moon (including the televising of the first "live" pictures from the moon); the first successful recovery of a space vehicle from orbit; the first interplanetary probe (to Venus); and the first manned flight (including a "group flight").

Apart from the claims to military and technological strength that were based on these achievements, some of them appear to have been timed to coincide with certain events considered to be politically significant for East-West relations. For example, the impacting of Lunik II on the moon occurred just prior to Khrushchev's visit to the United States,[51] while the second manned flight coincided with the Warsaw Pact meeting in 1961 at which the decision to close the East Berlin border was taken. These events were punctuated on several occasions by Soviet cosmonauts, as well as Khrushchev himself, publicly rattling the missile against any actual or potential adversary. These threats became progressively less vociferous as the so-called "missile gap" between the USSR and the West was closed by parallel developments in the United States.[52]

The publicity given by the Soviet Union to its space effort was of course rigidly controlled and selective.[53] Only those disclosures were made which had some propaganda value; furthermore, announcements only of successful experiments were made. This applies also to present-day Soviet policy on the disclosure of activities in outer space.

U.S. policy on disclosure is much less restrictive, and public announcements are made of almost all experiments, whether or not they are successful. The open nature of the U.S. information policy on space activities, demonstrated, for example, by live television coverage of manned space flights (including that of the first manned landings on the moon and the more recent launchings and returns of the space shuttle), has its own advantages of drama and even prestige which cannot be matched by selective disclosures.[54]

The desire of successive U.S. administrations to foster the public sharing of information along with international cooperation in space has caused a certain amount of tension between departments within the government. For example, in 1961 the State Department cosponsored a resolution in the UN Committee on the Peaceful Uses of Outer Space calling for international cooperation in space and public disclosure of space launches.[55] This conflicted with the Defense Department's policy of strict nondisclosure of the launching of military satellites.[56] However, the fact that the Department of Defense has a space program is a matter of public knowledge,[57] whereas the Soviet Union, by its policy of disclosing only those projects which are nonmilitary and of no intelligence value, sought until the early 1960s to convey the impression that it had no military program of its own in space. It endeavored to reinforce this impression at the political level in several ways—e.g., by taking a public stand in favor of the "peaceful" uses of outer space, and by contrasting this with the allegation that U.S. policy in space is essentially "aggressive."[58] Several motives for such tactics have been attributed to the USSR: to discourage other countries from assisting the U.S. space effort—e.g., through the provision of bases outside the U.S. for ground tracking facilities; to provide justification for Soviet noncooperation in the international control of space activities; and to provide justification for the Soviets' military space program, should they be forced to disclose it eventually.[59]

The publicly acknowledged separation between the civilian and the military aspects of the American space program may be contrasted with the absence of any official acceptance by the Soviet Union of such a separation in its space program. There is therefore little disclosure of military involvement in space, and when there is such a disclosure, it is deliberate and is calculated to serve particular aims of Soviet foreign policy. Khrushchev's early claims to military superiority arising from the first sputnik launchings are one example. Another is the disclosure in 1961 that the first two Soviet manned space flights (Vostok I and II) were launched by military personnel; this disclosure was made by the Soviet commander of strategic rocket forces to lend credibility to his claim of the combat readiness of his missile-launching crews.[60]

Since no distinction is made in the USSR between the military and the civilian aspects of the space program, there can be no interdepartmental tension within the government, of the kind occurring in the

United States. Such outward inconsistencies as may become apparent in the space program (e.g., if it conflicts with the official stand in favor of "peaceful" activities in space) are explained in terms of the dialectics of peace and war.[61] Military strength is well publicized, but it is stressed as being purely defensive, thus implying that it is pointless to arm in preparation for war against the Soviet Union because it has no aggressive intentions in the first place and because, if attacked, its missile technology provides more than adequate means for defense.

It is in this framework that the Soviet Union in 1962, acknowledged for the first time that it was using space for military purposes. A military commentator said: "It would be a mistake to allow any superiority whatever to the imperialist camp in the sphere [of the military uses of outer space]. It is necessary to oppose the imperialists with more effective means and methods of using space for military defense."[62] In the same year, a leading Soviet authority on space law, Zhukov, affirmed that nothing in the UN Charter, regarded as applicable to outer space, prevented the use of space for self-defense under Article 51.[63]

The above strategy is complemented by public advocacy of total demilitarization of outer space. Thus, on the one hand the defensive role of Soviet armaments is stressed, and on the other, a sustained propaganda campaign contrasts this to the allegedly "aggressive" purpose of Western arms policy. The support for total disarmament—apart from its propaganda value—is designed to give greater credibility to the other two aspects of the USSR's public verbal strategy on arms control.[64]

B. THE MILITARY POTENTIAL OF OUTER SPACE

Space-based weapons systems would have certain advantages which each space power will have to balance against possible disadvantages before arriving at a decision on whether or not to commit itself to a long-term strategic military program in space.[65] A space-based weapons system would mean that the nation owning it would potentially have one more strike force on which to rely, in addition to its land- and sea-based strategic forces. The greater the diversity within a country's offensive and retaliatory forces, the greater their overall deterrent value. A space-based system also complicates the coordination of the enemy's strike forces; if in addition to tracking down and destroying a highly mobile underwater force, it had to keep track of space forces that constantly varied and shifted their orbits at different points around the globe, or even possibly remained "parked" in a hidden orbit on the far side of the moon, it would make immensely more difficult and expensive the task of ensuring the total elimination of the rival's retaliatory force.[66] On the other hand, simultaneous attack from three fronts (land, sea, and space) would impose such a strain on the enemy's defense apparatus that penetration of its defenses would be made easier[67]—so much easier that the total of offensive and retaliatory capacity goes beyond assured destruction of the enemy to the point of "overkill."[68]

Just as a mobile seaborne weapons system can be used for purposes of demonstrative posturing in crisis situations, a space weapon such as a satellite bombardment system could be deliberately positioned above a target state to demonstrate military strength. A war fought in outer space would have the further advantage of having little or no repercussions on the earthly environment, provided that the conflict did not spill over into the terrestrial realm.[69] The chances that this would happen could be minimized through international agreement on the rules of space warfare. It may further be noted that a nation whose weapons were attacked only in outer space might, in order to avoid initiating a mutual destruction of civilian populations, confine its counteraction to the enemy's outer space weapons.[70] It is, however, possible that, even though the targets may be in space, the *launching* of the offensive missile might take place on earth, thus opening up the possibility of retaliation against such land-based targets as launch pads, silos, etc. Finally, a strategic war in space would presumably involve few, if any, civilian casualties. This, it has been observed, may render more real the possibility of limited strategic war.[71]

It can be seen, therefore, that if the space powers make any serious moves to militarize outer space, the following are among the weapons that could eventually be deployed: orbiting nuclear and conventional bombardment satellites, communications and observation satellites for monitoring the bombardment satellites or for other purposes, orbiting antimissile and antisatellite systems, reconnaissance satellites, manned space stations, and ground control facilities as well as tracking stations dotted all over the globe. Both powers have been developing antisatellite and bombardment systems since the late 1960s.[72] The Soviet Union has been developing a Fractional Orbital Bombardment System (FOBS),[73] as well as an antisatellite weapon known as a "directed energy weapon," capable of destroying targets with an intense beam of charged atomic particles.[74] The United States has been developing a Multi-Orbital Bombardment System (MOBS) and antisatellite weapons using laser beams.[75]

The feasibility of space weapons will depend very much on the two key questions of deterrence and vulnerability. Reconnaissance satellites may prove useful in giving advance warning of ground troop movements, gathering intelligence on the location of enemy missile sites, etc. But they may be of little use in providing advance warning of an impending missile attack; warning of such an attack would be possible only after the missiles have been fired.[76] However, if the opponent's deterrent forces are invulnerable, due to their diversity, their numbers, their mobility, the difficulty of detecting them, and so on, they may prevent such an attack in the first place—in which case a satellite warning system may not be needed. Reconnaissance vehicles could, however, be programmed to operate against bombardment satellites (assuming that the latter can be satisfactorily identified in space). It is even possible that such vehicles could be equipped with antisatellite missiles. Their effectiveness would, however, again depend on the vulnerability of bombardment satellites.

It should be noted that the vulnerability of terrestrial strategic weapons is not inversely linked to the invulnerability of bombardment satellites—i.e., increases in the invulnerability of bombardment satellites do not necessarily render earth weapons more targetable. The vulnerability of earth weapons depends on other, independent factors, such as their numbers, mobility, and effective concealment. However, regardless of the vulnerability of either terrestrial or space weapons, the existence of a satellite bombardment system per se would provide offensive capability as well as greater deterrent diversity. Greater deterrent diversity, as indicated above, would contribute to the invulnerability of the deterrent force as a whole. This, in turn, would improve first-strike capability, insofar as the attacking state felt confident in predicting a favorable outcome from a first strike. It is in this context that the regime of arms control in outer space must be assessed.

C. THE 1967 SPACE TREATY

(1) The General Scope of Prohibition

Following the soft landing of the Soviet Union's Luna IX on the moon in February 1966, the two space powers entered into negotiations within the UN framework. A draft treaty was produced, and it was adopted by the General Assembly in December 1966, was opened for signature in January 1967, and came into force in October 1967. The most significant provision of this Space Treaty is Article IV:

> State Parties to the Treaty undertake not to place in orbit around the Earth any objects carrying nuclear weapons or any other kinds of weapons of mass destruction, install such weapons on celestial bodies, or station such weapons in outer space in any other manner.
>
> The Moon and other celestial bodies shall be used by all States Parties to the Treaty exclusively for peaceful purposes. The establishment of military bases, installations and fortifications, the testing of any type of weapons and the conduct of military manoeuvres on celestial bodies shall be forbidden. The use of military personnel for scientific research or for any other peaceful purposes shall not be prohibited. The use of any equipment or facility necessary for peaceful exploration of the Moon and other celestial bodies shall also not be prohibited.[77]

This article gives the prima facie impression that for purposes of demilitarization, outer space and celestial bodies are to be treated differently. First of all, there is no express reservation of the use of outer space "exclusively for peaceful purposes," as in the case of the moon and other celestial bodies. Secondly, the ban on the "establishment of military bases, installations and fortifications, the testing of any type of weapons and the conduct of military manoeuvres" applies to celestial bodies only; the ban was not extended in haec verba to the space surrounding the earth, where only nuclear weapons and other weapons of mass destruction are prohibited. Thirdly, the ban on the military uses of celestial bodies is more wide-ranging than that which appears in the first paragraph of Article IV. While this paragraph—dealing primarily with outer space "around" the earth—also makes reference to celestial bodies, the second paragraph—dealing with the moon and other celestial bodies—makes no reference whatsoever to outer space.

In short, Article IV seems to preserve the present state of total non-militarization of celestial bodies,[78] but achieves only *partial* demilitarization of circumterrestrial space. It is possible to argue that, since in this area only nuclear weapons and other weapons of mass destruction are prohibited, the deployment of conventional weapons, including nonnuclear antisatellite weapons, is permissible.[79] The difficulty here is that there would be no way of verifying whether, for example, an antisatellite system claimed to be nonnuclear was not in fact equipped with some kind of nuclear weapon, such as the particle beam weapon.[80]

The second paragraph of Article IV requires total nonmilitarization of activities "on" the moon and celestial bodies, with a simultaneous injunction that they be used "exclusively for peaceful purposes." In this context it is arguable that the intention is that all activities *on the surface* of the moon and other celestial bodies must be "nonmilitary," an interpretation that would leave unaffected the legal status of activities *around* celestial bodies. That is, if the ban is construed strictly, or if the second sentence of the second paragraph of Article IV is interpreted literally, the ban can be said to apply only to surface activity and not to orbital activity.

It may be noted in this regard that Article III of the 1979 Agreement Governing the Activities of States on the Moon (the Moon Treaty),[81] after reaffirming the use of the moon "exclusively for peaceful purposes," provides:

> 3. States Parties shall not place in orbit around or other trajectory to or around the moon objects carrying nuclear weapons or any other kinds of weapons of mass destruction or place or use such weapons on or in the moon.
> 4. The establishment of military bases, installations and fortifications, the testing of any type of weapons and the conduct of military manoeuvres on the moon shall be forbidden.[82]

Thus, paragraph 3 prohibits nuclear and mass destruction weapons *on and around* the moon; paragraph 4 prohibits all other weapons, installations, etc., *"on* the Moon,"[83] but it does not expressly prohibit deployment of such (conventional and non-mass-destruction) weapons *around* the moon. Both the Space Treaty and the Moon Treaty maintain a peculiar silence on circumlunar activity involving nonnuclear and non-mass-destruction weapons.[84]

To justify the view that there is to be total nonmilitarization of the moon one is forced to rely on the arguments that (a) total nonmilitarization has been prescribed *on* the moon; (b) the moon is to be used "exclusively for peaceful purposes"; (c) the deployment of non-mass-destruction weapons in circumlunar space would not be an "exclusively peaceful" use of the moon; and (d) such weapons make uncertain and temporary an otherwise clear, unambiguous, and permanent regime of nonmilitarization on the moon.

(2) Surveillance and Verification

The Space Treaty did not tackle the problem of verification with the boldness with which it dealt with the nonmilitarization of celestial bodies. Its verification provision, Article XII, represents the characteristically timid approach of international inspection schemes. It is consensual and reciprocal:

> All stations, installations, equipment and space vehicles on the Moon and other celestial bodies shall be open to representatives of other State Parties to the Treaty on a basis of reciprocity.

The article also seems to reinforce the dichotomy between outer space and celestial bodies: verification is reserved only where total nonmilitarization is prescribed—i.e., on celestial bodies (including the moon) but not in outer space nor for that matter on earth-based centers for, say, launchings, communications, tracking, etc.[85] It may also be noted in this connection that verification would not be possible *at all* with respect to the ban on nuclear and mass-destruction weapons under paragraph 1 of Article IV. Even if the term "on the Moon and other celestial bodies" in Article XII were interpreted to include all stations, installations, and equipment in orbit *around* the moon and celestial bodies, the verification arrangements of the treaty do not measure up to the standard required by the far-reaching ban in Article IV, paragraph 2.

For these reasons, states will be forced to develop what means they can at the national level to monitor compliance with the treaty by rival parties. After the signing in 1963 of the Treaty Banning Nuclear Weapons Tests in the Atmosphere, in Outer Space, and Under Water, nuclear radiation and blast sensing devices were developed which accurately identify the location of the blast, its yield, and, in the case of atmospheric tests, what materials were used, the type of nuclear design, etc. Similarly, with regard to space activity, orbital inspection and control systems in satellites have been developed using optical, radar, infrared, ultraviolet, and other sensing devices which not only are able to pinpoint locations of factories, launch complexes, etc. but also can indicate the build-up and range of activities at such factories and complexes during day and night. Satellite surveillance systems such as MIDAS (Missile Defense Alarm System) and SAMOS (Satellite and Missile Observation System) were launched by the United States in the early 1960s.[86] These systems were designed to monitor enemy missile bases on earth as well as to provide early warning of the launching of missile-carrying rockets.[87] Despite the asymmetry caused by the unavailability of Soviet sources on such matters, as compared to American sources, the Soviet Union is known to have similar devices and has publicly hinted that it, too, has launched "spy" satellites.[88] Furthermore, the space powers have been developing networks of land-based sensing devices that work in conjunction with earth-orbiting satellites, making it almost impossible to launch any type of orbital payload or to conduct underground blasts without detection.[89] In the absence of a strong scheme for the international verification of activities in outer space, such devices will continue to be developed at the national level.

It is perhaps because of the immediacy of this problem that the Committee on the Peaceful Uses of Outer Space recommended in July 1977 that its Legal Sub-committee consider the legal implications of remote sensing of the earth from space as a matter of "high priority."[90] The following year, the sub-committee presented a set of draft principles on remote sensing.[91]

Although the verification clause of the Moon Treaty, Article XV, still appears to restrict inspection to only those vehicles, stations, etc., that are "*on* the moon," it nevertheless represents an improvement over the verification clause of the 1967 Space Treaty. Its advances are that (a) inspection is not based on reciprocity, (b) a request for consultations creates a binding obligation on the party receiving the request, (c) any party may participate in these consultations, and (d) any state party may unilaterally seek the "assistance" of the secretary general "in order to resolve the controversy." The secretary general, however, is given no express power to compel a settlement.

Since the militarization of celestial bodies has not occurred, the consideration of concrete future possibilities in this field is in the realm of pure conjecture, making it difficult for the lawyer to suggest specific rules. It is, however, clear that effective guarantees for the ban under paragraph 2 of Article IV will require bilateral and multilateral verification arrangements, utilizing listening and monitoring devices and other early warning systems in space.

(3) The Principle of "Common Interests"

Some writers have argued that all activities in outer space, including those under paragraph 1 of Article IV of the Space Treaty must be "nonmilitary."[92] This reasoning is based on a literal and somewhat simplistic interpretation of Article I, paragraph 1, of the treaty, which provides that "[t]he exploration and use of outer space, including the moon and other celestial bodies, shall be carried out for the benefit and in the interests of all countries, irrespective of their degree of economic and scientific development, and shall be the province of all mankind." The inference, it is said, is that "the principle of use in the interests of all countries," hitherto a "nonbinding" principle, has by this article been converted into "a perfect legal norm."[93] Article I in effect has forbidden any activity in outer space tht does not constitute a use in the interest of all countries.[94] Thus, since defensive military activity in space by a state to protect its own security would not be a use in the interest of *all* states, it would for that reason alone be unlawful.

There are several objections to this argument. First, it ignores the legislative history of the principle of the use of outer space for the benefit of all mankind. Since the early days of space activity the nonspace powers have been concerned that the space powers may appropriate space for their own benefit and might even use it to the *detriment* of the nonspace powers.[95] For this reason, expressions such as the "common interest of mankind," the "use of outer space for the benefit of all countries," the "equality" of access to space and celestial bodies for all states, the "scientific" purposes to which space activity is restricted— all these expressions were used in the Committee on the Peaceful Uses of Outer Space and in formal resolutions of the General Assembly to emphasize the nondiscriminatory use of space and to preclude its use by one space power against the other or by one or both powers against the nonspace powers.[96] Lipson and Katzenbach also note the fear of the small states "that the two space powers might act immoderately with regard to each other, or might do things in space which nonspace powers regard as inimical to their interests."[97] Article I can thus be seen to be nothing more than the reaffirmation by the parties of the traditional principles of equality, free access, nondiscrimination, and nonappropriation. If the article is read as a whole to gauge the proper context of the verbal formulae used therein, and if due consideration is given to their legislative roots, there is nothing in it which is consistent with the interpretation that if a particular activity is not specifically designed to be of general benefit to the world, or is not designed to benefit the interests of all countries, it is unlawful.

The Soviet Union has always resisted the argument that the "common heritage of mankind" principle, paraphrased in Article I, implies legally binding obligations. Dudakov, for example, points out that it is too early to speculate about common benefit and common sharing of profits arising from space activity, because space activity has not yet reached that stage. Attempts to define this principle would, in his opinion, be analogous to an attempt "to sell the bearskin before someone has caught the bear."[98]

To adopt the reasoning that defensive activity in outer space is unlawful under Articles I and IV(1) because it would not be, in the wording of Article I, "for the benefit and in the interests of all countries" would mean smuggling the terminology of Article IV(2) into Article IV(1) under the guise of the "common interests" principle and ignoring the express words of Article IV(1) which, as explained above, clearly envisage military activity in near-earth space. In fact, during the negotiations preceding the emergence of the final draft of the Space Treaty, India's proposal that the term "exclusively for peaceful purposes" as used in Article IV(2) be extended to *all* outer space areas was rejected.[99]

Too liberal a use of the "common interests" argument would prohibit pioneering space activity even in the nonmilitary field if it were of no direct benefit to or not in the interests of *all* countries, quite apart from the innumerable difficulties of defining what is a "benefit" and what is an "interest." How, for example, did activities such as the launching of the world's first sputnik, or the launching of dogs, rats, and spiders into space "benefit" all countries and advance their "interests"? It is quite reasonable to suppose that projects which lead to some tangible or measurable benefits in a nonaggressive manner to a specific country or group of countries could coexist with other projects of general benefit to all states. Neither Article IV nor the treaty as a whole forbids specific nonaggressive projects for the benefit of individual countries merely because they do not benefit other countries as well.[100]

The argument that all activity in space must be nonmilitary would not be consonant with current space-power behavior. The existence of a military dimension within the American space program is a matter of public knowledge.[101] While the Soviet Union refuses to publicly acknowledge any military activity in space, there can be no doubt that it is engaged in such activity.[102] According to American reports, both powers have been conducting antisatellite tests since the 1960s, and the USSR has been reported to have developed a "hunter-killer" system which can intercept and destroy satellites in space.[103] It it further impossible to believe that the Soviet Union has not taken *at least* such steps as the launching of satellites for purposes of surveillance,[104] military communication, and intelligence-gathering—steps which are not per se regarded as illegal by the United States.[105] Thus, it appears that neither power regards the use of outer space at least for military defense as inconsistent with the principle of common interests. Indeed, there have been indications that, since 1967, even the Soviet Union has moved toward the view that not every military activity in space is unlawful, and that it does not interpret the common interests principle or even Article I of the Space Treaty generally in a way that prohibits all military activity in outer space.[106]

Several arguments can be given to justify the current use by the space powers of reconnaissance satellites: that in the absence of compulsory international inspection, space reconnaissance is the only available confidence-building mechanism that can allay mutual fears of surprise attack and of other treaty violations; that reconnaissance is a peaceful activity in the sense of being nonaggressive;[107] that even if reconnaissance infringes the laws of national states it is not an international crime; and that in any case, reconnaissance satellites orbit in a zone beyond the reach of national/municipal law, so that their operation is literally "above law," i.e., without restrictions.[108]

Thus, in view of the fact that both powers are using outer space for at least some military purposes, they should not be too readily presumed to have intended, through a principle as vague as that of "common interests," to ban all military activity in space by signing the Space Treaty, in the absence of clear and unambiguous wording in the treaty to support such a construction.

3

CONCLUDING REFLECTIONS

An attempt has been made to examine the regimes of demilitarization in the oceans (including the ocean floor) and in outer space (including celestial bodies). It was seen that these regimes do not purport to achieve complete demilitarization, and in some instances they prohibit that which is under no immediate need of prohibition. For example, the 1971 Seabed Treaty ban on nuclear weapons on the seabed is not a set-back for the strategic forces of either of the two military powers. Because it permits mobile underwater weapons systems, and because it fails to regulate activity in those maritime zones falling into the traditional categories of national waters, territorial sea, contiguous zone, and the continental shelf, the treaty will not have much impact on the preservation of the oceans from the arms race. Since UNCLOS does not purport to change the existing regime of sovereignty over these zones, it too makes no new contribution: It does not restrict the traditional freedoms of the high seas (e.g., navigation and the immunity of warships). The scheme of verification under the Seabed Treaty, conducted on a national rather than an international level, has an inherent disability. With the signing of UNCLOS, wide zones of exclusive national jurisdiction will emerge, consisting chiefly of 12-mile territorial seas and 200-mile exclusive economic zones. The wider the zones of national jurisdiction, the more difficult it becomes for any scheme of national or international verification to operate effectively.

The verification procedures under the Space Treaty are also open to criticism. It has been pointed out that this treaty, while seeking to preserve the present state of *total* nonmilitarization of celestial bodies, achieves only *partial* demilitarization of circumterrestrial space. Verification is possible on the moon and other celestial bodies, but not in outer space or on earth-based centers.[109] It is ironic that verification of compliance with the ban on nuclear and mass-destruction weapons under paragraph one of Article IV of the Space Treaty would not be possible *at all*. Where verification *is* possible, it is with respect to a ban which, again, is not of much importance to the strategic forces of the space powers. The peculiar silence on circumlunar activity in both the Space and the Moon treaties applies to verification as well.

In view of both the provisions of and the loopholes in the existing regime of demilitarization and verification in outer space, the space powers are likely (a) to refrain, for the foreseeable future, from militarizing the moon and other celestial bodies (almost as much because of the technological and fiscal difficulties as because of the treaty prohibition); (b) to develop their own early warning surveillance and detection devices; (c) to resort to overt or covert defensive activities on or around the earth for nonaggressive purposes; (d) to eventually extend these activities to celestial bodies; and (e) to continue to search for mutually satisfactory verification arrangements that guarantee certainty and reliability.

The conclusions regarding the Space Treaty therefore seem similar to those regarding the Seabed Treaty. By signing the Space Treaty, the powers concerned agreed to refrain from doing something which did not show much potential for immediate strategic use; indeed, the prohibited activity was something which the powers had never even engaged in. One of the activities prohibited by the Space Treaty—the testing of nuclear weapons on celestial bodies—had in fact already been prohibited by the 1963 Test Ban Treaty. On the other hand, in both treaties, the powers stopped short of complete demilitarization of all activity: they left themselves freedom, under the Seabed Treaty, in the development of mobile underwater armament systems and related activities within the territorial sea and, under the Space Treaty, in the development and deployment in circumterrestrial space of orbital weapons systems.[110] In fact, as seen previously, by virtue of the silence of the Space Treaty and the Moon Treaty on circumlunar activity, the case can be made that the deployment of orbital weapons systems around the moon is lawful. Also missing from the Space Treaty are provisions regulating the development and use of land-based weapons systems capable of launching missiles which pass through space en route to targets on land.

The foregoing review also suggests, however, that peace cannot be simply legislated into place through a reform of the existing treaty law. Enthusiasm for reform will have to be tempered by a sober apprecia-

tion of the fact that, under the present system of international organization, that which is desirable may not always be practicable. Among the
best guides to what *is* practicable are actual state conduct (and the reasons and policies behind it) and acceptance of the practice of legitimizing competing state claims according to the degree to which they
approximate or deviate from the commonly accepted ideal of peace and
justice.[111] From this basic premise flows the proposition that state conduct is an important guide in the interpretation of the present law of
peace on the high seas and in outer space.

Observation of the present system of international relations shows
that international peace and order rest, in many important respects, on
a balance of power and mutual deterrence between states. In the absence of a strong central authority charged with the responsibility of
enforcing international peace, the development of offensive and defensive weapons systems on land, in the seas, and in space must be recognized as an important dynamic in the preservation of this balance of
power in the world. This cannot be "abolished" by treaty law. The
most that has been attempted, and without much success, is a freezing
of the status quo, with the option of achieving demilitarization and disarmament in stages in the future.[112] It has therefore been necessary to
show in some detail why the Space Treaty should not be interpreted to
have achieved total demilitarization in outer space or to have prohibited
all military uses of outer space. Such an interpretation would create
another glaring discrepancy between "law in action" and "law in the
books." The actualities of state behavior in space are not consistent
with the principle of total demilitarization.

The study of the issue of demilitarization under Article IV(1) of the
Space Treaty indicates, first, that the evolution of international conduct, or the emergence of an international convention or "norm" as an
aggregate of conduct, can occur independently of the individual or collective desire of the actors themselves. Thus, one or the other space
power or even both of them might think it desirable to prohibit all military activity in space, but a combination of political, economic, military, and strategic factors compels them to pursue such activity nevertheless and to refrain from agreeing to a comprehensive ban on the
stationing of all weapons (nuclear and conventional) in space. The
same applies to weapons at sea. A lawyer surveying the scene should
accordingly take heed of the possibility that the normative process un-

der observation is not necessarily the product of diligent legislators or even of the free will of the actors themselves.

Second, study of the above issue shows that overzealous enthusiasm may lead to the prescription of standards of behavior which are doomed to be ignored because the prescriber is misled by a conviction that norms of conduct between sovereign actors are always the product of their free will and therefore consonant with their conception of what is just and desirable. Conversely, this leads to the mistaken conclusion that if a particular prescription is desirable (in some universalistic sense because, e.g., it will reduce the risk of war), the actors will conform to it. The interpretation of Article IV of the Space Treaty as prohibiting all military activity in outer space is an example. As seen above, it has involved the use of a specious form of circumlocution whereby several words used in Article I are employed to color the meaning of the words actually used in Article IV. These words are thereby given a meaning thought to be more "desirable" than the one that the words in question would otherwise have.

The use of the behaviorist approach to the study of normative behavior would have a restraining effect on such tendencies. It reveals that actual state practice before and after the Space Treaty has been so patently inconsistent with such an interpretation that the actors cannot and will not adopt it. Abstraction of a norm from actual observed behavior also teaches the lawyer something about the evolution of a normative system which he may be studying—i.e., that it may in certain respects evolve in ways different from or even contrary to the subjective hopes and desires of the actors themselves, and that the lawyer should focus his attention on the real causes of the behavior (why states act the way they do), so that he can predict future patterns of behavior for purposes of creating a stable pattern of expectations and of minimizing conflict. If rules emerge through a process that is not entirely within the control of the actors, and if the actors are compelled to adopt certain uniformities of behavior that are at variance with their own conception of a "just," "ideal," or "morally desirable" order, then the lawyer is put on notice that neither vociferous advocacy of idealistic "codes" nor ingenious methods of interpreting existing ones to make them conform to some higher ideal will change behavior. It is one thing to say that particular normative patterns codified in a treaty are for some reason not conducive to peace and therefore undesirable, but it is quite another to ignore clearly discernible patterns of behavior which the treaty was actually intended to reflect and, by a process of "interpretation," to discover a norm in the treaty that does not reflect actual practice.

Municipal experience has proved the value of creative interpretation, but, even there, the change that this judicial tool can induce is at best modest and incremental. Its ability to do so is influenced by such factors as the independence and integrity of the judiciary, the power of judicial review, the presence or absence of political interference, shifts in public opinion in favor of or against the particular interpretation proposed, etc. Thus, there are always operational limits on the creative and innovative powers of lawyers and judges.

At the international level, as pointed out in chapter III, these operational limits are even more restricting. First of all, there is no judiciary with entrenched powers whose decisions bind all actors. Some would argue that there is not even much of a judiciary at all, let alone one that commands the awe and respect of its subjects. Secondly, the jurisdiction of such international judicial tribunals that do exist is not compulsory. Thirdly, there is no effective international enforcement machinery. Thus, the decision to resort to and comply with judicial settlement is a political one, and consequently the scope of action of international law-making agencies, as well as of international lawyers and judges, is not very wide.

One can identify several possible reasons to explain why the two powers have chosen not to achieve complete demilitarization and seem to have conceded reciprocal rights to each other to engage in some military activity in the oceans and in outer space: mutual suspicion between the rivals, compounded by weak inspection machinery, making it necessary to take precautionary military measures of a defensive nature; the insecurities caused by the rapid pace of technological advances in terrestrial and underwater armaments; the desire of one power to seek a military advantage in one sphere (e.g., sea or space) to neutralize the advantage of the rival in another sphere (e.g., land or underwater) or even to seek an overall military advantage over the rival; and fear that the rival may acquire an advantage and thereby upset the balance of power. Here again, the behaviorist approach proves itself to be value-neutral as well as empirical: value-neutral because it permits the abstraction of behavioral norms even though they may be thought to be undesirable from particular moral or ethical standpoints, and empirical because it is grounded in the actual observed behavior of the actors in question.

In the light of the foregoing, the following concluding observations concerning the future legal regimes on the high seas and in outer space may be made:

The norms of arms control on the high seas are evolving under circumstances that are different from those operative in the control and limitation of land-based armaments. The uniqueness of the former process is underlined by the fact that state economic and military activity underwater and on the seabed has been very modest in comparison to land-based activity. The result has been an almost total absence of a structured regime for the maintenance of law and order in that environment. The principle of the freedom of the high seas is in fact the epitome of this unstructured system, leaving states largely free from the control of any international authority. As undersea activity increases, the possibility of conflict increases correspondingly to the point where the need for a structured regime is not only obvious but also urgent, leading states to engage in a frantic search for such a regime at several large-scale multilateral conferences in the last few years. The freedom of states on the high seas is likely to be steadily eroded as economic and military activity increases, especially in the fields of the prevention of nuclear and chemical pollution, the prevention of nuclear and other accidents, the limitation of nuclear and conventional arms together with appropriate verification arrangements, and, finally, the rational economic exploitation of the resources of the seas.

State activity in outer space is, if anything, even less structured, and it does not even have a body of customary law such as that guiding activity on the high seas. Although outer space and celestial bodies have been repeatedly declared to be open to all states on an equal basis, no principle of "freedom of outer space" parallel to the "freedom of the seas" has been asserted in space. But this is unlikely to mean that states will be more amenable to international controls on their activities in outer space. In fact, the emergence of international constabularies and verification agencies for activities in outer space will be slower than it is apt to be in the case of undersea activities. This is not only because of the absence of customary law restrictions bearing directly on outer space activity, but also because the technological threshold for the verification of activity in outer space is far higher than for verification on land, underwater, or on the seabed. For this reason, in addition to such methods as satellite reconnaissance from outer space, verification of outer space activity may take place elsewhere than in outer space—e.g., at launching pads, at storage and testing sites, or in designated sections inside or outside space centers.

Insofar as verification at sea is technologically a more complex problem than on-site inspection on land, it is possible that some of the verification of ocean activity may take place on land rather than at sea—e.g., in shipyards, harbors, and similar facilities. Another unique characteristic of the evolving regime of arms control in hydrospace is the sudden increase in the economic and strategic significance of hydrospace itself. Outer space activity so far has not yielded any economic rewards, and while its strategic potential could conceivably increase in the future, it is not currently of as keen military interest as the oceans. This does not mean, however, that research in the development of space technology will not continue. Insofar as economic well-being and military prowess are in this age so much a function of technology, and since the resources of the earth are finite, it is only a matter of time before the search for economic and military security breaks away from the confines of this planet.

It is possible that an initial two-power verification agency may be an attractive idea to the space powers, not only because of its administrative simplicity but also because its maintenance would be far less expensive and compromises would be easier. The two space powers should be able to appreciate better than other states the close links between the military and nonmilitary applications of space technology. They would also possess the knowledge and expertise necessary to decide what kinds of space activity should be permitted, so as not to stifle interest and initiative in the nonmilitary application of space technology, and what kinds of research and development pose too great a military risk.

If the superpowers chose to leave room in the Space Treaty for some military activity in space, it could only be because the present international legal system, due to certain structural weaknesses such as ineffective machinery for inspection, verification, and enforcement, fails to provide an appropriate degree of security. As in other spheres of unregulated superpower activity, it is possible to discern the beginnings of a regime of tacitly conceded rights to engage in certain kinds of military activity in space, based on the principle of reciprocity. The most important example is the use of military reconnaissance satellites. The shift in the verbal strategy of the Soviet Union on this issue means not merely that it is using this method of intelligence gathering but also that it finds such use to be in its best interest. There are signs indicating that reconnaissance will move from being a tacitly and reciprocally accepted activity to being an explicitly sanctioned aspect of defense policy. In the absence of other guarantees, it seems to be the best method of ensuring that neither party acquires an advantage in armaments that might upset the balance of power on land, on the seas, or in outer space. The principle of reciprocity has already crystallized into a recognized precondition in respect of inspection under Article XII of the Space Treaty.

The international lawyer should therefore be aware that, although it may be desirable to have legal regimes for outer space and for the high seas that do not impede the exploitation of economic resources, that proscribe both nuclear and conventional weapons and both stationary and mobile armaments, and that provide strict and compulsory verification, a pragmatic policy for developing such regimes will be one that provides an accommodation between these goals and the principles of reciprocity and consensus. Such a policy should assist in the creation of a more or less stable pattern of expectations between the actors, without disturbing the existing balance of power. McDougal and Lipson adopt an essentially behaviorist line when they observe that the future law of space will evolve through "the slow building of expectations, the continued accretion of repeated instances of tolerated acts, the gradual development of assurance that certain things may be done under promise of reciprocity and that other things must not be done on pain of retaliation."[113]

CHAPTER V

Conclusions

Among the popular beliefs about law and legal systems is the belief that they encourage or promote, if indeed they do not create, a more or less stable pattern of expectations between the actors concerned. Viewed thus, law appears essentially as a list of prohibitions that concretize and reinforce a pattern of expectations of what one should not do. In the interests of preserving the status quo, or at least not altering the distribution of a particular set of power relationships, it is easier and mutually advantageous for the actors concerned to agree on what not to do, even if they cannot agree on what they *should* do. In fact, very often agreement on the latter is indirectly and partially reached by agreement on the former, because this by implication delimits the range of permissible activity.

This "negative community of interest" may arise through deliberate legislative planning or out of crisis management on an ad hoc basis. At the international level, the former process is exemplified by such laboriously drafted pieces of legislation as the 1963 Test Ban Treaty, the 1967 Space Treaty, the 1971 Seabed Treaty, the 1974 definition of aggression, and the Helsinki Final Act of 1975. All these prohibited certain types of activities, leaving open the possibility that what was not expressly prohibited was intended to be permitted. Thus, the Space Treaty, by providing two separate regimes of demilitarization in space (one on the moon and other celestial bodies and the other in circumterrestrial space) and by prescribing total nonmilitarization in only one of them, makes possible the argument that something short of complete nonmilitarization was intended in the other. Consistent with this interpretation, it is arguable that such military but nonaggressive uses of circumterrestrial space as remote sensing and satellite surveillance of earth are permissible. A further argument is that, by banning only nuclear and mass-destruction weapons around the earth, the treaty permits conventional weapons in orbit around the earth. Finally, even if the treaty is taken to have banned all orbital weapons around the earth, it cannot be understood to have banned those bombardment systems that employ nuclear missiles that pass through space en route to targets on earth without completing a full orbit.

The 1971 Seabed Treaty is another attempt to serve common interests through prohibition. The interest in question is keeping the seabed, the ocean floor, and its subsoil free of nuclear weapons and other weapons of mass destruction, the significance of which is obvious not only for coastal states but also for the impending commercial exploitation of the oceans. On the other hand, by prohibiting only nuclear and mass-destruction weapons, this treaty seems to permit the stationing of nonnuclear weapons that are not "weapons of mass destruction." Similarly, by apparently prohibiting only "fixed" weapons, it implicitly permits a wide range of mobile weapons systems, including submarines equipped with nuclear missiles. Finally, as stated previously, by juxtaposing two maritime zones (the 12-mile zone under the Geneva Convention and the ocean space beyond it) and by declaring the prohibited zone to end at the 12-mile zone, the treaty gives the impression that activity within the 12-mile zone was intended to be left entirely unfettered.

The most prominent example of proscriptions that have arisen not through deliberate legislation but through spontaneous and often hazardous experience of ad hoc crisis management is the law of interbloc reciprocity, discussed in chapter III. The norm of mutual noninterference in bloc affairs has emerged as the fundamental principle of contemporary superpower coexistence. Just as in the case of the Seabed and Space treaties, this proscription can be interpreted as implying the *permissibility* of certain acts. Thus, nonintervention in bloc affairs implies that a breach of bloc solidarity is a matter for *intrabloc* determination. And just as with the treaties, this "implied right" can be stretched to encompass more extreme interpretations—for example, as the Hungarian, Cuban, Czechoslovak, and Dominican interventions show, that it is the *leader* of the bloc that decides whether or not there exists a threat to bloc solidarity, and, as shown by the Hungarian and Cuban cases, that the leader of the bloc has a *unilateral competence* to take countermeasures.

The principle that regionalism has precedence over the UN Charter is another norm of interbloc reciprocity serving the same negative community of interests. The corollary to this principle was seen to be the denial of competence to individual nations to decide for themselves in what ways their own security is threatened and in what ways their own activities threaten regional solidarity. It also implies that individual bloc members cannot voluntarily withdraw their membership and pursue policies that are independent of the bloc. The Soviet Union has been far less tolerant than the United States on the question of independence and diversity within its bloc. This prompted the protest from Yugoslavia, for example, that while the Soviet Union advocates peace and peaceful coexistence outside its bloc, it suppresses such pleas *within* the bloc on the ground that they are "revisionist," and takes steps against them when they do appear.

However, even the minimal function of intrabloc measures to preserve existing power balances, whether taken by the Soviet Union or by the United States, is the product of the interplay of complex policy considerations that involve assessment of the nature of the threat, of the probable consequences if no countermeasures are taken, and of the probable impact of these measures on the rival party if they are taken. After this, there still remain the questions of the actual impact of the measures on the rival party and, finally, of the latter's own image of the intentions of the former. Depending on the facts and circumstances of each particular case, there are linkages between the proportionality or severity of a countermeasure and the nature of the perceived threat, and between proportionality and impact prediction. The Korean crisis, discussed in chapter II, and the Cuban crisis, discussed in chapter III, illustrate the principle of linkage. These two cases also show that miscalculation of impact or proportionality can result in a sudden and unexpected change in the direction that a dispute takes. This is of particular importance in zones of overlapping interest, such as Korea and Cuba. The Cuban case further delineates the boundaries within which the rule of nonintervention in bloc affairs is operative: Each power has a free hand in regulating intrabloc affairs as long as it does not affect the interests, goals, and security of the rival bloc. It also implies that the power to decide on the use of nuclear weapons is to be restricted to the ultimate policymakers in each bloc. The missiles in Cuba created the possibility of Cuban participation in any such future decision-making, which was unacceptable to the United States.

Finally, the Cuban case provides an especially clear illustration of the balance-of-power orientation of interbloc relations and the negative prescriptions which govern them. It will be recalled that during the negotiations following the Cuban quarantine, the Soviet Union made the removal of its missiles in Cuba conditional upon the removal of NATO missiles from Turkey, as well as upon a U.S. guarantee against future attacks on Cuba. The United States responded by offering to lift the quarantine and by giving a pledge of nonaggression, but it made no reference to the Turkish missiles. That the Soviet Union was prepared to accept this as sufficient for the removal of the missiles without further insistence on the removal of the missiles in Turkey can indicate only that these were regarded by both powers as an already established part of the political and military status quo in Europe, which should not be changed, while at the same time the Cuban missiles would have had a destabilizing influence on the power balance insofar as they constituted a sudden military advantage by one side deep inside the sphere of influence of the other.

These considerations show that a regime of negative prescriptions, even one oriented toward the status quo, does not comprise simply a list of rigid prohibitions within a static system, but is a complex network of interlocking policy considerations which, because of their frequency and regularity, have acquired normative status. The genesis of this empirically based regime suggests that it is something more than a temporary truce between two rival blocs, but is rather a dynamic and expanding regime in which norms are being generated and concretized at a level and pace that are commensurate with the intensity of cooperation and conflict between the two principal actors. The more or less spontaneous evolution of this regime further shows that it is not deliberately planned by the actors whose relations it governs, is in fact neutral to their value systems, and provides solutions to specific interbloc disputes without inquiry as to which side has the "just" cause and without requiring that the dispute be settled by some higher authority.

Contemporary superpower relations show that the two powers have had to grapple with several issues simultaneously. The degree of agreement on particular issues varies widely; on some, agreement is reached readily, yet on others there is total disagreement, the disparity of viewpoints being so wide as to render illusory any hope of agreement. In view of this concatenation of international issues confronting the two powers, their relations have been characterized by a unique form of *simultaneous* conflict and cooperation. Differences over one issue do not necessarily preclude agreement on other issues; on the other hand, willingness to cooperate or negotiate over a particular conflict does not guarantee that that conflict will be resolved. The fact that differences of opinion cannot be resolved by direct agreement does not, however, deny the possibility of settlement through processes other than direct agreement.

Every instance of interbloc conflict or cooperation shows that the procedure for settlement is in each case *problem-oriented*. This is true whether the settlement is achieved through deliberate legislation or through ad hoc crisis management. The law of interbloc reciprocity discussed in chapter III, together with the trouble situations described there, developed case by case. Each crisis was resolved in a manner suitable to its own special facts and circumstances. Indeed, even the rules of severity and proportionality of force, the assessment of probable consequences, and impact prediction were seen to necessitate a highly differentiated approach to each crisis.

Even norms created through deliberate legislation or codification were arrived at through the same step-by-step, problem-solving approach. Thus, the 1963 Partial Test Ban Treaty was agreed to after a summit meeting between the Soviet Union, the United States, and Great Britain. There, the sides confronted each other and had an opportunity to negotiate directly with each other on a specific topic. The Space Treaty was the product of similar negotiations, and the Seabed Treaty was a unique example of the step-by-step approach: unilateral draft proposals were exchanged, joint efforts were resumed after several rejections by other members of the UN until, finally, a much-amended version won approval.

The willingness of the Soviet Union to negotiate topic by topic with the United States is a significant concession to the Western preference for the handling of issues on the basis of priority and in a pragmatic manner, instead of through general acts of codification of the sort preferred by the Soviet Union. The problem-oriented nature of norm creation has meant that norms can emerge only ad hoc, the method of changing rules or of introducing new ones being *gradual* or *incremental*. A regime based on the status quo almost by definition cannot introduce more than incremental change.

Another characteristic closely connected to the gradualist nature of the approach is that it is *consensual*, in that both powers appear to recognize the desirability of negotiation and bargaining for purposes of reaching mutually acceptable normative arrangements. In other instances, consent is demonstrated by acquiescence or reciprocally tolerated acts. Finally, the approach may also be described as *unilateral-reciprocal*, insofar as contemporary interbloc (and international) law-making is a process in which one power unilaterally proposes a draft treaty on a matter affecting the interests of both powers, in the hope that the other power will reciprocate either by accepting the draft or by proposing a counterdraft that would then lead to negotiations and to eventual consensus—a process described by Khrushchev as the "politic of mutual example."

With regard to the evolution of norms through crisis management, certain unilaterally asserted claims by one side have been seen to create precedents for later parallel claims from the other, thus creating a new body of doctrine coexisting with a pattern of reciprocally condoned acts. While this doctrine treats ideological considerations as highly important, it would be incorrect to say that superpower relations are governed solely by ideological criteria. Several other considerations can be identified as of equal importance—e.g., the mutual fear of destruction, national security, economic interests, regional/hemispheric commitments, and even common interests. There is also considerable overlap among these considerations, and none operates to the total exclusion of the others. With one exception, there is no particular hierarchy or order of importance in the operative variables governing contemporary superpower relations. The exception is the mutual fear of annihilation, which has been seen to have led to determined efforts by both sides to limit the deployment of nuclear weapons on land, the seabed, and in outer space.

Having arrived at a de facto regime of noninterference with unilateral action taken within spheres of influence, the two powers appear to have delimited the extent to which they may pursue purely ideological goals outside national boundaries. Finally, ideological enmity has not precluded all possibilities of agreement or cooperation in matters of common interest. The anti-Hitler alliance is a good example. Others are the U.S.-Soviet agreement on the exchange of data gathered from certain activities in space and the treaty on the rescue of astronauts.

By way of conclusion, a few remarks may be made on the behaviorist approach to the study of international law. Apart from the fact that it is empirically based and value-neutral, it illuminates the numerous areas of international law in which there are discrepancies between the law-in-the-books and the law-in-action. This, in turn, serves several useful functions. First, it delineates for the international lawyer or judge the operational limits of his role, which is a particularly delicate question because of the absence of a strong and entrenched international judiciary with compulsory powers of adjudication regardless of the subject matter of the dispute. The urge for creative interpretation of written international legal documents must therefore be tempered by a sober evaluation of the extent to which existing state practice supports or is likely to support it. Too "radical" an interpretation—even if judicially upheld—can be easily cast aside and ignored in the absence of effective law-enforcing machinery. Such occurrences can only create further uncertainty within an already fragile and delicately balanced system.

In evaluating the extent to which existing state practice is likely to support a particular interpretation, the lawyer and judge must bear in mind that a legal system may in some respects evolve in ways contrary to the free will of the actors themselves. This may force them to focus on the actual causes of state conduct, which would vary from case to case. Thus, for example, even though the complete demilitarization of circumterrestrial space may be desirable to one or both powers, actual practice indicates that there is at least defensive military activity, and among the causes of such conduct may be mutual suspicion heightened by weak international inspection systems, technological advances, the danger of one side trying to gain an advantage over its rival, etc. Depending on the number, frequency, and cogency of the motives of state conduct, the lawyer and judge should be able to gauge to what extent particular interpretations are likely to be tolerated by the actors in question.

This approach also provides a warning against the dangers of sweeping acts of general codification. There would be little point in proclaiming idealistic codes that state practice shows no sign of accepting, quite apart from the ambiguities and semantic confusion that can often arise when two contending legal philosophies try to interpret the same document. The behaviorist approach proves Jellinek's dictum (uttered in a different context) that the factual reinforces the normative. Viewed in that way, observed behavior can actually operate as a guide to the interpretation of written codes. It has been seen how state practice relating to the use of outer space for satellite surveillance and other defensive military activity reinforces the argument that the particular verbal formulae in Article IV of the Space Treaty do not permit the interpretation that the article proscribes all military activity in space. This, in turn, as was pointed out earlier in this chapter, complements the regime of the negative community of interests by indicating the permissible range of activity, which under the present system of international organization is the only way of ensuring that neither side is clandestinely preparing any sudden moves to upset the power balance.

Apart from serving as an interpretive aid and performing a cautionary function in the drafting of legal codes of general application, the behaviorist approach reveals the nature and substance of the "living law" of power politics. It reveals that while force is in many instances the antithesis of law, the use of force in international relations does not mean that there is no international "law." The living law of power politics means that law pertains to particular subgroups; it does not "float around" in society at large, to use Pospíšil's phrase.[1] Thus, simultaneous membership of one state in two different subgroups (e.g., an ideological bloc and the society of nations under the UN Charter) may subject it to two different and sometimes contradictory regimes. A superficial examination of behavior from the point of view of only one subgroup may give an impression of lawlessness, whereas that same behavior, if examined in the context of an appropriate subgroup, may reveal a complex normative system which seems to be still evolving.

APPENDIX I

An Enumerative Definition of the Soviet Concept
of Peaceful Coexistence*

1. The Principle of Self-Determination

This principle has acquired cardinal importance in the present era of transition from capitalism to socialism, an era highlighted by the decisive influence of the world socialist system and by tremendous victories on the part of peoples fighting for national independence and social progress. Self-determination implies the inalienable right of every nation to a free choice of political, economic, social and cultural system, form of government and state structure; it means that no state may impose any system or form of government on any other nation, and affirms the right of every people to develop the political, economic and social order it has chosen.

All nations, great and small, including those still under foreign domination or colonial rule, have the right to self-determination.

2. The Principle of Non-Interference

Any form of direct or indirect interference, including subversive activity, is an encroachment on the sovereign rights of a people or state. It creates a threat to a country's independence, freedom and normal political, economic, social and cultural development, and jeopardizes world peace.

No state has the right to interfere directly or indirectly in the internal or foreign affairs of another state for any reason whatever.

Neither the United Nations nor any other international organization has the right to interfere in a country's internal affairs or to demand that its members submit such affairs for consideration by an international organization with the exception of cases when the Security Council takes enforcement actions under Chapter VII of the United Nations Charter.

International law condemns not only armed intervention but also all other forms of intervention directed against a state's sovereign rights or against its political, economic or cultural institutions.

Peaceful coexistence requires non-intervention (direct or indirect) in one another's internal or foreign affairs, respect for the systems chosen by nations, and no hostile propaganda that incites hatred among nations. States shall re-

*Source: G. ZADOROZHNY, PEACEFUL COEXISTENCE: CONTEMPORARY INTERNATIONAL LAW OF PEACEFUL COEXISTENCE 304–12 (V. Schneierson trans. 1968).

frain from aiding, abetting, financing, encouraging or organizing civil strife or subversive activities in another state, from committing terrorist acts with the aim of forcibly changing its system, and from organizing irregular troops or armed groups with the object of invading another state.

3. The Principle of Sovereignty

Observance of the above demands of international law is connected with the principle of sovereignty, which connotes the political independence of every people and state in its internal and external affairs, and independence from any foreign state. In international relations, sovereignty is the right of every state to participate in the solution of all international matters relating to its lawful interests through international treaties, conferences and organizations.

4. The Principle of Sovereign Equality

Peaceful coexistence means that all states enjoy legal equality in international relations and in international organizations and conferences, and have an equal right to protection in conformity with international law. Each state shall respect the legal competence of other peoples and states. No considerations of a political, social, economic, geographical, historical, racial or any other nature may restrict the legal capacity of a people or state with regard to its equal rights and duties as a subject of international law. All survivals of colonialism, including segregation and discrimination, shall be abolished. The only states whose rights may be restricted are aggressor states that have perpetrated international crimes.

5. The Principle of Territorial Inviolability

States are truly sovereign in internal affairs when they possess supreme authority on their territory, particularly, the right to deal freely with their national wealth and natural resources, and also the right to close down all foreign military bases on their territories.

The exercise of supreme authority does not imply that peoples or states may inflict damage on any other countries by experiments or actions liable to produce harmful consequences or jeopardize their security.

Respect for the territorial integrity and inviolability of each state rules out the use of force in resolving territorial disputes and frontier problems; it implies that territories under colonial rule shall be given their freedom.

6. The Principle of Human Rights and Fundamental Freedoms. The Banning of Racial Discrimination.

True equality of peoples and states is inconceivable without the equality of great and small nations and races. This, in turn, is inconceivable without the equality of all men, without human rights and fundamental freedoms for all. International law prohibits racial restrictions of any kind designed to destroy or curtail the recognition or equal exercise of human rights and fundamental freedoms in the political, economic, social, cultural and other spheres.

Recognition of the dignity of all members of the human family and of men's equal and inalienable rights is the foundation of freedom, justice and universal peace. The ideal of free human beings enjoying freedom from fear and want can only be achieved if conditions are created whereby everyone may enjoy his political, economic, social, civic and cultural rights.

Peaceful coexistence calls for the abolition of racial discrimination, which is an obstacle to peaceful relations between nations and can lead to a breach of international peace; it also demands the prevention and eradication of racist theory and practice, in order to promote mutual understanding between races and create an international community free from all forms of racial segregation and racial discrimination. International law prohibits discrimination, that is, any distinction, exclusion, restriction or privilege on account of race, color, or tribal, national or ethnic origin, aiming at, or resulting in, the abolition or curtailment of the recognition or equal exercise of human rights and fundamental freedoms in the political, economic, social, cultural or other spheres.

Effective implementation of human rights and fundamental freedoms strengthens world peace and friendship among nations.

It is impermissible for any state to impose on any other state privileges for foreigners or to grant foreigners greater rights than to its own citizens, although the state can exempt foreigners from certain liabilities such as military services, taxes, etc.

7. The Principle of Peace, Non-Aggression and the Banning of Aggression

An armed attack by one state on another, or the use of armed force in any other form contrary to the United Nations Charter is aggression, the gravest of all international crimes and the most dangerous encroachment on the rights of sovereign peoples and states. Armed intervention is synonymous with aggression.

The preparation of aggressive wars is an international crime which entails political and material responsibility, like aggression itself, for the state or states concerned and criminal responsibility for persons guilty of such a crime, irrespective of the statute of limitations.

Armed measures of repression against peoples fighting against colonialism, and also the use of force with the object of depriving peoples of the form of their national existence, are likewise international crimes.

8. The Principle of Self-Defense and the Lawfulness of National Liberation Wars

While branding aggressive wars as an international crime, international law recognizes as legitimate the use of armed or other force against aggressors and against colonial rule in pursuance of the right of self-determination. Peoples fighting against colonial rule, for their freedom and self-determination enjoy the right of individual and collective self-defense, just as states do.

9. The Principle of International Security and Collective Self-Defense

Struggle against aggression should be real and effective. In the event of an aggression, every state has the right of individual or collective self-defense in conformity with the principle of the indivisibility of the world (an attack on one state is regarded as an attack on all states) and the principle of collective security (assistance by other states to a victim of aggression and the suppression of aggression) within the framework of a universal security organization.

Peoples subjected to colonial oppression have the right to appeal for, and to receive, every support in their struggle.

10. The Principle of Banning the Use or Threat of Force

No state may apply or encourage political, economic or any other coercive measures to curtail the sovereign rights of another state or to obtain any benefits from it, except in case of preventive measures undertaken by the Security Council in accordance with Chapter VII of the United Nations Charter.

Any use or threat of force in international relations that contradicts the United Nations Charter is forbidden.

In this sense the term "force" embraces not only armed force but also any form of coercion, violence or pressure, including political, economic, social or psychological pressure, against the territorial integrity or political independence of a state. This outlaws the "positions of strength" and cold war policy, and all economic, political and other pressure that prejudices the sovereign rights of peoples and states, including any direct or indirect compulsory actions that deprive people under foreign domination of their right to self-determination, freedom, independence, and the form of their national existence.

11. The Principle of Banning War Propaganda

International law bans all propaganda of war, incitement to war or the fanning of war, in particular, propaganda of preventive war or strike-first nuclear war.

12. The Principle of the Peaceful Settlement of International Disputes

By virtue of the ban on the use or threat of force in international relations, states are obliged to adjust their international disputes so as not to jeopardize international peace, security and justice. Disputes of this kind should be settled by negotiation and other peaceful means agreed between the parties and consistent with the circumstances and nature of the dispute, in a spirit of mutual understanding and without any form of pressure. The parties to a dispute are obliged to take steps to reduce international tension, strengthen peace and encourage friendly relations and co-operation between states.

While employing peaceful means, all states must refrain from any actions that might exacerbate the situation.

13. The Principle of Disarmament

The ban on the use of force in international relations makes the armaments drive, which creates a threat to peace and is an unbearable burden on the peoples, unlawful and senseless. General and complete disarmament of all states under effective international control is the most desirable form of disarmament. This does not exclude such preliminary steps as the establishment of nuclear-free zones, non-proliferation of nuclear weapons, a complete ban on nuclear testing, the dismantling of foreign military bases on the territory of other countries, a ban on the use of weapons of mass destruction and destruction of the means of their delivery, etc.

14. The Principle of Mutual Advantage

The peaceful settlement of international disputes—which rules out unlawful use of force, threat of force and all forms of pressure and intimidation—implies that a search for agreed, mutually advantageous decisions is the only basis on which international problems may be resolved without imperilling international peace and security and without prejudicing mutual interests. Only in this case states are able to assume stable and enduring international commitments of their own free will.

15. The Principle of the Observance of International Commitments

Decisions reached on a mutually advantageous basis acquire the force of international contract obligatory for all states that accepted them of their own free will or agreed with them. Furthermore, every state must strictly observe the universally recognized standards of international law, in particular, the principles of international law postulating the peaceful coexistence of states and governing international law and order. Therefore, observance of justice and of commitments voluntarily undertaken, implicit in international treaties and other sources of international law, as well as the principle that international treaties are sacred, is a key principle of international relations. Peaceful coexistence creates conditions in which states are able to respect justice and observe commitments arising from treaties and other sources of international law, provided the commitments do not contradict the principles of peaceful coexistence of the United Nations Charter.

16. The Principle of Universal International Co-operation

In the world of today, countries having different socio-economic systems cannot live in isolation from one another. International co-operation envisages systematic actions by the states of different systems to eliminate everything that might jeopardize world peace or friendly relations among nations. The states of the two systems should co-operate not only in maintaining international peace and security but also in the economic, social and cultural spheres, as well as in science and technology, in order to further the progress of mankind and to eliminate the causes of international tension.

Peaceful coexistence connotes broad, fruitful and mutually advantageous international co-operation.

All states, great and small, bear responsibility for the development of good-neighbourly relations and the establishment of an atmosphere of co-operation on a regional scale as well, particularly among states with different social and political systems, inasmuch as all mutual understanding, including the improvement of bilateral relations, has a positive influence on international relations as a whole.

17. The Principle of the Universality of International Organizations

The modern system of relations between people and states in conformity with international law is not based on the establishment of any supra-national bodies of world government. It requires that all international organizations be used to promote the economic and social progress of all peoples, as centers for the co-ordination of actions by states belonging to different socio-economic systems.

Modern international law and order recognizes the right of every subject of international law to take part in the decisions of international organizations or conferences on international problems that concern its legitimate interests, and to become a party to any international treaties that affect these interests.

18. The Principle of Peaceful Competition Between the Two Systems

The peaceful coexistence of capitalist and socialist states connotes not simply all-round international co-operation between states of the two systems, but also a competition in which the winner will be the most progressive social system, the one that provides the higher living standard, the maximum of democratic rights and freedoms and a real abundance of material and spiritual blessings.

Conference on Security & Co-Operation in Europe: Final Act

DECLARATION OF PRINCIPLES GUIDING RELATIONS BETWEEN PARTICIPATING STATES *

The participating States,

Reaffirming their commitment to peace, security and justice and the continuing development of friendly relations and co-operation;

Recognizing that this commitment, which reflects the interest and aspirations of peoples, constitutes for each participating State a present and future responsibility, heightened by experience of the past;

Reaffirming, in conformity with their membership in the United Nations and in accordance with the purposes and principles of the United Nations, their full and active support for the United Nations and for the enhancement of its role and effectiveness in strengthening international peace, security and justice, and in promoting the solution of international problems, as well as the development of friendly relations and co-operation among States;

Expressing their common adherence to the principles which are set forth below and are in conformity with the Charter of the United Nations, as well as their common will to act, in the application of these principles, in conformity with the purposes and principles of the Charter of the United Nations;

Declare their determination to respect and put into practice, each of them in its relations with all other participating States, irrespective of their political, economic or social systems as well as of their size, geographical location or level of economic development, the following principles, which all are of primary significance, guiding their mutual relations:

---

* Adopted Aug. 1, 1975, at Helsinki, Finland, by the representatives of: Austria, Belgium, Bulgaria, Canada, Cyprus, Czechoslovakia, Denmark, Finland, France, the German Democratic Republic, the Federal Republic of Germany, Greece, the Holy See, Hungary, Iceland, Ireland, Italy, Liechtenstein, Luxembourg, Malta, Monaco, the Netherlands, Norway, Poland, Portugal, Romania, San Marino, Spain, Sweden, Switzerland, Turkey, the Union of Soviet Socialist Republics, the United Kingdom, the United States of America, and Yugoslavia. The Declaration of Principles constitutes section 1(a) under the heading "Questions relating to Security in Europe" in the Final Act. For the complete text of the act, see 73 DEP'T ST. BULL. 323 (1975); 14 INTERNATIONAL LEGAL MATERIALS 1292 (1975).

I. Sovereign equality, respect for the rights inherent in sovereignty

The participating States will respect each other's sovereign equality and individuality as well as all the rights inherent in and encompassed by its sovereignty, including in particular the right of every State to juridical equality, to territorial integrity and to freedom and political independence. They will also respect each other's right freely to choose and develop its political, social, economic and cultural systems as well as its right to determine its laws and regulations.

Within the framework of international law, all the participating States have equal rights and duties. They will respect each other's right to define and conduct as it wishes its relations with other States in accordance with international law and in the spirit of the present Declaration. They consider that their frontiers can be changed, in accordance with international law, by peaceful means and by agreement. They also have the right to belong or not to belong to international organizations, to be or not be a party to bilateral or multilateral treaties including the right to be or not to be a party to treaties of alliance; they also have the right to neutrality.

II. Refraining from the threat or the use of force

The Participating States will refrain in their mutual relations, as well as in their international relations in general, from the threat or use of force against the territorial integrity or political independence of any State, or in any other manner inconsistent with the purposes of the United Nations and with the present Declaration. No consideration may be invoked to serve to warrant resort to the threat or use of force in contravention of this principle.

Accordingly, the participating States will refrain from any acts constituting a threat of force or direct or indirect use of force against another participating State. Likewise they will refrain from any manifestation of force for the purpose of inducing another participating State to renounce the full exercise of its sovereign rights. Likewise they will also refrain in their mutual relations from any act of reprisal by force.

No such threat or use of force will be employed as a means of settling disputes, or questions likely to give rise to disputes, between them.

III. Inviolability of frontiers

The participating States regard as inviolable all one another's frontiers as well as the frontiers of all States in Europe and therefore they will refrain now and in the future from assaulting these frontiers.

Accordingly, they will also refrain from any demand for, or act of, seizure and usurpation of part or all of the territory of any participating State.

IV. Territorial integrity of States

The participating States will respect the territorial integrity of each of the participating States.

Accordingly, they will refrain from any action inconsistent with the purposes and principles of the Charter of the United Nations against the territorial integrity, political independence or the unity of any participating State, and in particular from any such action constituting a threat or use of force.

The participating States will likewise refrain from making each other's territory the object of military occupation or other direct or indirect measures of force in contravention of international law, or the object of acquisition by means of such measures or the threat of them. No such occupation or acquisition will be recognized as legal.

V. Peaceful settlement of disputes

The participating States will settle disputes among them by peaceful means in such a manner as not to endanger international peace and security, and justice.

They will endeavor in good faith and a spirit of co-operation to reach a rapid and equitable solution on the basis of international law.

For this purpose they will use such means as negotiation, enquiry, mediation, conciliation, arbitration, judicial settlement or other peaceful means of their own choice including any settlement procedure agreed to in advance of disputes to which they are parties.

In the event of failure to reach a solution by any of the above peaceful means, the parties to a dispute will continue to seek a mutually agreed way to settle the dispute peacefully.

Participating States, parties to a dispute among them, as well as other participating States will refrain from any action which might aggravate the situation to such a degree as to endanger the maintenance of international peace and security and thereby make a peaceful settlement of the dispute more difficult.

VI. Non-intervention in internal affairs

The participating States will refrain from any intervention, direct or indirect, individual or collective, in the internal or external affairs falling within the domestic jurisdiction of another participating State, regardless of their mutual relations.

They will accordingly refrain from any form of armed intervention or threat of such intervention against another participating State.

They will likewise in all circumstances refrain from any other act of military, or of political, economic or other coercion designed to subordinate to their own interest the exercise by another participating State of the rights inherent in its sovereignty and thus to secure advantages of any kinds.

Accordingly they will, inter alia, refrain from direct or indirect assistance to terrorist activities, or to subversive or other activities directed towards the violent overthrow of the regime of another participating State.

VII. Respect for human rights and fundamental freedoms, including the freedom of thought, conscience, religion or belief

The participating States will respect human rights and fundamental freedoms, including the freedom of thought, conscience, religion or belief, for all without distinction as to race, sex, language or religion.

They will promote and encourage the effective exercise of civil, political, economic, social, cultural and other rights and freedoms all of which derive from the inherent dignity of the human person and are essential for his free and full development.

Within this framework the participating States will recognize and respect the freedom of the individual to profess and practice, alone or in community with others, religion or belief acting in accordance with the dictates of his own conscience.

The participating States on whose territory national minorities exist will respect the right of persons belonging to such minorities to equality before the law, and will afford them the full opportunity for the actual enjoyment of human rights and fundamental freedoms and will, in this manner, protect their legitimate interests in this sphere.

The participating States recognize the universal significance of human rights and fundamental freedoms, respect for which is an essential factor for the peace, justice and well-being necessary to ensure the development of friendly relations and co-operation among themselves as among all States.

They will constantly respect these rights and freedoms in their mutual relations and will endeavor jointly and separately, including in co-operation with the United Nations, to promote universal and effective respect for them.

They confirm the right of the individual to know and act upon his rights and duties in this field.

In the field of human rights and fundamental freedoms, the participating States will act in conformity with the purposes and principles of the Charter of the United Nations and with the Universal Declaration of Human Rights. They will also fulfil their obligations as set forth in the international declarations and agreements in this field, including inter alia the International Covenants on Human Rights, by which they may be bound.

VIII. Equal rights and self-determination of peoples

The participating States will respect the equal rights of peoples and their right to self-determination, acting at all times in conformity with the purposes and principles of the Charter of the United Nations and with the relevant norms of international law, including those relating to territorial integrity of States.

By virtue of the principle of equal rights and self-determination of peoples, all peoples always have the right, in full freedom, to determine, when and as they wish, their internal and external political status, without external interference, and to pursue as they wish their political, economic, social and cultural development.

The participating States reaffirm the universal significance of respect for and effective exercise of equal rights and self-determination of peoples for the development of friendly relations among themselves as among all States; they also recall the importance of the elimination of any form of violation of this principle.

IX. Co-operation among States

The participating States will develop their co-operation with one another and with all States in all fields in accordance with the purposes and principles of the Charter of the United Nations. In developing their co-operation the participating States will place special emphasis on the fields as set forth within the framework of the Conference on Security and Cooperation in Europe, with each of them making its contribution in conditions of full equality.

They will endeavor, in developing their co-operation as equals, to promote mutual understanding and confidence, friendly and good-neighborly relations among themselves, international peace, security and justice. They will equally endeavor, in developing their co-operation, to improve the well-being of peoples and contribute to the fulfilment of their aspirations through, inter alia, the benefits resulting from increased mutual knowledge and from progress and achievement in the economic, scientific, technological, social, cultural and humanitarian fields. They will take steps to promote conditions favorable to making these benefits available to all; they will take into account the interest of all in the narrowing of differences in the levels of economic development, and in particular the interest of developing countries throughout the world.

They confirm that governments, institutions, organizations and persons have a relevant and positive role to play in contributing toward the achievement of these aims of their co-operation.

They will strive, in increasing their co-operation as set forth above, to develop closer relations among themselves on an improved and more enduring basis for the benefit of peoples.

X. Fulfilment in good faith of obligations under international law

The participating States will fulfil in good faith their obligations under international law, both those obligations arising from the generally recognized principles and rules of international law and those obligations arising from treaties or other agreements, in conformity with international law, to which they are parties.

In exercising their sovereign rights, including the right to determine their laws and regulations, they will conform with their legal obligations under international law; they will furthermore pay due regard to and implement the provisions in the Final Act of the Conference on Security and Co-operation in Europe.

The participating States confirm that in the event of a conflict between the obligations of the members of the United Nations and under the Charter of the United Nations and their obligations under any treaty or other international agreement, their obligations under the Charter will prevail, in accordance with Article 103 of the Charter of the United Nations.

All the principles set forth above are of primary significance and, accordingly, they will be equally and unreservedly applied, each of them being interpreted taking into account the others.

The participating States express their determination fully to respect and apply these principles, as set forth in the present Declaration, in all aspects, to their mutual relations and co-operation in order to ensure to each participating State the benefits resulting from the respect and application of these principles by all.

The participating States, paying due regard to the principles above and, in particular, to the first sentence of the tenth principle, "Fulfilment in good faith of obligations under international law," note that the present Declaration does not affect their rights and obligations, nor the corresponding treaties and other agreements and arrangements.

The participating States express the conviction that respect for these principles will encourage the development of normal and friendly relations and the progress of co-operation among them in all fields. They also express the conviction that respect for these principles will encourage the development of political contacts among them which in turn would contribute to better mutual understanding of their positions and views.

The participating States declare their intention to conduct their relations with all other States in the spirit of the principles contained in the present Declaration.

APPENDIX III

The 1974 General Assembly Definition of Aggression*

Article 1

Aggression is the use of armed force by a State against the sovereignty, territorial integrity or political independence of another State, or in any other manner inconsistent with the Charter of the United Nations, as set out in this definition.

Explanatory note: In this definition the term "State":

(a) Is used without prejudice to questions of recognition or to whether a State is a Member of the United Nations;

(b) Includes the concept of a "group of States" where appropriate.

Article 2

The first use of armed force by a State in contravention of the Charter shall constitute *prima facie* evidence of an act of aggression although the Security Council may, in conformity with the Charter, conclude that a determination that an act of aggression has been committed would not be justified in the light of other relevant circumstances including the fact that the acts concerned or their consequences are not of sufficient gravity.

Article 3

Any of the following acts, regardless of a declaration of war, shall, subject to and in accordance with the provisions of Article 2, qualify as an act of aggression:

(a) The invasion or attack by the armed forces of a State, or any military occupation, however temporary, resulting from such invasion or attack, or any annexation by the use of force of the territory of another State or part thereof;

(b) Bombardment by the armed forces of a State against the territory of another State or the use of any weapons by a State against the territory of another State;

(c) The blockade of the ports of coasts of a State by the armed forces of another State;

(d) An attack by the armed forces of a State on the land, sea or air forces, or marine and air fleets of another State;

(e) The use of armed forces of one State, which are within the terri-

---

*Adopted as G.A. Res. 3314, 29 U.N. GAOR Supp. (No. 31), U.N. Doc. 9890 (1974). Explanatory notes on Articles 3 and 5 are to be found in the report of the Special Committee (A/9619, para. 20).

tory of another State with the agreement of the receiving State, in contravention of the conditions provided for in the agreement or any extension of their presence in such territory beyond the termination of the agreement;

(f) The action of a State in allowing its territory, which it has placed at the disposal of another State, to be used by that other State for perpetrating an act of aggression against a third State;

(g) The sending by or on behalf of a State of armed bands, groups, irregulars or mercenaries, which carry out acts of armed force against another State of such gravity as to amount to the acts listed above, or its substantial involvement therein.

Article 4

The acts enumerated above are not exhaustive and the Security Council may determine that other acts constitute aggression under the provisions of the Charter.

Article 5

No consideration of whatever nature, whether political, economic, military or otherwise, may serve as justification for aggression.

A war of aggression is a crime against international peace. Aggression gives rise to international responsibility.

No territorial acquisition or special advantage resulting from aggression is or shall be recognized as lawful.

Article 6

Nothing in this definition shall be construed as in any way enlarging or diminishing the scope of the Charter, including its provisions concerning cases in which the use of force is lawful.

Article 7

Nothing in this definition, and in particular Article 3, could in any way prejudice the right to self-determination, freedom and independence, as derived from the Charter, of peoples forcibly deprived of that right and referred to in the Declaration of Principles of International Law concerning Friendly Relations and Co-operation among States in accordance with the Charter of the United Nations, particularly peoples under colonial and racist regimes or other forms of alien domination; nor the right of these peoples to struggle to that end and to seek and receive support, in accordance with the principles of the Charter and in conformity with the above-mentioned Declaration.

Article 8

In their interpretation and application the above provisions are interrelated and each provision should be construed in the context of the other provisions.

Notes

Citations to sources conform to the rules in A UNIFORM SYSTEM OF CITA-
TION, *13th ed. (1981)*.

CHAPTER I

1. Lipson, *International Law*, in HANDBOOK OF POLITICAL SCIENCE 415,
430 (Greenstein & Polsby eds. 1975). See also McWhinney, *"Peaceful
Co-Existence" and Soviet-Western International Law*, 56 AM. J. INT'L L. 951
(1962) [hereinafter cited as *Soviet-Western International Law*].

2. Y. KOROVIN, INTERNATIONAL LAW OF THE TRANSITIONAL PERIOD (in
Russian), translation from Snyder & Bracht, *Coexistence and International
Law*, 7 INT'L & COMP. L.Q. 54, 56 (1958) [hereinafter cited as Snyder &
Bracht]; J. HILDEBRAND, SOVIET INTERNATIONAL LAW: AN EXEMPLAR FOR
OPTIMAL DECISION THEORY ANALYSIS 24 (1968); I. LAPENNA, STATE AND
LAW: SOVIET AND YUGOSLAV THEORY 22–23 (1964), cited in *id.*; P. CORBETT,
LAW IN DIPLOMACY 91 (1959); Lapenna, *The Legal Aspects and Political Sig-
nificance of the Soviet Concept of Co-Existence*, 12 INT'L & COMP. L.Q. 737,
754 (1963) [hereinafter cited as *Legal Aspects of Soviet Co-Existence*].

3. L. Trotsky, *cited in* I. DEUTSCHER, THE PROPHET UNARMED: TROTSKY
1879–1921 145, at 158 (1970).

4. Snyder & Bracht, *supra* note 2, at 62; R. HIGGINS, CONFLICT OF INTER-
ESTS: INTERNATIONAL LAW IN A DIVIDED WORLD 138 (1965).

5. Pashukanis, *The Soviet State and the Revolution in Law*, in SOVIET
LEGAL PHILOSOPHY 244 (H. Babb trans. 1951); HILDEBRAND, *supra* note 2, at
28; McWhinney, *Soviet-Western International Law*, *supra* note 1, at 960–61.
Pashukanis was soon to fall into official disfavor, but he was later rehabilitated
posthumously; *see* Hazard, *Pashukanis Is No Traitor*, 51 AM. J. INT'L L. 385
(1957).

6. Lerner, *The Historical Origins of the Soviet Doctrine of Peaceful Coexistence*, in THE SOVIET IMPACT ON INTERNATIONAL LAW 21, at 25 (H. Baade
ed. 1965) [hereinafter cited as Baade].

7. Radek, *The Bases of Soviet Foreign Policy*, 12 FOREIGN AFF. 193,
198–99 (1933–34). *See also* J. Hazard, *Introduction* to SOVIET LEGAL PHI-
LOSOPHY, *supra* note 5, at xxxii; R. HIGGINS, *supra* note 4, at 133–40;
Lapenna, *Legal Aspects of Soviet Co-Existence*, *supra* note 2, at 758–59.

8. Vyshinskii, *The Fundamental Tasks of the Science of Soviet Legal Phi-

152   NOTES TO PAGE 3

losophy, in SOVIET LEGAL PHILOSOPHY, *supra* note 5, at 303, 325, 331. *See also* HILDEBRAND, *supra* note 2, at 35.

9. Krylov, *Les Notions Principales du Droit des Gens (La Doctrine Sovietique du Droit International)*, 1 RECUEIL DES COURS, ACADÉMIE DE DROIT INTERNATIONAL DE LA HAYE 406, 420 (1947). *See also* Krylov, *Shifting the Blame*, 51 AM. J. INT'L L. 771 (1957); Hazard, *The Soviet Union and International Law*, 1 SOVIET STUDIES 192 (1950); Snyder & Bracht, *supra* note 2, at 64, 70; Lapenna, *Legal Aspects of Soviet Co-existence*, *supra* note 2, at 760.

10. Lapenna, *Legal Aspects of Soviet Co-existence*, *supra* note 2, at 759. *See also* I.LAPENNA, CONCEPTIONS SOVIETIQUES DE DROIT INTERNATIONAL PUBLIQUE, 112–22 (1954). In 1938, at a conference of Soviet theorists, Vyshinskii delivered a major address, "The Fundamental Tasks of the Science of Soviet Socialist Law," in which he branded Pashukanis a "traitor" and a "wrecker": SOVIET LEGAL PHILOSOPHY, *supra* note 5, at 331; *cf.* Hazard, *Pashukanis Is No Traitor*, *supra* note 5.

11. Kozhevnikov, *International Law*, in GREAT SOVIET ENCYCLOPEDIA 636 (1940), *cited in* Snyder & Bracht, *supra* note 2, at 65. *See also* McWhinney, *Soviet-Western International Law*, *supra* note 1, at 955–57; R. HIGGINS, *supra* note 4, at 143–47. *See generally* J. TRISKA & R. SLUSSER, THE THEORY, LAW AND POLICY OF SOVIET TREATIES 26 *et seq.* (1962); Tunkin, *The United Nations 1945–1965 (Problems of International Law)*, 4 SOVIET L. & GOV'T 5–6 (1965–66).

12. Tunkin, *The 22nd Congress of the C.P.S.U. and the Tasks of the Soviet Science of International Law*, 1 SOVIET L. & GOV'T 18, 21, 25 (1962–63); *see also* Korovin, Zadorozhny & Kozhevnikov, *A Restatement of the Thesis of Peaceful Coexistence*, Izvestia, Apr. 18, 1962, at 5, *reprinted in* 14 CURRENT DIG. SOVIET PRESS 8–9 (No. 15, May 9, 1962); Kozhevnikov & Blishchenko, *Socialism and Contemporary International Law*, 9 SOVIET L. & GOV'T 207 (1970).

13. G. TUNKIN, THEORY OF INTERNATIONAL LAW 35–37, 40, 42, 44 (W. Butler trans. 1974). *See also* G. ZADOROZHNY, PEACEFUL COEXISTENCE 15 *et seq.* (V. Schneierson trans. 1968); Hazard, *Legal Research on "Peaceful Co-existence,"* 51 AM. J. INT'L L. 63, 71 (1957).

14. G. TUNKIN, THEORY OF INTERNATIONAL LAW, *supra* note 13, at 35–44; statement by I. Lukashuk, in REPORT OF THE 50TH CONFERENCE OF THE I.L.A. (Brussels) 272 (1962); Lukashuk, *The USSR and International Treaties*, in SOVIET Y.B. OF INT'L L. 27 (1960); statement by S. Krylov, in REPORT OF THE 47TH CONFERENCE OF THE I.L.A. (Dubrovnik) 42 (1956); G. ZADOROZHNY, *supra* note 13, at 15–35, 304–12; Karpov, *The Soviet Concept of Peaceful Coexistence and Its Implications for International Law*, in Baade, *supra* note 6, at 14, 16. For a detailed enumeration of the contemporary Soviet formulation of peaceful coexistence, see appendix I.

15. Lipson, Comments, Panel I, 1959 AM. SOC'Y INT'L L. PROCEEDINGS
42. *See also* E. MCWHINNEY, THE INTERNATIONAL LAW OF DETENTE: ARMS
CONTROL, EUROPEAN SECURITY AND EAST-WEST CO-OPERATION 12-14
(1978) [hereinafter cited as INTERNATIONAL LAW OF DETENTE].

16. INTERNATIONAL LAW: A TEXTBOOK FOR USE IN LAW SCHOOLS 7
(F. Kozhevnikov ed., D. Ogden trans. 1957). Almost identical definitions have
been given by Levin and Kalyuzhnaya in 1960, by Korovin in 1961, and by
Tunkin in 1958, 1959, and 1970. *See* G. TUNKIN, THEORY OF INTERNATIONAL
LAW, *supra* note 13, at 233-37; Lapenna, *Legal Aspects of Soviet Co-Exis-
tence*, *supra* note 2, at 761; Tunkin, *Co-existence and International Law*, 95
RECUEIL DES COURS, ACADÉMIE DE DROIT INTERNATIONAL DE LA HAYE I,
34-36 (1958).

17. See text accompanying note 16, *supra*.

18. Tunkin, *Co-existence and International Law, supra* note 16, at 35.
Tunkin cautions that the "co-ordinated wills" of states do *not* merge into a
"single will" but mutually condition each other's wills. In this way, he asserts,
agreement between states is based on the principle of "interconditionality."

19. G. TUNKIN, THEORY OF INTERNATIONAL LAW, *supra* note 13, at 42.

20. *Id.*

21. Lenin, *cited in id.* at 16.

22. Resolution of Feb. 24, 1918, of the Moscow Regional Bureau, *cited in*
V. LENIN, ON THE FOREIGN POLICY OF THE SOVIET STATE 40 (1973) [herein-
after cited as FOREIGN POLICY].

23. *See* V. LENIN, *Strange and Monstrous*, in FOREIGN POLICY, *supra* note
22, at 39-47; also published in Pravda, Nos. 37 & 38, Feb. 28 and Mar. 1, 1918,
and in V. LENIN, 27 COLLECTED WORKS 68-75 (1965). (This and all future
citations of V. LENIN, COLLECTED WORKS, refer to the English edition, 1965.)

24. V. LENIN, FOREIGN POLICY, *supra* note 22, at 43 (emphasis in the original). *See also* G. ZADOROZHNY, *supra* note 13, at 144.

25. V. LENIN, FOREIGN POLICY, *supra* note 22, at 43 (emphasis in the
original).

26. Lenin, *"Left-Wing" Childishness and Petty Bourgeois Mentality, reprinted in id.* at 69, 71, 73, 76-77; also published in Pravda, Nos. 88, 89, &
90, May 9, 10, and 11, 1918, and in V. LENIN, 27 COLLECTED WORKS,
325-33 (1965).

27. Speech on the Foreign and Domestic Position and the Tasks of the
Party, delivered to the Moscow Gubernia Conference of the R.C.P. (B) (Nov.
21, 1920), in V. LENIN, FOREIGN POLICY, *supra* note 22, at 283, 289-90; also
published in CURRENT QUESTIONS OF THE PARTY'S PRESENT WORK, MOSCOW
Committee R.C.P. (B) (1920), and in V. LENIN, 31 COLLECTED WORKS
408-15 (1966).

28. Report to the Tenth Congress of the R.C.P. (B) (March 8-16, 1921),

in V. LENIN, FOREIGN POLICY, *supra* note 22, at 338, and V. LENIN, 32 COL-
LECTED WORKS 179–83 (1965). Lenin appears to have stressed the benefits to
Russia as his primary reason for cooperating with nonsocialist countries.

29. V. LENIN, *Strange and Monstrous*, in FOREIGN POLICY, *supra* note 22,
at 42; *see also* G. ZADOROZHNY, *supra* note 13, at 34–35, 37, 42.

30. New York Evening Journal, No. 12671, Feb. 21, 1920, *quoted in*
V. LENIN, FOREIGN POLICY, *supra* note 22, at 198, and Pravda, No. 112,
Apr. 22, 1950; V. LENIN, 30 COLLECTED WORKS 365–67 (1965), *cited in id.*
See also G. ZADOROZHNY, *supra* note 13, at 24–25, 32.

31. *Cited in* AMERICAN BAR ASSOCIATION, PEACEFUL COEXISTENCE: A
COMMUNIST BLUEPRINT FOR VICTORY XV (1964).

32. G. Tunkin, THEORY OF INTERNATIONAL LAW, *supra* note 13, at 15, 42;
Kozhevnikov & Blishchenko, *supra* note 12, at 213.

33. *See* Fifield, *The Five Principles of Peaceful Co-existence*, 52 AM. J.
INT'L L. 504, 508 (1958); Aaron & Reynolds, *Peaceful Coexistence and
Peaceful Cooperation*, 3–4 POL. STUD. 293, 294–95 (1955–56); *see also*
A. BERZINS, THE TWO FACES OF COEXISTENCE 254–58 (1967).

34. Lipson, *The Rise and Fall of "Peaceful Coexistence" in International
Law*, 1 PAPERS ON SOVIET L. 6, 7 (L. Lipson & V. Chalidze eds. 1977).

35. G. TUNKIN, THEORY OF INTERNATIONAL LAW, *supra* note 13, at 38.

36. Lenin, *"Left-Wing" Childishness and Petty Bourgeois Mentality*, in
V. LENIN, FOREIGN POLICY, *supra* note 22, at 75–76 (emphasis in the
original).

37. It is not without reason that some Western scholars, such as Lipson,
Lerner, and Higgins, have questioned whether the Soviet concept of peaceful
coexistence is not just a modern replay of an old and familiar Soviet cold-war
tactic of supporting peace only when revolution is, for one reason or another,
inexpedient: *see* Lipson, *Peaceful Coexistence*, in Baade, *supra* note 6, at
34–35; Lerner, *supra* note 6, at 22; R. HIGGINS, *supra* note 4, at 114–18. *See
also* Kux, *Soviet Offensive Against the United States Bases Abroad*, 10 SWISS
REV. WORLD AFF. 3 (Feb. 1961), and Achilles (then the special assistant to the
U.S. Undersecretary of State for Political Affairs), *Peaceful Coexistence and
U.S. National Security*, 46 DEP'T ST. BULL. 324, 325 (1962). The North
Korean attack on South Korea was interpreted by the U.S. in this light: *see*
Robertson, *Our Victory in Korea*, 30 DEP'T ST. BULL. 149, 151–52 (1954).

38. See text accompanying notes 21–33, *supra*.

39. Khrushchev, *On Peaceful Coexistence*, 38 FOREIGN AFFAIRS 1, 5
(1959).

40. Ordinance on Penal Law of the People's Commissar for Justice of the
RSFSR, 1919, s.1, *cited in* Snyder & Bracht, *supra* note 2, at 56 n.4.

41. See text accompanying note 16, *supra*. See also generally text accompanying notes 16–18, *supra*.

42. Tunkin, *The United Nations 1945–1965, supra* note 11, at 5–6, 8; *see also* Tunkin, *The 22nd Congress of the C.P.S.U., supra* note 12, at 18.

43. *See* "Declaration of Rights of the Working and Exploited People," adopted by the Third All-Russian Congress of Soviets, Jan. 1918, published in V. LENIN, FOREIGN POLICY, *supra* note 22, at 25–27.

44. *See generally* Decree on Peace, adopted by the Second All-Russian Congress of Soviets, Nov. 8, 1917; for text, *see* MILESTONES OF SOVIET FOREIGN POLICY 1917–1967, at 27 (D. Skvirsky trans. 1967); also reprinted in V. LENIN, FOREIGN POLICY, *supra* note 22, at 11. *See also* appendix I.

45. *See also* Tunkin, *The 22nd Congress of the C.P.S.U., supra* note 12, at 18. *See generally* Kozhevnikov & Blishchenko, *supra* note 12, at 207–08.

46. E. McWHINNEY, INTERNATIONAL LAW OF DETENTE, *supra* note 15, at 148–66; E. KAUFMAN, THE SUPERPOWERS AND THEIR SPHERES OF INFLUENCE: THE UNITED STATES AND THE SOVIET UNION IN EASTERN EUROPE AND LATIN AMERICA 24 (1976); Griffith, *East-West Detente in Europe*, in UNCERTAIN DETENTE 12 (A. von Geusau ed. 1979) [hereinafter cited as von Geusau]; Russell, *The Helsinki Declaration: Brobdingnag or Lilliput?*, 70 AM. J. INT'L L. 242, 246, 249; Hopmann, *Asymmetrical Bargaining in the Conference on Security and Cooperation in Europe*, 32 INT'L ORG. 141, 170 (1978). *See generally* BEYOND DETENTE: PROSPECTS FOR EAST-WEST COOPERATION AND SECURITY IN EUROPE (N. Andren & K. Birnbaum eds. 1976); Byrnes, *United States Policy Toward Eastern Europe: Before and After Helsinki* 37 REV. POL. 435 (1975).

47. See appendix II.

48. For the complete text of the Final Act, see 14 INT'L LEGAL MATERIALS 1292 (1975). For text of the Declaration of Principles Guiding Relations Between Participating States, see appendix II.

49. Resolution of the Central Committee of the CPSU adopted in April 1973, Pravda and Izvestia, Apr. 28, 1973; complete text *reprinted in* 25 CURRENT DIG. SOVIET PRESS 3 (No. 17, May 23, 1973). *See also* Rakhmaninov, *Europe: Principles of Security and Cooperation*, 2 INT'L AFF. (Moscow) 41 (Feb. 1976).

50. See appendix II.

51. *See* Russell, *supra* note 46, at 255. *See also* Howard, *Helsinki Reconsidered: East-West Relations Two Years After the "Final Act"*, 267 ROUND TABLE 241, 243 (1977). *Cf.* McWhinney, who suggests that the view that the Final Act may have somehow, *sub silentio*, abolished the Brezhnev Doctrine "seems advanced more in whimsy than with any serious thought that substantive legal changes . . . were either intended at Helsinki or to be expected as logically flowing from the language of the Helsinki Final Act itself." E. McWHINNEY, INTERNATIONAL LAW OF DETENTE, *supra* note 15, at 244 n.20. *See also id.* at 126–27. The Brezhnev Doctrine itself is discussed in chapter III.

52. Rakhmaninov, *supra* note 49.

53. S. Vishnevsky, Remarks over Radio Moscow (Aug. 29, 1973), *quoted in* A. WEEKS, THE TROUBLED DETENTE 14 (1976). In February 1976, barely seven months after the signing of the Helsinki Final Act, Brezhnev reaffirmed this view before the 25th Congress of the Communist Party of the Soviet Union. See text accompanying note 62, *infra*.

54. V. Ghebali, *Les Dix Principes D'Helsinki: Interpretations et Mise en Oeuvre*, in von Geusau, *supra* note 46, at 57, 63.

55. Zakharov, *The World Revolutionary Process and Peaceful Coexistence*, 4 INT'L AFF. (MOSCOW) 80, 87 (1978).

56. Meissner, *The Soviet Concept of Coexistence and the European Security Conference*, 19 MODERN AGE 364, 368 (1975). Arguing against a "freezing" of the status quo, Brezhnev has stated: "As for the ultra-leftist assertions that peaceful coexistence is . . . 'freezing the socio-political *status quo*', our reply is this: Every revolution is above all a natural result of the internal development of the given society." Report to 25th Party Congress, February 1976, *reprinted in* SOVIET NEWS, Mar. 2, 1976, at 77.

57. Meissner, *supra* note 56, at 367.

58. Kovalev, *Sovereignty and the Internationalist Obligations of Socialist Countries*, Pravda, Sept. 26, 1968, at 4, *reprinted in* 20 CURRENT DIG. SOVIET PRESS 10, 11 (No. 39, Oct. 16, 1968).

59. Lipson, *supra* note 34, at 7. *See generally* Khrushchev, *supra* note 39, at 1.

60. Weeks, *supra* note 53, at 15.

61. *Id.*

62. SOVIET NEWS, Mar. 2, 1976, at 77. *See also generally* Podolsky, *Detente: The Battle of Ideas*, 2 INT'L AFF. (Moscow) 12 (Feb. 1981). For a cogently argued view that detente and contacts between East and West have actually weakened socialist claims and, in particular, have undermined Soviet authority in Eastern Europe, see Byrnes, *supra* note 46, at 443–54, 461–63.

63. See text accompanying note 58, *supra*.

64. "X" [Kennan], *The Sources of Soviet Conduct*, 25 FOREIGN AFF. 566 (1947).

65. Kennan, *Peaceful Coexistence: A Western View*, 38 FOREIGN AFF. 171, 173 (1960).

66. *See* Khrushchev, *supra* note 39, at 15.

67. Kennan, *supra* note 65, at 185–86.

68. *Id.* at 176.

69. *Id.* at 178.

70. *Id.* at 179.

71. *Id.* at 183.

72. Lerner, *supra* note 6, at 26. *See also* Lipson, *Peaceful Coexistence*, *supra* note 37, at 33–35.

73. Lerner, *supra* note 6, at 23.

74. Kennan, *supra* note 65, at 179–80.

75. Report of the Committee on Peaceful Coexistence, Proceedings and Committee Report of the American Branch of the I.L.A. 85, at 91 (1957–58) [hereinafter cited as Report of the American Branch, I.L.A.).

76. Truman declared that "the whole world should adopt the American system" because it could survive "only if it became a world system." J. WARBURG, PUT YOURSELF IN MARSHALL'S PLACE 46 (1948).

77. But see Hazard, who believes that coexistence is threatened "more because of emotionalism than the difference between economic systems." Emotionalism is, in his opinion, generated by lack of information for the general public about their own decision-making processes, together with the belief of certain leaders in the inability of the general public to make decisions. Statement by Hazard, in REPORT OF THE 48TH CONFERENCE OF THE I.L.A. (New York) 417, 428–29 (1958).

78. Report of the American Branch I.L.A., *supra* note 75, at 86–87.

79. *Id.*

80. *Id.* at 92.

81. *Id.* at 91.

82. Statement by Lipson, in REPORT OF THE 50TH CONFERENCE OF THE I.L.A. (Brussels) 260, 285 (1962).

83. *Id.*

84. Report of the American Branch, I.L.A., *supra* note 75, at 93.

85. *Id.* (emphasis added).

86. *Id.*

87. Statement by Hazard, *supra* note 77, at 427.

88. Statement by Nagorski (U.S.A.), in REPORT OF THE 48TH CONFERENCE OF THE I.L.A. (New York) 434 (1958).

89. Statement by McDougal, in REPORT OF THE 48TH CONFERENCE OF THE I.L.A. (New York) 423 (1958).

90. *Id.*

91. *Id.* at 440.

92. *Id.* at 438.

93. *See* Lipson, *International Law, supra* note 1, at 433.

94. Statement by McDougal at the 48th Conference of the I.L.A., *supra* note 89, at 438.

95. Hart, *Positivism and the Separation of Law and Morals*, 71 HARVARD L. REV. 593, 603 (1958).

96. Fuller, *Positivism and Fidelity to Law—A Reply to Professor Hart*, 71 HARVARD L. REV. 630, 642 (1958).

97. See statements by Lipson, Hazard, Baxter, and Sohn (U.S.), Lauterpacht and Bowett (U.K.) and McWhinney (Canada), for the Western view, and statements by Tunkin and Lukashuk (USSR) and Cristescu (Romania), for the

socialist view, in REPORT OF THE 50TH CONFERENCE OF THE I.L.A. (Brussels) 263, 264, 266, 268, 270, 272, 284, 288, 296, 348 (1962); see also statement by Hazard in REPORT OF THE 49TH CONFERENCE OF THE I.L.A. (Hamburg) 341 (1960).

98. Statement by Tunkin in REPORT OF THE 50TH CONFERENCE OF THE I.L.A. (Brussels) 264 (1962).

99. See appendix I.

100. Lipson, *supra* note 37, at 27.

101. Statement by Baxter, in REPORT OF THE 50TH CONFERENCE OF THE I.L.A. (Brussels) 268, 291 (1962); *see also* Report and Draft Code of the American Branch of the I.L.A., *id.* at 340. This tension first became evident in 1954 at a UNESCO Conference in Paris; *see* Hazard, *Legal Research on Peaceful Coexistence*, 51 AM. J. INT'L L. 63, 65 (1957). *See also* Lipson, *supra* note 37, at 28–29; Crane, *Basic Principles of Soviet Space Law: Peaceful Coexistence, Peaceful Cooperation and Disarmament*, in Baade, *supra* note 6, at 99, 102–03. Crane reports that Soviet scholars object to "peaceful cooperation" on the ground that the term obscures the theme of class struggle between socialist and capitalist states. *See also* Hazard, *Co-existence Codification Reconsidered*, 57 AM. J. INT'L L. 88 (1963), and McWhinney, *Soviet-Western International Law, supra* note 1, at 953.

102. *See* McWhinney, *The "New" Countries and the "New" International Law: The United Nations' Special Conference on Friendly Relations and Co-operation Among States*, 60 AM. J. INT'L L. 1, 2, 29 (1966) [hereinafter cited as *"New" International Law*]; McWhinney, INTERNATIONAL LAW OF DETENTE, *supra* note 15, at 23–27.

103. In 1963 the UN General Assembly established the Special Committee on Principles of International Law Concerning Friendly Relations and Co-operation Among States in Accordance with the Charter of the United Nations, G.A. Res. 1966, 18 U.N. GAOR Supp. (No. 15) at 70, U.N. Doc. A/5515 (1963).

104. G.A. Res. 2625, 25 U.N. GAOR Supp. (No. 28) at 121, U.N. Doc. A/8028 (1971). For background on the early work of the Special Committee, see Houben, *Principles of International Law Concerning Friendly Relations and Co-operation Among States*, 61 AM. J. INT'L L. 703 (1967); McWhinney, *Soviet-Western International Law, supra* note 1, at 951; McWhinney, *Friendly Relations and Co-operation Among States: Debate at the Twentieth General Assembly, United Nations*, 60 AM. J. INT'L L. 356 (1966) [hereinafter cited as *Friendly Relations*].

105. This criticism was, ironically, expressed by Czechoslovakia, a member of the Soviet bloc: statement by Dr. Vratislav Pechota, Sixth Committee, Nov. 8, 1965, *cited in* McWhinney, *Friendly Relations, supra* note 104, at 357–58.

106. McWhinney, *"New" International Law, supra* note 102, at 7, 16, 21, 26.

107. *See* Rosenstock, *The Declaration of Principles of International Law Concerning Friendly Relations: A Survey*, 65 AM. J. INT'L L. 713 (1971).

108. Statement by Baxter and Franck, in REPORT OF THE 50TH CONFERENCE OF THE I.L.A. (Brussels) 268–70, 281–83 (1962).

109. *Id.* at 270–71.

110. Statement by Lipson, in REPORT OF THE 50TH CONFERENCE OF THE I.L.A. (Brussels) 286–87 (1962).

111. For example, the Declaration on Principles of International Law Concerning Friendly Relations and Co-operation Among States in Accordance with the Charter of the United Nations, G.A. Res. 2625, *supra* note 104; the Declaration on the Inadmissibility of Intervention in the Domestic Affairs of States and the Protection of Their Independence and Sovereignty (1965), G.A. Res. 2131, 20 U.N. GAOR Supp. (No. 14) at 11, U.N. Doc. A/6014 (1966); the General Assembly Definition of Aggression (1974) (reprinted in appendix III of this work); and the Helsinki Declaration of Principles Guiding Relations Between Participating States of the European Security Conference (1975) (reprinted in appendix II of this work).

112. One commentator has warned that "any list of principles arrived at in this way by purely *a priori* methods would be mere exercises in cloudiness and semantic confusion, flowing from the normative ambiguity existing between the different legal systems to be involved in any such grand declaration or code." McWhinney, *"New" International Law, supra* note 102, at 29. *See also* McWhinney, *Changing International Law: Method and Objectives in the Era of Soviet-Western Detente*, 59 AM. J. INT'L L. 1, 11 (1965).

113. K. LLEWELLYN & E. HOEBEL, THE CHEYENNE WAY 284–86 (1961); E. HOEBEL, THE LAW OF PRIMITIVE MAN 28 (1954); O. LIPPS, THE NAVAJOS 28 (1956); L. POSPÍŠIL, ANTHROPOLOGY OF LAW: A COMPARATIVE THEORY 65–78 (1974).

114. L. POSPÍŠIL, *supra* note 113, at 95 (emphasis added).

115. *Id.* at 31–37.

116. The Soviet Union is particularly insistent on this principle.

117. Munch of the Federal Republic of Germany observed in 1960 that "the maximum of coexistence of states is the federal state where you have a merger of sovereignty; the minimum of coexistence, chaos, is the absence of any legal obligation, that is, the fullest sovereignty in the sense it had in the past century." Statement in REPORT OF THE 49TH CONFERENCE OF THE I.L.A. (Hamburg) 349, 350 (1960).

118. *See* Pospíšil, *supra* note 113, at 52–65.

119. Statement by Lipson, in REPORT OF THE 50TH CONFERENCE OF THE I.L.A., *supra* note 110, at 286–87.

CHAPTER II

1. The containment doctrine was enunciated in 1947 by George Kennan and became widely accepted as the considered justification of the U.S. Department of State for its policy. *See* "X" [Kennan], *The Sources of Soviet Conduct*, 25 FOREIGN AFF. 566, 571 *et seq.* (1947); *see also* note 10, *infra*, and N. LEITES, A STUDY OF BOLSHEVISM 45 *et seq.* (1953).

2. J. WARBURG, PUT YOURSELF IN MARSHALL'S PLACE 12, 46, 47-48 (1948).

3. D. FLEMING, 1 THE COLD WAR AND ITS ORIGINS 540 (1961), *quoting* State Paper NSC 68.

4. U.N. SCOR (473d mtg.) at 4, U.N. Doc. S/1501 (1950).

5. U.N. SCOR (474th mtg.) at 5, U.N. Doc. S/1511 (1950).

6. D. FLEMING, 2 THE COLD WAR AND ITS ORIGINS 602 (1961).

7. MacArthur Hearings, Part 3, at 1991, *cited by* D. FLEMING, *supra* note 6, at 604. *But see* Hitchcock, *North Korea Jumps the Gun*, 20 CURRENT HIST. 136-44 (Mar. 1951). Hitchcock argues that it could not have been in Moscow's interest to order the attack and that it was executed by North Korea without Russia's knowledge.

8. Y. Hudson, *The Rise of Communist Power in The Far East*, in THE COLD WAR: A RE-APPRAISAL 62, 73 (E. Luard ed. 1964).

9. *See* Statements of John Foster Dulles, Consultant to the Secretary, 23 DEP'T ST. BULL. 88, 89 (July 17, 1950), and *id.* at 207 (Aug. 7, 1950).

10. Hudson, *supra* note 8, at 79. *See also* President Truman's statement of Dec. 1, 1950, *in* 23 DEP'T ST. BULL. 925-26.

11. George, *American Policy-Making and the North Korean Aggression*, 7 WORLD POL. 209, 213 (1955).

12. Kennan's concept of containment had included agreements against "threats or blustering or superficial gestures of outward 'toughness'" against the Soviet Union and in favor of "the adroit and vigilant application of counter-force at a series of constantly shifting geographical and political points, corresponding to the shifts and manoeuvres of Soviet policy." "X", *supra* note 1, at 576.

13. President Truman's Message to Congress, Mar. 12, 1947, *reprinted in* J. WARBURG, *supra* note 2, at 47-48. *See also* chapter I, note 76.

14. *See* George, *supra* note 11, at 211-15, for a more detailed statement of these explanations.

15. J. LUKACS, A HISTORY OF THE COLD WAR 127-36 (1961).

16. J. RADVANYI, HUNGARY AND THE SUPERPOWERS: THE 1956 REVOLUTION AND REALPOLITIK 12 (1972).

17. Declaration by the Government of the USSR On the Principles Underlying the Development and Further Consolidation of Friendship and Cooperation Between the Soviet Union and Other Socialist Countries, Oct. 30, 1956,

reprinted in MILESTONES OF SOVIET FOREIGN POLICY 1917–1967, at 166, 168 (D. Skvirsky trans. 1967).

18. D. FLEMING, *supra* note 6, at 798.

19. For text of the declaration, see MILESTONES OF SOVIET FOREIGN POLICY, *supra* note 17, at 166, 168–69.

20. J. LUKACS, *supra* note 15, at 134; *see also* J. RADVANYI, *supra* note 16, at 12–13.

21. D. FLEMING, *supra* note 6, at 843, 847.

22. For further background on the Middle East crisis of the 1950s, see Luard, *supra* note 8, at 140, and J. LUKACS, *supra* note 15, at 148 *et seq.*

23. For more background on the crisis in Lebanon and Jordan vis-à-vis the Eisenhower Doctrine, see Raleigh, *The Middle East in 1957—A Political Survey*, 9 MIDDLE EASTERN AFF. 86, 90 *et seq.* (1958); Raleigh, *Middle East Politics: The Past Ten Years*, 10 MIDDLE EASTERN AFF. 3, 11 *et seq.* (1959); Wright, *United States Intervention in the Lebanon*, 53 AM. J. INT'L L. 112 (1959); Martin, *A Decade of Cold War*, 10 MIDDLE EASTERN AFF. 95 (1959).

24. Leites had written in 1953 concerning Soviet conduct that "if an area becomes a no-man's land between the two world blocs, the Politburo [could be expected to] proceed on the assumption that the enemy will incorporate it unless it does so first." Leites, *supra* note 1, at 44.

CHAPTER III

1. For text of the definition, see appendix III of this work; and see generally B. FERENCZ, DEFINING INTERNATIONAL AGGRESSION: THE SEARCH FOR WORLD PEACE, A DOCUMENTARY HISTORY AND ANALYSIS (2 vols. 1975).

2. *See* Lipson, *Peaceful Coexistence*, in THE SOVIET IMPACT ON INTERNATIONAL LAW 28, 31 (H. Baade ed. 1965) [hereinafter cited as Baade].

3. *See* appendix I of this work; G. ZADOROZHNY, CONTEMPORARY LAW OF PEACEFUL COEXISTENCE 308 (V. Schneierson trans. 1968); *see also* chapter I, *supra*; E. MCWHINNEY, PEACEFUL CO-EXISTENCE AND SOVIET-WESTERN INTERNATIONAL LAW 36 (1964); B. RAMUNDO, PEACEFUL COEXISTENCE: INTERNATIONAL LAW IN THE BUILDING OF COMMUNISM 116 (1967).

4. INTERNATIONAL LAW: A TEXTBOOK FOR USE IN LAW SCHOOLS 402 (F. Kozhevnikov ed., D. Ogden trans. 1957) [hereinafter cited as Kozhevnikov].

5. Lenin, *On Britain, cited in* Kozhevnikov, *supra* note 4, at 401.

6. Karpov, *The Soviet Concept of Peaceful Coexistence and Its Implications for International Law*, in Baade, *supra* note 2, at 16, 19.

7. This policy is, of course, said to be that of the ruling class; see Kozhevnikov, *supra* note 4, at 7, 14–15.

8. S. OZHEGOV, SLOVAR' RUSSKOGO YAZYKA (1952), *cited in* J. GA-

WENDA, THE SOVIET DOMINATION OF EASTERN EUROPE IN THE LIGHT OF IN-
TERNATIONAL LAW 119 (1974).

9. Lenin, *cited in* Kozhevnikov, *supra* note 4, at 402; *see also* B. RA-
MUNDO, *supra* note 3, at 122.

10. Starushenko, *Abolition of Colonialism and International Law*, in CON-
TEMPORARY INTERNATIONAL LAW: A COLLECTION OF ARTICLES 91 (G. Tunkin
ed., Ivanov-Mumjiev trans. 1969) (emphasis added). *See also* B. RAMUNDO,
supra note 3, at 122–23, 132–33.

11. Starushenko, *supra* note 10, at 91. Starushenko also asserts that colonial peoples are "subjects of international law and as such enjoy the right of
self-defense [i.e., against colonialism]." *Cf.* Freeman, *Some Aspects of Soviet
Influence on International Law*, 62 AM. J. INT'L L. 710, 719 (1968).

12. Starushenko, *supra* note 10, at 92.

13. *Id.* at 95. *See* Anand, *Attitude of the Asian-African States Toward Certain Problems of International Law*, 15 INT'L & COMP. L.Q. 55 (1966) (a nonsocialist view of colonialism as "aggression").

14. Starushenko, *supra* note 10, at 95; *see also* G. ZADOROZHNY, *supra*
note 3, at 308–09. For a critique of this type of argument, see Dugard, *The
O.A.U. and Colonialism: An Inquiry into the Plea of Self-Defence as a Justification for the Use of Force in the Eradication of Colonialism*, 16 INT'L &
COMP. L.Q. 157 (1967).

15. The assistance given by the U.S. to El Salvador since September 1981
is an example. The pledge given by the U.S. to the Sudan, following the assassination of Egyptian president Sadat, is another example; the pledge was
designed to counter threats from Libya, which was backed by the USSR. *See
Sudan's Leader Predicts an Invasion by Libyans: Soviet Role Is Seen*, N.Y.
Times, Oct. 13, 1981, at A1, col. 2; *Mideast Strategy: The 1950's Revived, id.*
at A14, col. 1. The latter report states that the Reagan administration's statements "suggest that it believes there is a new polarization in the Middle East
that resembles the divisions of the 1950's that produced the Eisenhower Doctrine in 1957, a commitment to aid any Middle East nation requesting help
'against overt armed aggression from any nation controlled by international
Communism.'" For background on the genesis of the Eisenhower Doctrine,
see chapter II, *supra*, nn. 20–22.

16. R. FALK, LEGAL ORDER IN A VIOLENT WORLD 508 (1968).

17. *Id.* at 498; *see also* Art. 3 of the 1974 definition, containing a detailed
list of the more "direct" forms of aggression, in appendix III.

18. R. FALK, *supra* note 16, at 498.

19. *Id.*

20. 16 U.N. SCOR (987th mtg.) at 10–11, U.N. Doc. S/P.V. 987 (1961).

21. Report of the Secretary General on the Question of Defining Aggression, U.N. Doc. A/2211 at 72 (1952), para. 414.

22. R. FALK, *supra* note 16, at 499.

23. *Id.* at 508.

24. *Id.*

25. *See* chapter I, section 5, Problems of Norm-creation and Norm-identification, *supra*.

26. B. MALINOWSKI, CRIME AND CUSTOM IN SAVAGE SOCIETY 24, 39, 45, 46 (1969).

27. L. POSPÍŠIL, ANTHROPOLOGY OF LAW: A COMPARATIVE THEORY 78 (1974).

28. *Id.* at 61, 65 *et seq.*

29. *See* Coates, *International Law and Political Authority*, 4 INT'L LAW 22, 36 (1969).

30. The fact that, as suggested by Hedley Bull, the two powers often exert a form of joint leadership over smaller states in maintaining world order seems only to reinforce the point that neither power acknowledges the leadership of the other over itself. *See* H. BULL, THE ANARCHICAL SOCIETY: A STUDY OF ORDER IN WORLD POLITICS 227–29 (1977).

31. DOCUMENTS ON BRITISH FOREIGN POLICY 1919–1939, at 251 (3d ser. 1953) (emphasis added). For the Anglo-French reaction to the proposal, see *id.* at 277, 309–11, 314, 319–20.

32. Report of the U.N. Special Committee on the Question of Defining Aggression, U.N. Doc. A/AC.66/L.2/Rev. 1 (1953).

33. 35 NEW TIMES, Sept. 4, 1968, at 1–2.

34. The reference is to the Dominican intervention, which will be discussed later in this chapter.

35. *C.I.A. Operations: A Plot Scuttled,* N.Y. Times, Apr. 28, 1966, at 1, col. 2, and at 28, col. 1 (series on C.I.A. operations); *see also* A. ULAM, THE RIVALS: AMERICA AND RUSSIA SINCE WORLD WAR II 203, 255 (1976); H. HUNT, UNDERCOVER: MEMOIRS OF AN AMERICAN SECRET AGENT 97–101 (1974).

36. Cablegram of June 19, 1954, from the Minister of External Relations of Guatemala to the President of the Security Council, U.N. Doc. S/3232 (1954); *see also* Letter of June 22, 1954, from the Representative of Guatemala to the Security Council, U.N. Doc. S/3241 (1954).

37. 9 U.N. SCOR (675th mtg.) at 29, U.N. Doc. S/P.V. 675 (1954).

38. 9 U.N. SCOR (676th mtg.) at 28–29, 31, U.N. Doc. S/P.V. 676 (1954).

39. 9 U.N. SCOR (675th mtg.) at 32, U.N. Doc. S/P.V. 675 (1954).

40. This declaration, often referred to as the Declaration of Caracas, was adopted by the Politico-Juridical Committee of the Tenth Inter-American Conference by a vote of 17-1; Guatemala voted against it, and Mexico and Argentina abstained. For full text, see 30 DEP'T ST. BULL. 420 (1954). See also statements of Mar. 5, 8, and 11, 1954, by Secretary of State Dulles, *id.* at 419, 423.

41. *Id.* at 420.

42. *Id.*

43. *Id. See also* W. Bowdler, *Report on the Tenth Inter-American Conference*, 30 DEP'T ST. BULL. 634 (1954).

44. 9 U.N. SCOR (676th mtg.) at 28, 29, 31, U.N. Doc. S/P.V. 676 (1954).

45. Franck & Weisband, *The Johnson and Brezhnev Doctrines: The Law You Make May Be Your Own*, 22 STAN. L. REV. 979, 992 (1970) (emphasis in the original).

46. Con. Res. 91, 100 CONG. REC. Part 7, Proceedings & Debates of the 83d Congress, 2nd Session, June 22, 1954–July 7, 1954, at 9176.

47. For full text, see MILESTONES OF SOVIET FOREIGN POLICY 1917–1967 at 166 (D. Skvirsky trans. 1967).

48. 9 U.N. SCOR (676th mtg.), *supra* note 44, at 28–31.

49. Declaration of Oct. 30, 1956, in MILESTONES, *supra* note 47, at 166.

50. *See generally* H. HUNT, *supra* note 35, at 128 *et seq.*; L. FITZSIMONS, THE KENNEDY DOCTRINE 18–71 (1972); A. ULAM, *supra* note 35, at 319, *et seq.*; A. SCHLESINGER, A THOUSAND DAYS: JOHN F. KENNEDY IN THE WHITE HOUSE 226 *et seq.* (1965).

51. Letter of July 11, 1960, from the Foreign Minister of Cuba to the President of the Security Council, U.N. Doc. S/4378 (1960).

52. 15 U.N. SCOR (874th mtg.) at 27, U.N. Doc. A/P.V. 874 (1960); *see also id.* at 1–27 (statement of Cuban representative Roa).

53. *Id.* at 32.

54. Declaration of San José, Costa Rica, *reprinted in* U.N. Doc. S/4480 at 5–6 (1960).

55. Final Act of the Eighth Meeting of Consultation of Ministers of Foreign Affairs, Serving as Organ of Consultation in Application of the Inter-American Treaty of Reciprocal Assistance, Punta del Este, Uruguay, Jan. 22–31, 1962, *reprinted in* U.N. Doc. S/5075 at 17 (1962). *See also* Statement of U.S. Ambassador Stevenson in the UN General Assembly, Feb. 14, 1962, and in the Security Council, Mar. 15 and 23, 1962, *reprinted in* 46 DEP'T ST. BULL. 553, 684, 691 (1962). In his address to the Security Council, Stevenson rejected Cuban charges that the Final Act of Punta del Este constituted "aggression" against Cuba.

56. 15 U.N. SCOR (874th mtg.) at 28, U.N. Doc. S/P.V. 874 (1960).

57. 15 U.N. SCOR (876th mtg.) at 16, U.N. Doc. S/P.V. 876 (1960).

58. For full text of the presidential address, entitled "The Soviet Threat to the Americas," see 47 DEP'T ST. BULL. 715 (1962).

59. S.J. Res. 230, 87th Cong., 2d Sess., 108 CONG. REC. 20,929, *reprinted in* 47 DEP'T ST. BULL. 597 (1962).

60. *Supra* note 58, at 716. See also the speech of the U.S. representative,

Adlai E. Stevenson, in the Security Council, Oct. 23, 1962, *reprinted in* 47 DEP'T ST. BULL. 723, 736 (1962).

61. *Supra* note 58, at 718.

62. For full text of the resolution, see 47 DEP'T ST. BULL. 722–23 (1962). For full text of the presidential proclamation, *Interdiction of the Delivery of Offensive Weapons to Cuba*, see *id.* at 717, *reprinted in* R. KENNEDY, THIRTEEN DAYS: A MEMOIR OF THE CUBAN MISSILE CRISIS 172 (1969).

63. Chayes, *The Legal Case for U.S. Action on Cuba*, 47 DEP'T ST. BULL. 763, 764 (1962) [hereinafter cited as Chayes, *Legal Case*]. *But see* A. CHAYES, THE CUBAN MISSILE CRISIS: INTERNATIONAL CRISES AND THE ROLE OF LAW 62–66 (1974), for his later reflections on the crisis and his reservations on self-defense as a justification for the Cuban quarantine.

64. Franck & Weisband, *supra* note 45, at 1003. Ulam reports that Secretary McNamara also saw "no difference between Soviet missiles in Cuba and those in the USSR": A. ULAM, *supra* note 35, at 333. *See also* Wright, *The Cuban Quarantine*, 57 AM. J. INT'L L. 546, 553, 560–63 (1963). Lipson, on the other hand, suggests that the Cuban missiles may have been intended to neutralize, by means of nearby short-range missiles, the U.S. lead in long-range ballistic missiles. Lipson, *Castro on the Chessboard of the Cold War*, in CUBA AND THE UNITED STATES: LONG-RANGE PERSPECTIVES 178, 192 (J. Plank ed. 1967).

65. McDougal, *The Soviet-Cuban Quarantine and Self-Defense*, 57 AM. J. INT'L L. 597, 600 (1963). *See also* Fenwick, *The Quarantine Against Cuba: Legal or Illegal?*, 57 AM. J. INT'L L. 588, 589 (1963); MacChesney, *Some Comments on the "Quarantine" of Cuba*, 57 AM. J. INT'L L. 592, 595 (1963).

66. G.A. Res. 2625, 25 U.N. GAOR Supp. (No. 28) at 121, U.N. Doc. A/8028 (1971). *See* chapter I *supra*, text accompanying nn. 101–07.

67. Statement of Mr. Khlestov (USSR), 19 U.N. GAOR (14th mtg.), UN Doc. A/AC.119/SR.14, at 11–12 (1964).

68. *Id.* The final text of the declaration got around the disagreement by providing that "[n]othing in the foregoing paragraphs shall be construed as enlarging or diminishing in any way the scope of the provisions of the Charter concerning cases in which the use of force is lawful." G.A. Res. 2625, *supra* note 66, at 123.

69. Franck, *Who Killed Article 2(4)? or: Changing Norms Governing the Use of Force by States*, 64 AM. J. INT'L L. 809, 827 (1970).

70. Chayes, *Legal Case*, *supra* note 63, at 765.

71. *Id.*

72. *Id.*

73. *See id.* at 763; Meeker, *Defensive Quarantine and the Law*, 57 AM. J. INT'L L. 515 (1963); Oliver, *International Law and the Quarantine of Cuba: A Hopeful Prescription for Legal Writing*, 57 AM. J. INT'L L. 373 (1963);

Chayes, *Law and the Quarantine of Cuba*, 41 FOREIGN AFF. 550 (1963) [hereinafter cited as Chayes, *Law and the Quarantine of Cuba*].

74. Wright, *supra* note 64, at 546.

75. Meeker (then the deputy legal advisor in the Department of State), *Defensive Quarantine and the Law*, 57 AM. J. INT'L L. 515 (1963). On another occasion, however, Meeker denied that legal arguments in support of the quarantine were after-the-fact rationalizations: Meeker, *Role of Law in Political Aspects of World Affairs*, 48 DEP'T ST. BULL. 83, 87 (1963) [hereinafter cited as Meeker, *Role of Law*]. McWhinney, on the other hand, observes that "[i]n the end result . . . the Western action in the October 1962 crisis may have been vindicated as international law, on more modest or traditional grounds, by the simple passage of events." E. McWHINNEY, PEACEFUL CO-EXISTENCE AND SOVIET-WESTERN INTERNATIONAL LAW 77 (1964) (footnote omitted); *see also id.* at 81, for the argument that the U.S. action actually made new law as other states acquiesced to the reasonableness of the action.

76. Chayes, *Law and the Quarantine of Cuba*, *supra* note 73, at 550.

77. 57 AM. SOC'Y INT'L L. PROCEEDINGS 11, 14 (1963).

78. Statement by President Johnson, Apr. 28, 1965, *reprinted in* 52 DEP'T ST. BULL. 738 (1965). For a description of the political background of the Dominican crisis, see R. BARNET, INTERVENTION AND REVOLUTION 153–80 (1968).

79. Statement of Apr. 30, 1965, *reprinted in* 52 DEP'T ST. BULL. 742 (1965).

80. Statement of May 2, 1965, *reprinted in id.* 744, 745.

81. *Id.* at 746; *see also* Statement of U.S. Representative Stevenson in the Security Council, 20 U.N. SCOR (1196th mtg.) at 16, U.N. Doc. S/P.V. 1196 (1965).

82. Franck & Weisband, *supra* note 45, at 1008.

83. Department of State, *Legal Basis for United States Actions in the Dominican Republic*, May 7, 1965, *reprinted in* 2 A. CHAYES, T. EHRLICH & A. LOWENFELD, INTERNATIONAL LEGAL PROCESS: MATERIALS FOR AN INTRODUCTORY COURSE 1179, 1180 (1969).

84. *Id.*

85. *Id.* at 1181. *See also* President Johnson's statement of May 2, 1965, *supra* note 80; Franck & Weisband, *supra* note 45, at 1008.

86. Meeker, *The Dominican Situation in the Perspective of International Law*, 53 DEP'T ST. BULL. 60, 62–63 (1965).

87. *Id.* at 64.

88. *Id.* at 64. *See generally* Nanda, *The United States Action in the 1965 Dominican Crisis: Impact on World Order—Part II*, 44 DEN. L.J. 225, 233–43 (1967).

89. Chayes, *Legal Case*, *supra* note 63, at 765.

90. Declaration of the Government of the USSR on the Principles Under-

lying the Development and Further Consolidation of Friendship and Co-
operation Between the Soviet Union and Other Socialist Countries, Oct.
30, 1956, in MILESTONES OF SOVIET FOREIGN POLICY, *supra* note 47, at 166, 168.

91. Statement of May 2, 1965, *supra* note 80, at 745.

92. TASS statement, Pravda and Izvestia, Aug. 21, 1968, at 1, *reprinted
in* 20 CURRENT DIG. SOVIET PRESS 3 (No. 34, Sept. 11, 1968).

93. TASS communique, Pravda and Izvestia, Aug. 22, 1968, at 1, *reprinted in id.*

94. Ragulin & Chushkov, *Adventurist Plans of the Pentagon and the
C.I.A.*, Pravda, July 19, 1968, at 4, *reprinted in* 20 CURRENT DIG. SOVIET
PRESS 6 (No. 29, Aug. 7, 1968).

95. *Id.*

96. 2 A. CHAYES, T. EHRLICH & A. LOWENFELD, *supra* note 83, at 1181.

97. Editorial, *Defense of Socialism Is the Highest Internationalist Duty*,
Pravda, Aug. 22, 1968, at 2–3; Izvestia, Aug. 23, 1968, at 3–4; *reprinted in*
20 CURRENT DIG. SOVIET PRESS 5, 6, 11 *et seq.* (No. 34, Sept. 11, 1968).
This editorial is a long and laborious attempt to catalog the events that allegedly threatened regional socialist solidarity. *See also Appeal to Citizens of
the Czechoslovak Socialist Republic*, Pravda and Izvestia, Aug. 24, 1968, at 1,
reprinted in id. at 15. For the pre-invasion press build-up against the developments in Czechoslovakia, cumulatively described as "creeping counter-
revolution," see *Is This Situation Normal?*, Izvestia, July 31, 1968, at 2, condensed text in 20 CURRENT DIG. SOVIET PRESS 11 (No. 31, Aug. 21, 1968);
see also Pomelov, *Common Principles and National Characteristics in the Development of Socialism*, Pravda, Aug. 14, 1968, at 3–4, *condensed text in* 20
CURRENT DIG. SOVIET PRESS 3 (No. 33, Sept. 4, 1968), and editorial, *International Duty of All Fraternal Peoples*, in Krasnaya Zvezda, July 20, 1968, at 1,
excerpts in 20 CURRENT DIG. SOVIET PRESS 10 (No. 29, Aug. 7, 1968).

98. Kovalev, *On "Peaceful" and Nonpeaceful Counterrevolution*, Pravda,
Sept. 11, 1968, at 4, *condensed text in* 20 CURRENT DIG. SOVIET PRESS 11
(No. 37, Oct. 2, 1968); *see id.* at 10–11 for further allegations about anti-
socialist forces engaged in "quiet counterrevolution." For an official rebuttal
of the view that developments in Czechoslovakia were an experiment in "liberalization," see *Counterrevolution Disguised as "Regeneration,"* Izvestia,
Aug. 25, 1968, at 3, *condensed text in* 20 CURRENT DIG. SOVIET PRESS 7–8
(No. 35, Sept. 18, 1968). For criticism of stands taken by Yugoslavia, Romania, and China, see *Peking Without Camouflage*, Izvestia, Aug. 30, 1968,
at 2, reprinted in 20 CURRENT DIG. SOVIET PRESS 21 (No. 35, Sept. 18, 1968).
For further criticism of the "liberalization" and "democratization" argument,
see *On the Communist Party's Leadership Role in the Construction of Socialism*, Pravda, Sept. 19, 1968, at 3–4, *condensed text in* 20 CURRENT DIG. SO-
VIET PRESS 10–12 (No. 38, Oct. 9, 1968).

168 NOTES TO PAGES 68-71

99. Bosch, as quoted by Ambassador Tabio of Cuba, 20 U.N. SCOR (1198th mtg.) at 21, U.N. Doc. S/P.V. 1198 (1965).

100. 23 U.N. SCOR (1445th mtg.) at 17, U.N. Doc. S/P.V. 1445 (1968).

101. *Id.* at 18. *See also* Goodman, *The Invasion of Czechoslovakia: 1968*, 4 INT'L LAW. 42, 61–63 (1969).

102. Franck & Weisband, *supra* note 45, at 1011.

103. *Sovereignty and the Internationalist Obligations of Socialist Countries*, Pravda, Sept. 26, 1968, at 4, *reprinted in* 20 CURRENT DIG. SOVIET PRESS 10 (No. 39, Oct. 16, 1968) *and in* 7 INT'L LEGAL MATERIALS 1323 (1968).

104. 20 CURRENT DIG. SOVIET PRESS, *supra* note 103, at 11.

105. *Id.*

106. Apparently in an attempt to justify these fears, Germany was accused of having designs on Czechoslovakia. *See Lessons of Munich*, Pravda, Sept. 29, 1968, *condensed text in* 20 CURRENT DIG. SOVIET PRESS 12–13 (No. 39, Oct. 16, 1968); *see also The Bridges Bonn is Building*, Pravda, Sept. 17 and 20, 1968, at 5; Sept. 23 and 30, 1968, at 4; Oct. 5, 1968, at 4, *condensed texts in* 20 CURRENT DIG. SOVIET PRESS 3–6 (No. 41, Oct. 30, 1968); Karagezyan, *What the Sudeten-German Revanchists Are Out For*, 35 NEW TIMES, Sept. 4, 1968, at 5.

107. Speech at the Fifth Congress of the Polish United Workers' Party, Pravda and Izvestia, Nov. 13, 1968, at 1–2, *condensed text in* 20 CURRENT DIG. SOVIET PRESS 3–5 (No. 46, Dec. 4, 1968).

108. *See* T. WOLFE, SOVIET POWER AND EUROPE 1945–1970, at 385 (1970); E. MCWHINNEY, INTERNATIONAL LAW OF DETENTE: ARMS CONTROL, EUROPEAN SECURITY AND EAST-WEST COOPERATION 122–23 (1978).

109. CURRENT DIG. SOVIET PRESS, *supra* note 103, at 11.

110. *Id.* at 11–12. *Cf.* Reis, *Legal Aspects of the Invasion and Occupation of Czechoslovakia*, 59 DEP'T ST. BULL. 394 (1968) (statements of U.S. representative in UN Special Committee on Principles of International Law). *See also id.* at 405 (Secretary Rusk's statement in the UN General Assembly, Oct. 2) and at 664 (statements of U.S. representative Cooper in the 6th Committee of the General Assembly), and Goodman, *supra* note 101, at 42 *et seq.*

111. T. WOLFE, *supra* note 108, at 387–91; Goodman, *supra* note 101, at 63–64. *See generally* J. VALENTA, SOVIET INTERVENTION IN CZECHOSLOVAKIA, 1968: ANATOMY OF A DECISION (1979).

112. *See* Lipson, *supra* note 64, at 194.

113. *See* chapter II, section 4, Impact Prediction and Proportionality of Force, *supra*.

114. For accounts of the actual impact of the intervention in Czechoslovakia on the West and its immediate reaction, see Cleveland, *NATO After the Invasion*, 47 FOREIGN AFF. 251, 256–59, 261–62 (1968–69); Shub, *Lessons of Czechoslovakia*, 47 FOREIGN AFF. 266, 273 (1968–69). On extrahemispheric

interventions—i.e., interventions in areas that are not within the pre-existing spheres of influence in the classical sense (e.g., the Soviet-Cuban intervention in Angola and the Soviet invasion of Afghanistan)—see the next section.

115. Attempts have been made in the past to abstract interbloc norms ex post facto from superpower behavior. These have, however, been limited to case studies of specific crisis situations, with no attempt so far to synthesize a comprehensive set of behavioral norms from a simultaneous comparison of the entire range of superpower trouble situations of the post–World War II era. See, in this respect, the useful beginning by McWhinney, who abstracts a set of norms—or "rules of the game"—from a case study of the Cuban crisis: McWhinney, *Soviet and Western International Law and the Cold War in the Era of Bipolarity: Inter-bloc Law in a Nuclear Age*, CANADIAN Y.B. INT'L L. 40, 63 (1963). *See also generally* T. FRANCK & E. WEISBAND, WORD POLITICS: VERBAL STRATEGY AMONG THE SUPERPOWERS (1971); Oglesby, *The Use of Force in Bloc Situations*, 2 GA. J. INT'L & COMP. L. 77 (1972); Franck & Weisband, *supra* note 45.

116. Under Secretary of State George W. Ball observed:

The most direct and obvious way would have been to eliminate the offensive weapons by force—through a sudden air strike or an invasion. Such a response might have seemed clean, surgical and definitive. We had ample power to achieve a decisive stroke with a minimum of cost.

But President Kennedy chose not to take such action. . . . He chose instead a more limited response—a quarantine, interdicting the build-up of offensive weapons in Cuba. Through that choice we could avoid resort to an immediate use of force that might have led the United States and the Soviet Union, and with them their allies, up an ascending scale of violence. (Ball, *NATO and the Cuban Crisis*, 47 DEP'T ST. BULL. 831, 831–32 [1962].)

117. R. KENNEDY, *supra* note 62, at 62–63; *see generally id.* at 34–35, 48–49, 51, 54. *See also* Lipson, *supra* note 64, at 193.

118. Meeker, *Role of Law, supra* note 75, at 87. It is of course self-evident that recognizing the USSR's miscalculation does not explain its actual motives in Cuba: The missiles could have been intended simply as a psychological prop for the Castro regime in the aftermath of the Bay of Pigs affair and perhaps to gain wider support in Latin America, or to narrow down the nuclear lead of the U.S. over the USSR, or perhaps, as Ulam has suggested, to "intimidate" both the U.S. and the People's Republic of China into signing a nuclear non-proliferation treaty with the USSR, to extract Western agreement to a peace treaty with Germany, and possibly even to force the withdrawal of American support for the Formosa regime. For more detail, see A. ULAM, EXPANSION AND CO-EXISTENCE: THE HISTORY OF SOVIET FOREIGN POLICY 1916–67, at 661–77 (1968); A. ULAM, *supra* note 35, 331. *See also* George, *The Cuban*

Missile Crisis 1962, in A. GEORGE, D. HALL & W. SIMON, THE LIMITS OF COERCIVE DIPLOMACY: LAOS, CUBA, VIETNAM 86, 95, 100 (1971); Horelick, *The Cuban Missile Crisis—An Analysis of Soviet Calculations and Behavior*, 16 WORLD POL. 363, 368-69, 375-76 (1963-64).

119. McDougal, *International Law, Power and Policy: A Contemporary Conception*, 1 RECUEIL DES COURS, ACADÉMIE DE DROIT INTERNATIONALE DE LA HAYE 137, 185 (1953).

120. Art. 53 provides, in part: "The Security Council shall, where appropriate, utilise such regional arrangements or agencies for enforcement action under its authority. But no enforcement action shall be taken under regional arrangements or by regional agencies without the authorization of the Security Council." Article 103 provides that "in the event of a conflict between the obligations of the Members of the United Nations under the present Charter and their obligations under any other international agreement, their obligations under the present Charter shall prevail."

121. Excerpts from President Ford's news conference on foreign policy, Sept. 16, 1974, 71 DEP'T ST. BULL. 471, 472 (1974).

122. *Id.* at 472. For further consideration of unilateral determinations by the U.S. of the "best interests" of target countries, see Falk, *President Gerald Ford, C.I.A. Covert Operations, and the Status of International Law*, 69 AM. J. INT'L L. 354 (1975).

123. R. WALTON, THE REMNANTS OF POWER: THE LAST TRAGIC YEARS OF ADLAI STEVENSON 170 (1968).

124. *Id.* Senator Fulbright also criticized the factual assumptions of the U.S. action: 111 CONG. REC. 23,855, 23,861 (1965).

125. Franck & Weisband, *supra* note 45, at 1005.

126. McWhinney, *supra* note 115, at 67.

127. *See* Khrushchev's letter to Kennedy, Oct. 27, 1962, *reprinted in* 47 DEP'T ST. BULL. 741 (1962).

128. Letter from Kennedy to Khrushchev, Oct. 27, 1962, *reprinted in id.* at 743.

129. *See* Lipson, *supra* note 64, at 193, 196.

130. Letter from the Central Committee of the Soviet Communist Party to the Central Committee of the Polish United Workers' Party, June 5, 1981; for full text of English translation, see N.Y. Times, June 11, 1981, at A8, col. 1. A commentary in Pravda subsequently declared that "[t]he preservation of the revolutionary gains of the Polish people is not only their domestic affair. It is a question that touches directly on the vital interests of all peoples and states that have chosen the path of socialism." *Soviet Bids Poles Act Against Union*, N.Y. Times, Oct. 14, 1981, at A5, col. 1.

131. *See* chapter I, section 3, The Soviet Concept of Coexistence after Helsinki, *supra*.

132. Voronov, *USSR-Poland: Traditions of Friendship and Revolutionary Solidarity*, 12 INT'L AFF. (Moscow) 75, 78 (1978).

133. Speech of Secretary of State Alexander Haig to the Foreign Policy Association, July 14, 1981, N.Y. Times, July 15, 1981, at A1, A11, col. 2.

134. For text of the official State Department summary of the Sonnenfeldt statement, made in London in December 1975 at a meeting of U.S. ambassadors in Europe, see N.Y. Times, Apr. 6, 1976, at A14, col. 4. The "Sonnenfeldt doctrine" gave rise to some controversy, but Secretary of State Kissinger affirmed that it did not go beyond what was already "the basic policy of the United States." 74 DEP'T ST. BULL. 543, 546 (1976) (questions and answers following a speech before the Foreign Policy Association and other organizations, Apr. 8, 1976). On the Grenada invasion, *see* Dore, *The Invasion of Grenada: The Johnson Doctrine Reaganized*, 20 STAN. J. INT'L L. (1984). This article examines the invasion in the context of the intrabloc interventions discussed in the previous section of this chapter.

135. *See* Marcum, *Lessons of Angola*, 54 FOREIGN AFF. 407, 412–13, 417 (1976).

136. Report at the 25th Congress of the C.P.S.U., *quoted in* Uralov, *Angola: The Triumph of the Right Cause*, 5 INT'L AFF. (MOSCOW) 51, 52 (1976).

137. *Id.* at 53; *see also* Marcum, *supra* note 135, at 414–16.

138. Uralov, *supra* note 136, at 55.

139. Marcum, *supra* note 135, at 419–20; *see also* N.Y. Times, Dec. 2, 1976, at A8, col. 1.

140. *See* 74 DEP'T ST. BULL. 76, 182–183 (1976) (President Ford's reactions to the Senate vote on funds for Angola).

141. *See* statement of U.S. Representative Moynihan in the UN General Assembly, *reprinted in* 74 DEP'T ST. BULL. 80 (1976). *See also* Secretary Kissinger's news conferences of Dec. 23, 1975, and Jan. 14 and Feb. 3, 1976, *id.* at 69, 125, 216; President Ford's letter of Jan. 27, 1976, to the Speaker of the House of Representatives, *id.* at 182; Secretary Kissinger's statement to the Subcommittee on African Affairs of the Senate Committee on Foreign Relations, Jan. 29, 1976, *id.* at 174. On Feb. 20, 1976, Sonnenfeldt declared the Angolan intervention an attempt to gain a "unilateral advantage," and in April he said that the "intervention in Angola [was] unacceptable and that its repetition in other areas of Africa or the world will be met with determination." *Id.* at 370, 581. This in itself implied that the U.S. was prepared to overlook the Soviet intervention this time. A similar statement was made by Secretary Kissinger: "The United States will not accept further Cuban military interventions abroad." *Id.* at 464.

142. Valenta, *The Soviet-Cuban Alliance in Africa and the Caribbean*, WORLD TODAY 45 (Feb. 1981).

143. *See, e.g.,* statement of Philip C. Habib, Under Secretary of State for

Political Affairs, before the Subcommittee on Africa of the House Committee on International Relations, Mar. 3, 1977, *Southern Africa in the Global Context*, 76 DEP'T ST. BULL. 318 (1977); *see also* address by Chester A. Crocker, Assistant Secretary of State for African Affairs, *Strengthening US-African Relations*, to the African-American Institute Conference, Wichita, Kan., June 20, 1981, *reprinted in* 81 DEP'T ST. BULL. 57 (1981).

144. *See* statement of Chester A. Crocker before the Subcommittee on Africa of the House Foreign Affairs Committee, June 17, 1981, *reprinted in* 81 DEP'T ST. BULL. 55 (1981).

145. *See* 76 DEP'T ST. BULL. 357, 361 (1977) (excerpts from President Carter's news conference of Mar. 24, 1977).

146. Heuer, *Analyzing the Soviet Invasion of Afghanistan: Hypotheses from Causal Attribution Theory*, 13 STUD. COMP. COMMUNISM 347, 348 (1980). *Cf.* Valenta, *Czechoslovakia and Afghanistan: Comparative Comments*, 13 STUD. COMP. COMMUNISM 332 (1980).

147. *See Western Hemisphere: Soviet Combat Troops in Cuba*, 79 DEP'T ST. BULL. 63–64 (1979).

148. Speech of President Carter, Oct. 1, 1979, *reprinted in* 79 DEP'T ST. BULL. 7, 8 (1979).

149. For further historical background, see A. FLETCHER, AFGHANISTAN: HIGHWAY OF CONQUEST (1965); D. SINGHAL, INDIA AND AFGHANISTAN 1876–1907: A STUDY IN DIPLOMATIC RELATIONS (1963); L. ADAMEC, AFGHANISTAN 1900–1923: A DIPLOMATIC HISTORY (1967).

150. Dupree, *Afghanistan Under the Khalq*, 28 PROB. COMMUNISM 34, 36 (1979).

151. *Id.* Dupree argues that Afghanistan became the "economic Korea" of the Soviet Union, on the theory that massive economic aid (on the pattern of the Marshall Plan) would give Russia the ability to influence the social and political institutions of Afghanistan.

152. *Id.* at 47.

153. Valenta, *The Soviet Invasion of Afghanistan: The Difficulty of Knowing Where to Stop*, 24 ORBIS 201, 205 (1980).

154. *Id.* at 207.

155. Dupree, *supra* note 150, at 50.

156. Valenta, *supra* note 153, at 210.

157. *See* statement of President Reagan, Apr. 24, 1981, 81 DEP'T ST. BULL. 41 (1981).

158. Reports indicated that, in 1981, 90 percent of the Afghan countryside was outside Soviet control. *Soviet Is Said to Reject U.S. Offer of Afghan Talks*, N.Y. Times, Aug. 7, 1981, at A1, col. 2, A4, col. 5. *See also Military Analysis: Afghanistan: New Outlook, id.* at A4, col. 1, (assessment of the military problems faced by the USSR in Afghanistan), and *Afghan Rebels Reported to Inflict Heavy Losses*, N.Y. Times, Apr. 28, 1982, at A7, col. 4.

159. Shchedrov, *The USSR and Afghanistan: The Firm Foundation of Friendship and Cooperation*, 1 INT'L AFF. (MOSCOW) 14, 16 (1981).

160. *See* appendix III, *infra*, for text.

161. Shchedrov, *supra* note 159, at 16.

162. Commenting on the trend to solve great-power problems in arenas other than the UN, McWhinney observes that the trend "may not be very good for the health of the United Nations Organization as a whole, . . . but it may still be a viable approach to World public order in an ideologically-divided World Community." McWhinney, *Ideological Conflict and the Special Soviet Approach to International Law*, U. TOL. L. REV. 215, 232 (1971).

163. Report of the Special Committee on the Question of Defining Aggression, 29 U.N. GAOR Supp. (No. 19) at 24, U.N. Doc. A/9619 (1974).

164. *Id*. at 37.

165. *Id*. at 23.

166. *Id*.

167. *Id*.

168. Sohn, *The Definition of Aggression*, 45 VA. L. REV. 697, 699 (1959).

169. McDougal, *supra* note 119, at 182–83.

170. L. POSPÍŠIL, ANTHROPOLOGY OF LAW: A COMPARATIVE THEORY 113 (1974). Pospíšil, Llewellyn, Hoebel, and other anthropologists have collected ethnographic data from several politically unstructured societies (e.g., the Kapauku Papuans, the Nunamiut Eskimo, the Cheyenne Indians, etc.) to illustrate the existence of smaller subgroups—with their own distinctive legal systems—within larger social units: *id*. at 106 *et seq.*; K. LLEWELLYN & E. HOEBEL, THE CHEYENNE WAY 28, 53 (1941).

171. L. POSPÍŠIL, *supra* note 170, at 112. *See also* A. GOULDNER, FOR SOCIOLOGY 226 (1973).

172. McDougal, *supra* note 119, at 183–84 (italics added).

173. Pospíšil, *supra* note 170, at 107.

174. Principles II, III, IV, and VI of the Declaration of Principles of the Final Act, appendix II.

175. U.N. CHARTER arts. 53, 103.

176. Declaration on the Inadmissibility of Intervention in the Domestic Affairs of States and the Protection of Their Independence and Sovereignty, Dec. 21, 1965, G.A. Res. 2131, 20 U.N. GAOR Supp. (No. 14) at 11, U.N. Doc. A/6014 (1966).

177. Declaration of Principles of International Law Concerning Friendly Relations and Cooperation Among States in Accordance with the Charter of the United Nations, in G.A. Res. 2625, *supra* note 66.

178. The Soviet Union alleged that certain powers were "seeking to impede the advance of history by aggressive acts and open intervention in the domestic affairs of sovereign States." 20 U.N. GAOR Annex 3 (Agenda Item 107) at 1, U.N. Doc. A/5977 (1965).

179. *See* Rosenstock, *The Declaration of Principles of International Law Concerning Friendly Relations: A Survey*, 65 AM. J. INT'L L. 713, 726 (1971).

180. *See generally* Onuf, *The Principle of Non-Intervention, the United Nations, and the International System*, 25 INT'L ORG. 209 (1971).

181. Gouldner argues that reciprocity emerges inevitably in any social arena in which there is continuous interaction, and that it provides overall systemic stability: Gouldner, *The Norm of Reciprocity: A Preliminary Statement*, 25 AM. SOC. REV. 161 (1960). For an argument that outright bloc interventions themselves promote systemic stability and overall world order, see Oglesby, *supra* note 115, at 88.

CHAPTER IV

1. R. PABST, MAJOR ISSUES OF THE LAW OF THE SEA 84–85, 108 (1976).

2. Ray, *Ecology, Law and the Marine Revolution*, in PACEM IN MARIBUS 8–9 (E. Borgese ed. 1972).

3. Charney, *The Equitable Sharing of Revenues from Seabed Mining*, in POLICY ISSUES IN OCEAN LAW 53, 69 (1975).

4. Johnson & Logue, *U.S. Economic Interests in Law of the Seas Issues*, in THE LAW OF THE SEA: U.S. INTERESTS AND ALTERNATIVES 37, 44–47 (C. Amacher & R. Sweeney eds. 1976).

5. Craven, *Ocean Arms Control*, in QUIET ENJOYMENT: ARMS CONTROL AND POLICE FORCES FOR THE OCEAN 76–83 (Center for the Study of Democratic Institutions, Proceedings of the Preparatory Conference on Arms Control and Disarmament, 1970).

6. *See* Kindt, *Offshore Siting of Nuclear Power Plants*, 8 OCEAN DEV. & INT'L L.J. 57, 64 (1980); Nanda, *The Legal Status of Surface Devices Functioning at Sea Other Than Ships*, 26 (Suppl.) AM. J. COMP. L. 233 (1978).

7. Reisman, *The Regime of Straits and National Security: An Appraisal of International Lawmaking*, 74 AM. J. INT'L L. 48, 48–50 (1980).

8. *Cf.* N. Brown, *Military Uses of the Ocean Floor*, in PACEM IN MARIBUS, *supra* note 2, at 285, 291. Thus, it has been suggested that ABMs be deployed in the oceans to intercept MIRVs before the warheads separate: *Id.* Another possible development is the deployment of the controversial MX missile system on hundreds of submarines. Early in January 1983, President Reagan formed a Commission on Strategic Forces to study U.S. land, sea, and air weapons systems. One of the commission's major purposes was to recommend a basing mode for the MX system, and indications at the time of writing point toward a land-based version. *See Next: Densetrack? Racepack?*, Time, Jan. 17, 1983, at 12, col. 1.

9. THE TIDES OF CHANGE: PEACE, POLLUTION AND POTENTIAL OF THE

OCEANS 78 (E. Borgese & D. Krieger eds. 1975); Reisman, *supra* note 7, at 48, 50.

10. E. BROWN, ARMS CONTROL IN HYDROSPACE: LEGAL ASPECTS, 12–14 (Woodrow Wilson International Center for Scholars, Ocean Series No. 301, 1971).

11. One study states the advantages of undersea weapons systems as follows:

The absorption of water with respect to light, high-energy particles, electro-magnetic radiation, heat and other known forms of energy is such that, except for acoustic radiation, none of the mechanisms postulated has a detection range potential which is significant when compared with the vast areas available in the ocean. The ultimate test in this regard is the ability of the submersible to blend with and be masked by the environment. At near zero speed this ought to be quite attainable. The hotel load for life support and weapons readiness is modest, and if, for example, power is supplied by fuel cell, the machinery associated with it should be extremely quiet. Drifting in the current, at great depth or at low speeds, the hydrodynamic wake would be insignificant. A further aid would be the capability to move very close to the bottom, rendering the submersible difficult to detect by long-range, active sonar. Ultimately, the underseas weapons systems could develop into something akin to a manned on-the-bottom, slowly mobile mine. (J. Craven, *Ocean Technology and Submarine Warfare*, in IMPLICATIONS OF MILITARY TECHNOLOGY INTO THE 1970's 38, 41–42 [Institute for Strategic Studies, Adelphi Paper No. 46, 1968].)

12. Reisman, *supra* note 7, at 52–53.

13. SIPRI YEARBOOK OF WORLD ARMAMENTS AND DISARMAMENTS, 1968/69, at 99–100 (1970).

14. *Id.*; Scoville & Hoag, *Ballistic Missile Submarines as Counterforce Weapons*, in THE FUTURE OF THE SEA-BASED DETERRENT 33 (K. Tsipis, A. Cahn & B. Feld eds. 1973).

15. N. Brown, *supra* note 8, at 285, 291. *See also* E. Brown, *The Legal Regime of Inner Space*, 22 CURRENT LEGAL PROBS. 181, 183 (1969).

16. Annual Report of the President on Marine Resources and Engineering Development and Report of the National Council on Marine Resources and Engineering Development, *cited in* SIPRI YEARBOOK OF WORLD ARMAMENTS AND DISARMAMENTS, 1969/70, at 95 (1971).

17. Ritchie-Calder, *In Quiet Enjoyment*, in PACEM IN MARIBUS, *supra* note 2, at 260, 262; *see also* E. Young, *Arms Control and Disarmament in the Ocean*, in *id.* 266, 268–69.

18. Treaty on the Prohibition of the Emplacement of Weapons of Mass De-

struction on the Seabed, Art. I, T.I.A.S. No. 7337, *reprinted in* 10 INT'L
LEGAL MATERIALS 146 (1971) [hereinafter cited as Seabed Treaty].

19. *See* Joyner, *Towards a Legal Regime for the International Seabed: The
Soviet Union's Evolving Perspective*, 15 VA. J. INT'L L. 871, 884 (1975). *See
also* Barry, *The Seabed Arms Control Issue 1967–71—A Superpower Sym-
biosis?*, 61 INT'L L. STUD. 572, 583 (R. Lillich & J. Moore eds. 1980). Con-
firmation was given within the Disarmament Committee by the U.S. delegate,
who said:

> [V]ehicles which can navigate in the water above the sea-bed and sub-
> marines should be viewed in the same way as any other ships; sub-
> marines would therefore not be violating the treaty if they were either
> anchored to, or resting on, the sea-bed. (U.N. Doc. CCD/PV.440 at 9).

20. Barry, *supra* note 19, at 583.

21. E. BROWN, *supra* note 10, at 58.

22. G. Smith, *Ambassador Smith Presents U.S. Views on Seabed Proposal
at Eighteen-Nation Disarmament Conference*, 60 DEP'T ST. BULL. 333, 336
(1969).

23. 1971 Seabed Treaty, *supra* note 18, Art. I.

24. *See* subsection of this chapter, Relationship to the Geneva Conventions, *infra*.

25. SIPRI YEARBOOK 1969–70, *supra* note 16, at 158.

26. *Id.*

27. *Id.* at 159. This interpretation would also seem to be a logical extension of the principle of freedom of the high seas, which has been said to give
states the right to use the seas for military purposes. Zedalis, *Military Uses of
Ocean Space and the Developing International Law of the Sea: An Analysis in
the Context of Peacetime ASW*, 16 SAN DIEGO L. REV. 575, 607 (1979); *see
also* Zedalis, *"Peaceful Purposes" and Other Relevant Provisions of the Revised Composite Negotiating Text: A Comparative Analysis of the Existing and
the Proposed Military Regime for the High Seas*, 7 SYRACUSE J. INT'L L. &
COM. 1, 4 (1979).

28. W. BURKE, OCEAN SCIENCE, TECHNOLOGY AND THE FUTURE INTER-
NATIONAL LAW OF THE SEAS 10–39 (1965). *See also* Barry, *supra* note 19, at
582; SIPRI YEARBOOK 1969–70, *supra* note 16, at 168.

29. *See* E. BROWN, *supra* note 10, at 85–86.

30. *Id.* at 84.

31. *Id.*

32. SIPRI YEARBOOK 1969/70, *supra* note 16, at 171.

33. *Id.*

34. M. McDOUGAL & W. BURKE, THE PUBLIC ORDER OF THE OCEANS 64
(1962).

35. Art. 5(2) provides in part:

Where the establishment of a straight baseline in accordance with Article 4 has the effect of enclosing as internal waters areas which previously had been considered as part of the territorial sea or the high seas, a right of innocent passage, as provided in Articles 14 to 23, shall exist in those waters. (Convention on the Territorial Sea, 516 U.N.T.S. 205 [1958].)

36. It should be noted that such restrictions are consensual and apply only to those states that are parties to the treaty in question.

37. Under Art. 14(6) of the Geneva Convention on the Territorial Sea and Art. 20 of the United Nations Convention on the Law of the Sea (UNCLOS), U.N. Doc. A/CONF. 62/122 (1982), submarines must both navigate on the surface and show their flag.

38. Geneva Convention on the Territorial Sea, Art. 16(4). The provisions of Art. 14(6) regarding submarines would seem to apply also to navigation through international straits forming part of the territorial sea. Such restrictions led the U.S. to demand the right of "free transit" rather than just "innocent passage" through international straits. In return, the U.S. indicated, at the Geneva Conferences of 1959 and 1960 on the law of the sea, that it would drop its insistence on a narrow territorial sea of 3 miles and accept a wider limit of 12 miles. The development of Soviet naval strength and of its fishing and merchant marine fleets led the USSR to support the U.S. position on narrow territorial seas and transit through straits. *See generally* M. McDougal & W. Burke, *supra* note 34, at 501, 504; Sulikowski, *Soviet Ocean Policy*, 3 Ocean Dev. & Int'l L.J. 69, 70–71 (1975); M. Janis & D. Daniel, The USSR: Ocean Use and Ocean Law 21 (Law of the Sea Institute, U. of Rhode Island, Occasional Paper Series No. 1, 1974); Hollick, *Bureaucrats at Sea*, in New Era of Ocean Politics 1, 4–5, 42–43 (Studies in International Affairs No. 22, 1974).

39. Art. 2 of UNCLOS, *supra* note 37. For a comprehensive examination of how the proposed regime of UNCLOS affects military uses of the high seas in general, see Dore, *International Law and the Preservation of Ocean Space and Outer Space as Zones of Peace: Progress and Problems*, 15 Cornell Int'l L.J. 1 (1982).

40. *See* text accompanying notes 7–11, *supra*.

41. *See* text accompanying notes 20–24 and 34–40, *supra*.

42. *See* text accompanying notes 77–79, *infra*.

43. *See* Editorial, *Leading on Earth and in Space*, 9 Int'l Aff. (Moscow) 3, 4 (1962).

44. Horelick, *The Soviet Union and the Political Uses of Outer Space*, in Outer Space in World Politics 43, 46, 56 (J. Goldsen ed. 1963).

45. Khrushchev's interview with James Reston of the N.Y. Times, Oct. 7, 1957, quoted in *id.* at 52.

46. Horelick, *supra* note 44, at 52, 56.

47. *Id.* at 53.

48. *Id.* Ironically, it was at a UN General Assembly debate on disarmament that Khrushchev publicly announced that the USSR was engaged in mass production of ICBMs. In the Soviet Union, he said, rockets were being mass-produced "like sausages from a sausage-machine." Statement by Khrushchev in the UN General Assembly, Oct. 11, 1960, 15 (1) U.N. GAOR (900th plen. mtg.) at 646, U.N. Doc. A/P.V. 900 (1960).

49. *See* Zhukov, *The Moon, Politics and Law*, 9 INT'L AFF. (Moscow) 32, 35 (1966).

50. Horelick, *supra* note 44, at 43, 58.

51. *Id.* at 59.

52. *Id.* at 54.

53. Kecskemeti, *Outer Space and World Peace*, in OUTER SPACE IN WORLD POLITICS, *supra* note 44, at 25, 31; *see also* Horelick, *supra* note 44, at 59–60.

54. Comparisons between U.S. and Soviet space activities became possible, of course, only after the U.S. space program was well established and had accumulated its own body of space data.

55. 16 U.N. GAOR Annex (Agenda Item 21), U.N. Doc. A/C.1/L.301 (1961).

56. *See* Kecskemeti, *supra* note 53, at 34.

57. *See* P. Thacher, *Arms Control and Outer Space in the United Nations*, in INTERNATIONAL COOPERATION IN OUTER SPACE 287, 309 (U.S. Senate, symposium prepared for the Committee on Aeronautical and Space Sciences, 1971). The U.S. space shuttle program has been publicly acknowledged to have a military component, although the precise details have not been disclosed: *Shuttle, Carrying Military Cargo, Blasts Off in Smoothest Start Yet*, N.Y. Times, June 28, 1982, at A1, col. 3, 13, col. 1.

58. *See, e.g.*, Teplinsky & Suprun, *The Missile Business in the U.S.A.*, 4 INT'L AFF. (Moscow) 37 (1960).

59. Horelick, *supra* note 44, at 67.

60. *Id.* at 53.

61. *Id.* at 62–63.

62. MILITARY STRATEGY 360–61 (V. Sokolovsky ed. 1962), *quoted in* Crane, *The Beginnings of Marxist Space Jurisprudence?*, 57 AM. J. INT'L L. 615, 617 (1963).

63. G. Zhukov, *Problems of Space Law at the Present Stage*, in PROCEEDINGS OF THE 5TH COLLOQUIUM ON THE LAW OF OUTER SPACE 1, 15, 20–21 (International Institute of Space Law [I.I.S.L.] of the International Aeronautical Federation [I.A.F.], 1962). The following quotation is an apt summary of the war/peace dialectic in Soviet armament policy:

The appearance of the dreadful power of nuclear-ballistic weapons in the hands of socialist states, which defend the law of peace and of peaceful coexistence, guarantees the possibility in an ever increasing degree to prevent both small and large misdemeanors and crimes by the imperialist states, and this consolidates and stabilizes the entire international legal order. (Lazarev, *Technical Progress and Contemporary International Law*, SOVETSKOYE GOSUDARSTVO I PRAVO, [1962], *quoted in* Crane, *supra* note 62, at 624.)

64. *See* Statement of Secretary of State Rusk, *New Frontiers of Science, Space, and Foreign Policy*, 46 DEP'T ST. BULL. 931, 934 (1962), for an official American criticism of Soviet political strategy in space.

65. The U.S. has already decided to establish a permanent, unified military command headquarters in space: *USAF's Space Command to be Established Sept. 1*, 116 AVIATION WEEK & SPACE TECH., June 28, 1982, at 30–31. *See also* Schelling, *The Military Uses of Outer Space: Bombardment Satellites*, in OUTER SPACE IN WORLD POLITICS, *supra* note 44, at 103.

66. For a futuristic but not entirely implausible description of the nature and strategy of possible "dogfights" in space, see Willenson & Clark, *War's Fourth Dimension*, NEWSWEEK, Nov. 29, 1976, at 46. *See also* Sherr, *Satellite Warfare*, N.Y. Times, Aug. 27, 1982, at 25, col. 3.

67. Schelling, *supra* note 65, at 103–04.

68. *See* Healey, *The Sputnik and Western Defence*, 34 INT'L AFF. 145, 146–47 (1958).

69. *See* Willenson & Clark, *supra* note 66, at 47, 48.

70. *Id.*

71. Schelling, *supra* note 65, at 97, 101. *See also* M. GOLOVINE, CONFLICT IN SPACE: A PATTERN OF WAR IN A NEW DIMENSION 113, 119 (1962).

72. Covault, *New Soviet Anti-satellite Mission Boosts Backing for U.S. Tests*, 112 AVIATION WEEK & SPACE TECH., Apr. 28, 1980, at 20.

73. S. LAY & H. TAUBENFELD, THE LAW RELATING TO ACTIVITIES OF MAN IN SPACE 27 (1970).

74. Robinson, *Soviets Push for Beam Weapons*, 106 AVIATION WEEK & SPACE TECH., May 2, 1977, at 16.

75. *Anti-satellite Laser Weapons Planned*, 112 AVIATION WEEK & SPACE TECH., June 16, 1980, at 244; Covault, *Anti-satellite Design Weapon Advances*, *id.* at 243; Gregory, *Military Power in Space*, 117 AVIATION WEEK & SPACE TECH., Oct. 18, 1982, at 7; Wulf, *Arms Control-Outer Space* 11 J. SPACE L. 67 (1983).

76. Knorr, *The International Implications of Outer-Space Activities*, in OUTER SPACE IN WORLD POLITICS, *supra* note 44, at 123.

77. Treaty on Principles Governing the Activities of States in the Exploration of Outer Space, Art. IV, 610 U.N.T.S. 205 (1967).

78. *Cf.* Zedalis, *Will Article III of the Moon Treaty Improve Existing Law?: A Textual Analysis*, 5 SUFFOLK TRANSNAT'L L.J. 53, 57 (1980), for the view that Art. IV(1) could be read as not prohibiting the installation of nuclear and mass-destruction weapons on celestial bodies on a *temporary* basis.

79. *See* Statement by Goedhuis, in REPORT OF THE 54TH CONFERENCE OF THE I.L.A. (The Hague) 422, 426 (1970).

80. *See generally* Zedalis & Wade, *Anti-satellite Weapons and the Outer Space Treaty of 1967*, 8 CAL. W. INT'L L.J. 454, 459 (1978).

81. U.N. Doc. A/34/664 (Nov. 12, 1979), *reproduced in* 18 INT'L LEGAL MATERIALS 1434 (1979).

82. Agreement Governing the Activities of States on the Moon, Art. III, paras. 3, 4, in *id.*

83. Emphasis added.

84. *See generally* Zedalis, *supra* note 78, at 56-61.

85. *See* N. Poulantzas, *The Outer Space Treaty of Jan. 27, 1967, and Its Aftermath*, in PROCEEDINGS OF THE 11TH COLLOQUIUM ON THE LAW OF OUTER SPACE 50, 55 (I.I.S.L. of the I.A.F., 1968).

86. S. LAY & H. TAUBENFELD, *supra* note 73, at 32.

87. *Id.*

88. J. MORENOFF, WORLD PEACE THROUGH SPACE LAW 65-66 (1967). *See also* W. HYMAN, A MAGNA CARTA OF SPACE 145 (1966).

89. *See* Shiffer & Snyders, *The Need for Enforcement for International Space Treaties*, in PROCEEDINGS OF THE 10TH COLLOQUIUM ON THE LAW OF OUTER SPACE 237, 238 (I.I.S.L. of the I.A.F., 1967).

90. Report of the Committee on the Peaceful Uses of Outer Space, 32 U.N. GAOR Supp. (No. 20), at 8, U.N. Doc. A/32/20 (1977). The other two matters of "high priority" were the question of a draft treaty relating to the moon and the elaboration of principles governing the use of satellites for direct television broadcasting. *See id.*, Report of the Scientific and Technical Subcommittee on Remote Sensing of the Earth from Space, 8-11. The latter report does not, however, broach the subject of military surveillance from space. *See generally* Polter, *Remote Sensing and State Sovereignty*, 4 J. SPACE L. 99 (1976).

91. Report of the Legal Sub-committee (17th sess.) to the Committee on the Peaceful Uses of Outer Space, U.N. Doc. A/AC.105/218 Annex 3 (1978). For draft principles on direct television broadcasting, see Annex 2, *id.*

92. For a discussion of the views of various authors, see Zedalis & Wade, *supra* note 80, at 470 *et seq. See also* Zedalis, *supra* note 78, at 62-63.

93. Markoff, *Disarmament and "Peaceful Purposes" Provisions in the 1967 Outer Space Treaty*, 4 J. SPACE L. 3, 7 (1976). *See also* G. GAL, SPACE LAW 155, 168 (1969); G. Gal, *"The Peaceful Uses of Outer Space"—After the Space Treaty*, in PROCEEDINGS OF THE 10TH COLLOQUIUM, *supra* note 90, at 132-33; Markov, *Implementing the Contractual Obligation of Article I, para-*

graph 1, of the Outer Space Treaty 1967, in Proceedings of the 17th Colloquium on the Law of Outer Space 136 *et seq.* (I.I.S.L. of the I.A.F., 1974); M. Niciu, *What is the Meaning of the Use of Cosmos Exclusively for Peaceful Purposes?*, in *id.* at 226; Markov, *Against the So-called "Broader" Interpretation of the Term "Peaceful" in International Space Law*, in Proceedings of the 11th Colloquium, *supra* note 85, at 73, 75; M. Lachs, The Law of Outer Space: An Experience in Contemporary Law Making 105–9 (1972).

94. Zedalis & Wade, *supra* note 80, at 472–73.

95. L. Lipson & N. Katzenbach, Report to the National Aeronautics and Space Administration on the Law of Outer Space 27 (1961).

96. G.A. Res. 1148, 12 U.N. GAOR Supp. (No. 18) at 3, U.N. Doc. A/3805 (1958), urges, in paragraph 1(f), "the joint study of an inspection system designed to ensure that the sending of objects through outer space shall be exclusively for peaceful and scientific purposes." *See also* G.A. Res. 1472, 14 U.N. GAOR Supp. (No. 16) at 5, U.N. Doc. A/4354 (1960); G.A. Res. 1721, 16 U.N. GAOR Supp. (No. 17) at 6–7, U.N. Doc. A/5100 (1962); G.A. Res. 1802, 17 U.N. GAOR Supp. (No. 17) at 5, U.N. Doc. A/5217 (1963); G.A. Res. 1962, 18 U.N. GAOR Supp. (No. 15) at 15, U.N. Doc. A/5515 (1964); G.A. Res. 1963, 18 U.N. GAOR Supp. (No. 15) at 16, U.N. Doc. A/5515 (1964); G.A. Res. 2222, 21 U.N. GAOR Supp. (No. 16) at 13, U.N. Doc. A/6316 (1967). All these resolutions consistently emphasize the theme of the common "interest" of mankind in space activity on the basis of equality and nonappropriation of space and celestial bodies.

97. L. Lipson & N. Katzenbach, *supra* note 95, at 27. The writers comment:

Hence their [*i.e.*, the small states'] emphasis on a legal regime which insists that uses of space be "peaceful," that space powers act "reasonably," that due regard be given to principles of "equality," and so forth. While they do not appear to desire a regime that would allow to each . . . state an unqualified veto . . . neither would they wholeheartedly approve a regime that authorized the space powers to decide unilaterally (or even, conceivably, bilaterally) what was permissible.

98. Dudakov, *The Outer Space Treaty and Subsequent Scientific Development of International Space Law*, in Proceedings of the 17th Colloquium, *supra* note 93, at 107, 108. Dudakov maintains that the specific rights and interests of the community of states as well as their obligations can arise only through "special agreements" between them: *id.* at 111. *See also* R. Dekanozov, *Juridical Nature of Outer Space, Including the Moon and Other Celestial Bodies*, in Proceedings of the 17th Colloquium 200.

99. U.N. Doc. A/AC 105/C.2/SR.66, at 6–7 (July 25, 1966). Another proposal to introduce the term "use for peaceful purposes" into the text of

Art. 1 also failed: U.N. Doc. A/AC 105/C.2/SR.65, at 11 (July 22, 1966). An attempt to include the term in the title of the treaty failed as well: U.N. Doc. A/ AC 105/C.2/SR.63, at 5 (July 20, 1966).

100. *See* Statement by Goedhuis, *supra* note 79, at 440. *See also* Fasan, *The Meaning of the Term "Mankind" in Space Legal Language*, 2 J. SPACE L. 125 (1974). Although Fasan argues that the term "mankind" has emerged as a new legal concept, he does not attempt to explain what kind of space activities are in the "interest" of "mankind" or for its "benefit," nor does he offer any guide for measuring "interest" or "benefit." For a more detailed outline of the uncertainties of the "benefit and interest" clause, see S. Gorove, *Limitations on the Principles of Freedom of Exploration and Use in the Outer Space Treaty: Benefit and Interests*, in PROCEEDINGS OF THE 13TH COLLOQUIUM ON THE LAW OF OUTER SPACE 74 (I.I.S.L. of the I.A.F., 1970). Zhukov, writing in 1969, makes several comments about the 1967 treaty. In a reference to Art. 1, which contains the "common use" principle, he observes:

> Since all states are sovereign and equal, outer space is open and free for the exploration and use by all states without discrimination of any kind and on a basis of complete equality. Granting the rights to all states freely to explore and use outer space is not confined to recognition of their specific rights. It also means the assumption of certain obligations on their part . . . that the states will not hamper one another in their space research. In other words they must respect one another's rights and interests in outer space and on celestial bodies. [Zhukov, *Fundamental Principles of Space Law*, in CONTEMPORARY INTERNATIONAL LAW: A COLLECTION OF ARTICLES 263, 267–68 (Ivanov-Mumjiev trans., G. Tunkin ed. 1969).]

An almost identical passage appears in a Soviet publication, INTERNATIONAL SPACE LAW 84 (B. Belitsky trans., A. Piradov ed. 1976). This interpretation not only does not suggest any qualification or modification of the regime of partial demilitarization under Art. IV(1), but by virtue of its emphasis on the principles of equality, nondiscrimination, and use of space in ways not prejudicial to the interests of other states engaged in space exploration, it is consistent with the interpretation being suggested here. For a parallel U.S. view, see the statement of U.S. Representative Plimpton before the UN Space Committee (Mar. 19, 1962), *reprinted in* 46 DEP'T ST. BULL. 809 (1962).

101. *See* text accompanying note 57, *supra*.

102. *See, e.g.*, Robinson, *Soviets Push for Beam Weapon*, AVIATION WEEK & SPACE TECH., May 2, 1977, at 16; NEWSWEEK, Nov. 29, 1976, at 46.

103. Report of Defense Secretary Harold Brown's News Conference, N.Y. Times, Oct. 5, 1977, at A11; Covault, *supra* note 72, at 20.

104. The Soviet Union was reported to have launched at least four sur-

veillance satellites (designated Cosmos 1172, 1173, 1176, and 1177) in April 1980. *Soviets Launch Surveillance Spacecraft*, 112 AVIATION WEEK & SPACE TECH., May 5, 1980, at 25; Covault, *supra* note 72, at 20.

105. *See, e.g.*, Lipson, *An Argument on the Legality of Reconnaissance Satellites*, 55 AM. SOC. INT'L L. PROCEEDINGS 174 (1961); Note, *Legal Aspects of Reconnaissance in Airspace and Outer Space*, 61 COLUM. L. REV. 1074 (1961); *see also* statement of Plimpton before the UN Space Committee, *supra* note 100; Meeker, *Observation in Space*, in LAW AND POLITICS IN SPACE 75 (M. Cohen ed. 1964). Morenoff argues that reconnaissance satellites may be used in pursuit of the "inherent" right of self-defense, including anticipatory self-defense: J. MORENOFF, *supra* note 88, at 232–37; *see also* Hosenball, *Current Issues of Space Law Before the United Nations*, 2 J. SPACE L. 5, 15, 17 (1974).

106. S. LAY & H. TAUBENFELD, *supra* note 73, at 187.

107. *Id.* at 98.

108. *See* McMahon, *Legal Aspects of Outer Space*, 38 BRIT. Y.B. INT'L L. 339, 367–69, 380 (1962); M. VAZGUEZ, COSMIC INTERNATIONAL LAW 165–71 (1965). Vazguez argues that, because satellite reconnaissance takes place outside municipal jurisdiction, it is inappropriate to compare it to aerial reconnaissance from conventional aircraft, which, he argues, is illegal if it violates national airspace: *id.* at 168. Vazguez further maintains that, in an age when radio waves from different countries constantly invade each other's airspace, satellite photography should be even less objectionable because it does not involve the transmission of any waves into territorial airspace; the satellite camera merely collects or receives light waves from the ground: *id.* at 171; *Cf.* G. GAL, SPACE LAW, *supra* note 93, at 178.

109. *See* text accompanying notes 79–80 and 85, *supra*.

110. Mankiewicz, taking a strongly pessimistic view, argues that the Space Treaty will not contribute toward law and order in space and is a mere "window-dressing" arrangement behind which the space powers will continue to pursue whatever activity they choose. Mankiewicz, *Interpretation of the Treaty on Outer Space*, PROCEEDINGS OF THE 11TH COLLOQUIUM, *supra* note 85, at 82–83.

111. M. McDOUGAL, LAW AND MINIMUM WORLD PUBLIC ORDER 57 (1961).

112. A recent example is the Strategic Arms Limitation Treaty of 1979 (SALT II). While the Seabed Treaty prohibits the emplacement of stationary nuclear weapons or missiles on the ocean floor, SALT II proposes to prohibit the development, testing, or deployment of stationary or mobile strategic nuclear missiles designed to be placed on, or able to move in contact with, any part of the ocean floor, including portions that are subjacent to internal waters. Art. IX of the proposed treaty (which has not, as of this writing, come into force) provides:

184 NOTESNOTES TO PAGES 127–135

1. Each Party undertakes not to develop, test, or deploy:

. . . .

(b) Fixed ballistic or cruise missile launchers for emplacement on the ocean floor, on the seabed, or on the beds of internal waters and inland waters, or in the subsoil thereof, or mobile launchers of such missiles, which move only in contact with the ocean floor, the seabed, or the beds of internal waters and inland waters, or missiles for such launchers. . . (Treaty on Limitation of Strategic Offensive Arms, June 18, 1979, U.S.-USSR, Selected Documents No. 12A, 26, 41 [Bureau of Public Affairs, Department of State].)

113. McDougal & Lipson, *Perspectives for a Law of Outer Space*, 52 AM. J. INT'L L. 407, 420 (1958).

CHAPTER V

1. L. POSPÍŠIL, ANTHROPOLOGY OF LAW: A COMPARATIVE THEORY 125 (1974).

Selective Bibliography

The purpose of the following list of works is to enable the interested reader to pursue further the subject matter of this book. The list contains pertinent and important works that have not been cited in the reference notes.

BOOKS

W. BUTLER, WRITINGS ON SOVIET LAW AND SOVIET INTERNATIONAL LAW. A BIBLIOGRAPHY OF BOOKS AND ARTICLES PUBLISHED SINCE 1917 IN LANGUAGES OTHER THAN EAST EUROPEAN (1966).

CONTEMPORARY SOVIET LAW: ESSAYS IN HONOR OF JOHN N. HAZARD (D. Barry, W. Butler & G. Ginsburgs eds. 1974).

CURRENT DIGEST OF THE SOVIET PRESS, Quarterly Indices, index heading "State and Law."

DIPLOMATICHESKII SLOVAR' (A. Vyshinskii & S. Lozovskii eds. 1948–50, 2 vols.) (2d ed. 1960–64) (3d ed. 1971–73). Encyclopedia devoted to diplomacy and international law, with particular attention to Soviet foreign policy. The first edition records interpretations of the late Stalin era. Many articles contain useful bibliographic data. All complement one another from an historical viewpoint.

FUNDAMENTALS OF MARXISM-LENINISM: MANUAL (trans. from the Russian, C. Dutt ed. 1960) (2d ed. 1963).

J. HAZARD & W. STERN, BIBLIOGRAPHY OF THE PRINCIPAL MATERIALS ON SOVIET LAW, AMERICAN FOREIGN LAW ASSOCIATION SERIES (1945).

INSTITUTE OF STATE AND LAW, U.S.S.R. ACADEMY OF SCIENCES, LITERATURE ON SOVIET LAW, INDEX OF BIBLIOGRAPHY (1960).

H. KELSEN, POLITICAL THEORY OF BOLSHEVISM: A CRITICAL ANALYSIS (1955).

H. KELSEN, THE COMMUNIST THEORY OF LAW (1955).

Y. KOROVIN, MEZHDUNARODNOE PRAVO PEREKHODNOGO VREMENI (1923). First edition of the first attempt to elucidate a Marxist theory of international law. Much criticized in later years, it nevertheless remains a landmark in Soviet international legal literature.

Y. KOROVIN, MEZHDUNARODNOE PRAVO PEREKHODNOGO VREMENI (2d ed. 1924). Revised edition of Korovin's introduction to international law of the transition period.

D. LEVIN, O SOVREMENNYKH BURZHUAZNYKH TEORIIAKH MEZHDUNAROD-
NOGO PRAVA (1959). Critical evaluation of contemporary bourgeois theories
of international law.

H. MARCUSE, SOVIET MARXISM, A CRITICAL ANALYSIS (1958).

N. MINASIAN, SUSHCHNOST' SOVREMENNOGO MEZHDUNARODNOGO PRAVA
(1962). Theoretical analysis of modern international law and peaceful
coexistence.

O BURZHUAZNYKH VLIIANIIAKH V SOVETSKOI MEZHDUNARODNO-PRAVOVOI
LITERATURE; DISKUSSIIA NA MEZHDUNARODMON OTDELENII MGU (1930).
Report of a meeting held at Moscow State University in 1929–30 to discuss
the problem of bourgeois influences in Soviet doctrinal literature on international law.

R. SCHLESINGER, SOVIET LEGAL THEORY: ITS SOCIAL BACKGROUND AND DE-
VELOPMENT (2d ed. 1951).

SOVIET LEGAL PHILOSOPHY (trans. H. Babb, 20th Century Legal Philosophy
Series, vol. 5, 1951).

V. TUMANOV, CONTEMPORARY BOURGEOIS LEGAL THOUGHT: A MARXIST
EVALUATION OF THE BASIC CONCEPTS (1974).

Z. ZILE, IDEAS AND FORCES IN SOVIET LEGAL HISTORY (1967) (2d ed. 1970).

ARTICLES

Afghan Crisis: Interview with Roy Medvedev, 121 NEW LEFT REV. 91
(1980).

Andelman, *Space Wars*, 44 FOREIGN POL'Y 94 (Fall 1981).

Anderson, *Justifications and Precedents as Constraints in Foreign Policy
Decision-Making*, 25 AM. J. POL. SCI. 738 (1981).

Aron, *From American Imperialism to Soviet Hegemonism*, 17 ATL. COMMU-
NITY Q. 489 (1979).

Asad, *Anthropology and the Analysis of Ideology*, 14 MAN 607 (1979).

Baldwin, *Interdependence and Power: A Conceptual Analysis*, 34 INT'L
ORG. 471 (1980).

Baldwin, *Power Analysis and World Politics: New Trends Versus Old Tendencies*, 31 WORLD POL. 161 (1979).

Barnet, *U.S.-Soviet Relations: The Need for a Comprehensive Approach*, 57
FOREIGN AFF. 779 (1979).

Beloff, *The Military Factor in Soviet Foreign Policy* [review article], 30
PROBS. COMMUNISM 70 (Jan.-Feb. 1981).

Berman, *The Challenge of Soviet Law*, 62 HARV. L. REV. 220 (1948–49).

Bienen, *Perspectives on Soviet Intervention in Africa*, 95 POL. SCI. Q. 29
(1980).

Binns, *The Changing Face of Power: Revolution and Accommodation in the Development of the Soviet Ceremonial System*, 14 MAN 585 (1979); 15 MAN 170 (1980).

Bodenheimer, *The Impasse of Soviet Legal Philosophy*, 38 CORNELL L.Q. 51 (1952).

Boyle, *The Law of Power Politics*, 1980 U. ILL. L.F. 901.

Brecher, *State Behavior in International Crisis: A Model*, 23 J. CONFLICT RESOLUTION 446 (1979).

Bridge, *International and Military Activities in Outer Space*, 13 AKRON L. REV. 649 (1980).

Bromke, *Poland: The Cliff's Edge*, 41 FOREIGN POL'Y 154 (Winter 1980–81).

Brzezinski, *American Foreign Policy in a Rapidly Changing World*, 17 ATL. COMMUNITY Q. 6 (1979).

Cammer, *Communications on: Tumanov and Terrar and Bourgeois Legal Thought (A Reply to Toby Terrar)*, 39 NAT'L LAW. GUILD PRAC. 15 (1982).

Charles, *The Changing Vision of the African Working Class—A Component of Soviet Strategy in Black Africa?*, 16 J. MOD. AFRICAN STUD. 695 (1978).

Chkhikvadze & Zivs, *New Trends in Legal Sovietology and Our Tasks*, 6 SOVIET L. & GOV'T 3 (Summer 1967).

Christol, *The American Bar Association and the 1979 Moon Treaty: The Search for a Position*, 9 J. SPACE L. 77 (1981).

Clarke, *Arms Control and Foreign Policy Under Reagan*, 37 BULL. ATOM. SCI. 12 (Nov. 1981).

Claude, *Just Wars: Doctrines and Institutions*, 95 POL. SCI. Q. 83 (1980).

Cleveland, *U.S. Foreign Policy: Illusions of Powerlessness and Realities of Power*, 20 ATL. COMMUNITY Q. 143 (1982).

Close, *Soviet Strategy, the Atlantic and the Defense of the West*, 18 ATL. COMMUNITY Q. 403 (1980–81).

Crocker & Lewis, *Missing Opportunities in Africa*, 35 FOREIGN POL'Y 142 (Summer 1979).

Cutler, *The Formation of Soviet Foreign Policy: Organizational and Cognitive Perspectives*, 34 WORLD POL. 418 (1982).

Dawisha, *Moscow's Moves in the Direction of the Gulf—So Near and Yet So Far*, 34 J. INT'L AFF. 219 (1980–81).

Dawisha, *Soviet Security and the Role of the Military: The 1968 Czechoslovak Crisis*, 10 BRIT. J. POL. SCI. 341 (1980).

de Mesquita, *An Expected Utility Theory of International Conflict*, 74 AM. POL. SCI. REV. 917 (1980); Discussion, 75 AM. POL. SCI. REV. 732 (1981).

Desfosses, *North-South or East-West? Constructs for Superpower African Policy in the Eighties*, 34 J. INT'L AFF. 369 (1980–81).

Dulles, *Soviet Concept of Legal Institutions*, 7 MERCER L. REV. 250 (1956).

Durch, *The Cuban Military in Africa and the Middle East from Algeria to Angola*, 11 STUD. COMP. COMMUNISM 34 (1978).

Eberwein, Hübner-Dick, Jagodzinski, Rattinger & Weede, *External and Internal Conflict Behavior Among Nations, 1966–1967*, 23 J. CONFLICT RESOLUTION 715 (1979).

Eorsi, *Comparative Analysis of Socialist and Capitalist Law*, 1964 CO-EXISTENCE 139.

Falk, *The Menace of the New Cycle of Interventionary Diplomacy*, 17 J. PEACE RESEARCH 201 (1980).

Fine, *Underlying Impetus for Soviet Invasion (Afghanistan)*, BUS. W. 62 (Sept. 29, 1980) (minerals trove).

Fink, *Afghan Invasion Likened to 1968 Action*, 113 AVIATION WEEK AND SPACE TECH. 20 (July 14, 1980).

Freedman, *Soviet Policy Towards the Middle East Since the Invasion of Afghanistan*, 34 J. INT'L AFF. 283 (1980–81).

Fuller, *Pashukanis and Vyshinsky: A Study in the Development of Marxian Legal Theory*, 47 MICH. L. REV. 1157 (1949).

Gallie, *Wanted: A Philosophy of International Relations* [review article], 27 POL. STUD. 484 (1979).

Garrett, *Afghanistan and Korea: Examining the Parallels*, 109 U.S.A. TODAY 15 (May 1981).

Garthoff, *American Reaction to Soviet Aircraft in Cuba, 1962 and 1978*, 95 POL. SCI. Q. 427 (1980).

Garthoff, *Soviet Views on the Interrelation of Diplomacy and Military Strategy*, 94 POL. SCI. Q. 391 (1979).

Gasser, *International Non-International Armed Conflicts: Cast Studies of Afghanistan, Kampuchea, and Lebanon* (Conference: Amer. Red Cross— Washington College of Law Conference: International Humanitarian Law) (Transcript), 31 AM. U.L. REV. 911 (1982).

Gilbert & Lauren, *Crisis Management: An Assessment and Critique* [with discussion], 24 J. CONFLICT RESOLUTION 641 (1980).

Gitelman, *Politics of Socialist Restoration in Hungary and Czechoslovakia*, 13 COMP. POL. 187 (1981).

Glos, *The Theory and Practice of Soviet International Law*, 16 INT'L LAW 279 (1982).

Goldstick, *Bourgeois Prejudices Versus the Philosophy of Marxism*, 25 WORLD MARXIST REV. 41 (Feb. 1982).

Gouré & McCormick, *Soviet Strategic Defense: The Neglected Dimension of the U.S.-Soviet Balance*, 24 ORBIS 103 (1980).

Gray, *The Most Dangerous Decade: Historic Mission, Legitimacy and Dynamics of the Soviet Empire in the 1980s*, 25 ORBIS 13 (1981).

Gregory, *The Afghan Puzzle*, 112 AVIATION WEEK & SPACE TECH. 11 (Jan. 21, 1980).

Griffiths, *Afghan Problems Stall Soviets*, 112 AVIATION WEEK & SPACE TECH. 18 (Apr. 21, 1980).

Guertner, *Strategic Vulnerability of a Multinational State: Deterring the Soviet Union*, 96 POL. SCI. Q. 209 (1981).

Guins, *East and West in Soviet Ideology*, 8 THE RUSSIAN REV. 271 (1949).

Haas, *Words Can Hurt You; or, Who Said What to Whom about Regimes*, 36 INT'L ORG. 207 (1982).

Hamilton, *To Link or Not to Link*, 42 FOREIGN POL'Y 127 (Fall 1981).

Hammer, *Law Enforcement, Social Control and the Withering of the State: Recent Soviet Experience*, 14 SOVIET STUD. 379 (1963).

Hannum & Lillich, *The Concept of Autonomy in International Law*, 74 AM. J. INT'L L. 858 (1980).

Harris & Espinosa, *Reform, Repression and Revolution in El Salvador*, 5 FLETCHER F. 295 (1981).

Hartley, *Afghan Invasion Prods Iraq Toward West*, 88 U.S. NEWS 43 (Feb. 25 1980).

Hawkesworth, *Ideological Immunity: The Soviet Response to Human Rights Criticism*, 2 UNIVERSAL HUM. RTS. 67 (1980).

Hazard, *Contrasting Principles in Soviet and Common Law*, University of Chicago Conferences Series No. 15 (Conferences on Jurisprudence and Politics, Apr. 30, 1954) 20 (1954).

Hazard, *The Future of Soviet Law*, 8 SYDNEY L. REV. 590 (1979).

Hazard, *Soviet Law and Its Assumptions*, in IDEOLOGICAL DIFFERENCE AND WORLD ORDER, 192 (F. Northrop ed. 1949).

Heggen & Cuzán, *Legitimacy, Coercion and Scope: An Expansion Path Analysis Applied to Five Central American Countries and Cuba*, 26 BEHAV. SCI. 143 (1981).

Henrikson, *Space Politics in Historical and Futuristic Perspective*, 5 FLETCHER F. 106 (1981).

Hinton, Higgons, Hassan, Schwebel & Ferencz, *Legal Responses to the Afghan-Iranian Crises*, 74 AM. SOC. INT'L L. PROC. 248 (1980).

Howard, *Return to the Cold War?*, 59 FOREIGN AFF. 459 (1981).

Husband, *Soviet Perceptions of U.S. Positions-of-Strength Diplomacy in the 1970s*, 31 WORLD POL. 495 (1979).

Hyland, *Brezhnev and Beyond*, 58 FOREIGN AFF. 51 (1979).

Hyland, *The Soviet Union and the United States*, 80 CURRENT HIST. 309 (1981).

Immerman, *Guatemala As Cold War History*, 95 POL. SCI. Q. 629 (1980–81).

Ioffe & Shargorodskii, *The Significance of General Definitions in the Study of Problems of Law and Socialist Legality*, 2 SOVIET L. & GOV'T 3 (Fall 1963).

Is Detente Dead? (Interviews by A. Balk: M. Tatu, U. Schiller, T. Prasuram), 27 WORLD PRESS REV. 19 (1980).

Jacobsen, *Changing American-Soviet Power Balance*, 79 CURRENT HIST. 65 (1980).

Jacobsen, *Soviet Strategic Objectives for the 1980s*, 35 WORLD TODAY 130 (1979).

Jaksetic, *Peaceful Uses of Outer Space: Soviet Views*, 28 AM. U.L. REV. 483 (1979).

Jaworskyj, *Soviet Critique of the "Bourgeois" Philosophy of Law*, 6 OST-EUROPA RECHT 11 (1960).

Jay, *Regionalism as Geopolitics*, 58 FOREIGN AFF. 485 (1980).

Jervis, *Deterrence Theory Revisited* [Review article], 31 WORLD POL. 288 (1979).

Jervis, *Impact of the Korean War on the Cold War*, 24 J. CONFLICT RESOLU-TION 563 (1980).

Jessop, *On Recent Marxist Theories of Law, the State, and Juridico-Political Ideology*, 8 INT'L J. SOC. L. 339 (1980).

Journes, *The Crisis of Marxism and Critical Legal Studies: A View from France*, 10 INT'L J. SOC. L. 2 (1982).

Joyner, *U.N. General Assembly Resolutions and International Law: Rethinking the Contemporary Dynamics of Norm-Creation*, 11 CAL. W. INT'L L.J. 445 (1981).

Kaiser, *U.S.-Soviet Relations: Goodbye to Detente*, 59 FOREIGN AFF. 500 (1981).

Kennan, *Imprudent Response to the Afghan Crisis?*, 36 BULL. ATOM. SCI. 7 (Apr. 1980).

Kennan, *Scholarship, Politics and the East-West Relationship*, 37 BULL. ATOM. SCI. 4 (May 1981).

Kirkpatrick, *Afghanistan: Implications for Peace and Security*, 144 WORLD AFF. 242 (1981).

Kirkpatrick, *East/West Relations: Toward a New Definition of a Dialogue*, 144 WORLD AFF. 14 (1981).

Kozicharow, *NATO Cautions Soviets on Invasion of Poland*, 113 AVIATION WEEK & SPACE TECH. 18 (Dec. 15, 1980).

Krasner, *Regimes and the Limits of Realism: Regimes as Autonomous Variables*, 36 INT'L ORG. 497 (1982).

Krasner, *Structural Causes and Regime Consequences: Regimes as Intervening Variables*, 36 INT'L ORG. 185 (1982).

Kratochwil, *On the Notion of Interest in International Relations*, 36 INT'L ORG. 1 (1982).

Krauthammer, *What's Good for General Motors: Reagan's Foreign Policy*, 20 POL'Y REV. 140 (1982).

Laqueur, *Containment for the 80s*, 70 COMMENTARY 33 (Oct. 1980).

Legvold, *Containment Without Confrontation*, 40 FOREIGN POL'Y 74 (Fall 1980).

LeoGrande, *Cuba Policy Recycled*, 46 FOREIGN POL'Y 105 (Spring 1982).

Levy, *Alliance Formation and War Behavior: An Analysis of the Great Powers, 1495–1975*, 25 J. CONFLICT RESOLUTIONS 581 (1981).

Lider, *The Correlation of World Forces: The Soviet Concept*, 17 J. PEACE RESEARCH 151 (1980).

Lipson, *Socialist Legality: The Road Uphill*, in RUSSIA UNDER KHRUSHCHEV 444 (A. Brumberg ed. 1962).

Lukes, *Hegel, Freedom and the Ideological Roots of Soviet Foreign Policy*, 5 FLETCHER F. 278 (1981).

Luttwak, *After Afghanistan, What?*, 69 COMMENTARY 40 (Apr. 1980).

Mackey, *Some Basic Considerations of Soviet Law and Socialist Legality*, 11 ALA. L. REV. 254 (1959).

Maclure, *Soviet International Legal Theory—Past and Present*, 5 FLETCHER F. 49 (1981).

McGeehan, *Is a New Detente Possible?*, 38 WORLD TODAY 207 (1982).

Mendlovitz, *International Conflicts, Law, and a Just World Order: The 1980 David Stoffer Lectures* [introduction], 33 RUTGERS L. REV. 397 (1981).

Milshtein, *The Present Military-Political Doctrine of the United States*, 23 WORLD MARXIST REV. 44 (Nov. 1980).

Minola, *The Moon Treaty and the Law of the Sea*, 18 SAN DIEGO L. REV. 455 (1981).

Mladenov, *Peaceful Coexistence Policy Today*, 23 WORLD MARXIST REV. 16 (Jan. 1980).

Mlynar, *Rules of the Game: The Soviet Bloc Today*, 50 POL. Q. 403 (1979).

Moon Treaty—Should the U.S. Become a Party, 74 AM. SOC. INT'L L. PROC. 152 (1980).

Moscow's Defensive Offensive [reaction to criticism of Afghanistan invasion], 115 TIME 38 (Feb. 11, 1980).

Moynihan, *Further Thoughts on Words and Foreign Policy*, 17 ATL. COMMUNITY Q. 346 (1979).

Murarka, *Afghanistan: The Russian Intervention: A Moscow Analysis*, 282 ROUND TABLE 122 (1981); Discussion, 283 ROUND TABLE 276 (1981).

Neal, *Afghanistan: A Created Crisis*, 36 BULL. ATOM. SCI. 10 (Oct. 1980).

Negaran, *Afghan Coup of April 1978: Revolution and International Security*, 23 ORBIS 93 (1979).

Neuman, *Book Review*, 64 POL. SCI. Q. 127 (1949) (reviewing A. Vyshinsky, LAW OF THE SOVIET STATE).

Newcombe, *Some Contributions of the Behavioural Sciences to the Study of Violence*, 30 INT'L SCI. J. 750 (1978).

Nicol, *Africa and the U.S.A. in the United Nations*, 16 J. MOD. AFRICAN STUD. 365 (1978).

Nincic, *Understanding International Conflict: Some Theoretical Gaps*, 19 J. PEACE RESEARCH 49 (1982).

Osgood, *East-West Global Equilibrium*, 17 ATL. COMMUNITY Q. 138 (1979).

Paul & Simon, *Poland Today and Czechoslovakia 1968*, 30 PROBS. COMMUNISM 25 (Sept./Oct. 1981).

Peaceful Uses of Outer Space, 74 AM. J. INT'L L. 421 (1980).

Petras & Selden, *Social Classes, the State of the World System in the Transition to Socialism*, 11 J. CONTEMP. ASIA 189 (1981).

Pfaltzgraff, *The Superpower Relationships and U.S. National Security Policy in the 1980s*, 457 ANNALS 186 (1981).

Pipes, *Soviet Global Strategy*, 69 COMMENTARY 31 (Apr. 1980).

Platig, *Crisis, Pretentious Ideologies and Superpower Behavior*, 25 ORBIS 511 (1981).

Ponomaryov, *Existing Socialism and Its International Significance*, 22 WORLD MARXIST REV. 22 (Feb. 1979).

Potter, *Perception and Misperception in U.S.-Soviet Relations* (review article), 29 PROBS. COMMUNISM 68 (Mar.–Apr. 1980).

Puchala & Hopkins, *International Regimes: Lessons from Inductive Analysis*, 36 INT'L ORG. 245 (1982).

Ra'anan, *Soviet Strategic Doctrine and the Soviet-American Global Contest*, 457 ANNALS 8 (1981).

Rabkin, *U.S.-Soviet Rivalry in Central America and the Caribbean*, 34 J. INT'L AFF. 329 (1980–81).

Rapkin, Thompson & Christopherson, *Bipolarity and Bipolarization in the Cold War Era: Conceptualization, Measurement and Validation*, 23 J. CONFLICT RESOLUTION 261 (1979).

Ratliff, *United States Policy Toward the Caribbean*, 17 WILLAMETTE L.J. 221 (1980).

Reed & Norris, *Military Use of the Space Shuttle, 13* AKRON L. REV. 665 (1980).

Reisman, *Critical Defense Zones and International Law: The Reagan Codicil*, 76 AM. J. INT'L L. 589 (1982).

Reisman, *Termination of the USSR's Treaty Right of Intervention in Iran*, 74 AM. J. INT'L L. 144 (1980).

Reshetar, *Search for Law in Soviet Legality* [review article], 28 PROBS. COMMUNISM 61 (July–Aug. 1979).

Responding to Soviet Power, 144 AMERICA 241 (Mar. 28, 1981).

Richardson, Kegley & Agnew, *Symmetry and Reciprocity as Characteristics of Dyadic Foreign Policy Behavior*, 62 SOC. SCI. Q. 128 (1981).

Richelson, *Soviet Responses to MX*, 96 POL. SCI. Q. 401 (1981).
Ro'i, *Moscow and the Third World: Ideology vs. Power Politics*, 28 PROBS. COMMUNISM 59 (Jan.–Feb. 1979).
Rood, *Cuba: Payment Deferred* [Soviet military aid since missile crisis], 33 NAT'L REV. 1401 (1981).
Rostow, *Law and the Use of Force by States: The Brezhnev Doctrine*, 7 YALE J. WORLD PUB. ORD. 209 (1981).
Roucek, *The Sociological Aspect of Soviet Legality*, 15 UKRAINIAN Q. 368 (1959).
Rubinstein, *The Last Years of Peaceful Coexistence: Soviet-Afghan Relations 1963–1978*, 36 MID. E.J. 165 (1982).
RUBINSTEIN, *Soviet Imperialism in Afghanistan*, 79 CURRENT HIST. 80 (Oct. 1980).
Rudden, *Law and Ideology in the Soviet Union*, 31 CURRENT LEGAL PROBS. 189 (1978).
Salter, *U.S. and U.S.S.R.: Convergence or Confrontation?*, 35 OKLA. BAR J. 1443 (1964).
Scherer, *Reinterpreting Soviet Behavior During the Cuban Missile Crisis*, 144 WORLD AFF. 110 (1981).
Schneider, *Preventing Star Wars*, 37 BULL. ATOM. SCI. 13 (Oct. 1981) (banning antisatellite weapons).
Schneyer & Barta, *Legality of U.S. Economic Blockade of Cuba Under International Law*, 13 CASE W. RES. J. INT'L L. 451 (1982).
Schwenninger, *The 1980s: New Doctrines of Intervention or New Norms of Nonintervention?* (1980 David Stoffer Lectures) (transcript), 33 RUTGERS L. REV. 423 (1981).
Seabury, *George Kennan vs. Mr. 'X'*, 185 NEW REPUB. 17 (Dec. 16, 1981) (views of G. F. Kennan in the *New Yorker*).
Simes, *Clash Over Poland*, 46 FOREIGN POL'Y 49 (Spring 1982).
Simes, *Disciplining Soviet Power*, 43 FOREIGN POL'Y 33 (Summer 1981).
Skilling, *The Soviet Impact on the Czechoslovak Legal Revolution*, 6 SOVIET STUD. 361 (1955).
Smith, *Military Space Systems Applications Increasing*, 114 AVIATION WEEK AND SPACE TECH. 83 (March 9, 1981).
Smolansky, *Soviet Policy in Iran and Afghanistan*, 80 CURRENT HIST. 321 (Oct. 1981).
Snow, *Lasers, Charged-Particle Beams, and the Strategic Future*, 95 POL. SCI. Q. 277 (1980).
Solzhenitsyn, *Misconceptions About Russia Are a Threat to America*, 58 FOREIGN AFF. 797 (1980); Discussion, 58 FOREIGN AFF. 1178 (1980); 59 FOREIGN AFF. 187 (1980).
Sonnenfeldt, *Implications of the Soviet Invasion of Afghanistan for East-West Relations*, 18 ATL. COMMUNITY Q. 184 (1980).

Spitz, *Space Law—Agreement Governing the Activities of States on the Moon and Other Celestial Bodies*, 21 HARV. INT'L L.J. 579 (1980).

Stein, *Coordination and Collaboration: Regimes in an Anarchic World*, 36 INT'L ORG. 299 (1982).

Steinberg, *Goals in Conflict: Escalation, Cuba, 1962*, 14 CAN. J. POL. SCI. 83 (1981).

Summerscale, *Eastern Europe in the Wake of Afghanistan*, 36 WORLD TODAY 172 (1980).

Symposium, *Problems Facing the Atlantic Alliance as a Result of Soviet Penetration into Africa*, 17 ATL. COMMUNITY Q. 257 (1979).

Talbott & Nelan, *View from Red Square* [reaction to Afghanistan invasion], 115 TIME 18 (Feb. 4, 1980).

Thompson, *Directed Energy Weapons and the Strategic Balance*, 23 ORBIS 697 (1979).

Thompson & Rapkin, *Collaboration, Consensus, and Detente: The External Threat-Bloc Cohesion Hypothesis*, 25 J. CONFLICT RESOLUTION 615 (1981).

Timasheff, *Is Soviet Law a Challenge to American Law?*, 19 FORDHAM L. REV. 182 (1950).

Toon, *The Soviet Threat: An Appropriate U.S. Response* (Symposium: International Law and Foreign Policy in the 1980's), 17 WILLIAMETTE L.J. 57 (1980).

Towster, *Vyshinsky's Concept of Collectivity* in CONTINUITY AND CHANGE IN RUSSIAN AND SOVIET THOUGHT 237 (E. Simmons ed. 1955).

Trofimenko, *The Third World and the U.S.-Soviet Competition: A Soviet View*, 59 FOREIGN AFF. 1021 (1981).

Tumanov, *Failure to Understand or Unwillingness to Understand? (On Harold Berman's "Justice in the USSR: An Interpretation of Soviet Law")*, 4 SOVIET L. & GOV'T 3 (No. 3, 1965–66).

Tunkin, *Contemporary Theory of Soviet International Law*, 31 CURRENT LEGAL PROB. 177 (1978).

Ulam, *How to Restrain the Soviets*, 70 COMMENTARY 38 (Dec. 1980).

Ulam, *U.S.-Soviet Relations: Unhappy Coexistence*, 57 FOREIGN AFF. 555 (1978).

U.S. Policy Toward Zaire, 26 AFRICA REP. 22 (1981).

Vagts & Vagts, *Balance of Power in International Law: A History of an Idea*, 73 AM. J. INT'L L. 555 (1979).

Valenta, *The Bureaucratic Politics Paradigm and the Soviet Invasion of Czechoslovakia*, 94 POL. SCI. Q. 55 (1979).

Valenta, *Soviet-Cuban Alliance in Africa and the Caribbean*, 37 WORLD TODAY 45 (1981).

Valenta, *Soviet-Cuban Intervention in the Horn of Africa: Impact and Lessons*, 34 J. INT'L AFF. 353 (1980–81).

Varga, *Towards a Sociological Concept of Law: An Analysis of Lukács' Ontology*, 9 INT'L J. SOC. L. 159 (1981).

Valkenier, *Great Power Economic Competition in Africa: Soviet Progress and Problems*, 34 J. INT'L AFF. 259 (1980–81).

Wallensteen, *Incompatibility, Confrontation and War: Four Models and Three Historical Systems*, 1816–1976, 18 J. PEACE RESEARCH 57 (1981).

Walsh, *Controversial Issues under Article XI of the Moon Treaty*, 6 ANNALS AIR & SPACE L. 489 (1981).

Ward, *Cooperation and Conflict in Foreign Policy Behavior: Reaction and Memory*, 26 INT'L STUD. Q. 87 (1982).

Weissman, *CIA Covert Action in Zaire and Angola: Patterns and Consequences*, 94 POL. SCI. Q. 263 (1979).

Wessell, *Soviet Views of Multipolarity and the Emerging Balance of Power*, 22 ORBIS 785 (1981).

Wessell, *Yugoslavia: Ground Rules for Restraining Soviet and American Competition*, 34 J. INT'L AFF. 311 (1980–81).

Wiarda, *U.S. and the Dominican Republic: Intervention, Dependency and Tyrannicide* [review essay], 22 J. INTERAM. STUD. 247 (1980).

Wilkenfeld, Hopple, Andriole & McCauley, *Profiling States for Foreign Policy Analysis*, 11 COMP. POL. STUD. 4 (1978); Discussion, 13 COMP. POL. STUD. 379 (1980).

Winn, *Western and Soviet Systems/Social Science Approaches to International Affairs: An Introductory Comparison*, 26 BEHAV. SCI. 281 (1981).

Wise, *Social Science and Global Law*, 14 CREIGHTON L. REV. 1355 (1981).

Wright, *Varieties of Marxist Conceptions of Class Structure*, 9 POL. & SOC. 323 (1979–80).

Young, *Regime Dynamics: The Rise and Fall of International Regimes*, 36 INT'L ORG. 277 (1982).

Young, *United States' Focus on Africa*, 5 S. U.L. REV. 5 (1978).

Zagoria, *Into the Breach: New Soviet Alliances in the Third World*, 57 FOREIGN AFF. 733 (1979).

Zellweger, *The Principle of Socialist Legality*, 5 J. INT'L COMMISSION JURISTS 163 (1964).

Zeray, *Afghanistan: The Beginning of a New Era*, 22 WORLD MARXIST REV. 103 (Jan. 1979).

Zhogin, *Vyshinsky's Distortions in Soviet Legal Theory and Practice*, 4 SOVIET L. & GOV'T 48 (No. 2, 1956), 6 SOVIET REV. 44 (Winter 1965–66).

Index